EDUCATIONAL MANAGEMENT IN ACTION

This reader comprises a collection of papers published in connection with the Open University course E828 'Educational Management in Action'. This course involves carrying out three small-scale investigations of management practice and making recommendations for improved practice.

This reader is one part of an Open University integrated teaching system and the selection is therefore related to other material available. The editors have nevertheless attempted to make it of value to all those concerned with undertaking small-scale investigations of professional practice. Opinions expressed in it are not necessarily those of the course team or of the University.

EDUCATIONAL MANAGEMENT IN ACTION
A Collection of Case Studies

EDITED BY

Megan Crawford
Lesley Kydd and Susan Parker

AT THE OPEN UNIVERSITY

Published in Association with
The Open University

P·C·P
Paul Chapman
Publishing Ltd

Paul Chapman Publishing Ltd
144 Liverpool Road
London
N1 1LA

British Library Cataloguing in Publication Data
Educational Management in Action:
Collection of Case Studies
  I. Crawford, Megan
  371.2

  ISBN 1-85396-276-7

Typeset by Hewer Text Composition Services, Edinburgh
Printed and bound by The Athenaeum Press Ltd, Gateshead, England

ABCDEFGH 987654

Contents

About the editors

MEGAN CRAWFORD is a lecturer in the Centre for Educational Policy and Management at The Open University. She has previously worked as a deputy headteacher and class teacher in primary schools.

LESLEY KYDD is a staff tutor at The Open University in Scotland. She has previously worked in secondary schools and at SCOTVEC.

SUSAN PARKER is a course manager in the School of Education at The Open University. She has previously taught science and mathematics in secondary schools and managed learning in adult education.

About the authors

GRAHAM ATTWELL has worked for the last six years in the further education sector in Wales. He has been involved in research and curriculum and staff development for a number of European and Welsh development projects and currently works for Gwent Tertiary College training shop.

TREVOR BURTON is a member of the senior management team in a city technology college. His main responsibilities include information technology, reporting to parents, and the management of the faculty of science, mathematics and physical education.

LESLEY BROOMAN has taught in Yorkshire, Northants and Birmingham and has experience of both primary and secondary schools. As a head of special needs and teacher counsellor she had much to do with schools' external relations. Since 1989 she has been deputy headteacher in a Birmingham comprehensive school.

JEANNE COBURN is head of the faculty of enterprise, marketing and the community at Charles Keene College, Leicester. She has previously worked as head of publicity and marketing at Doncaster College and marketing manager at Rotherham College of Art and Technology. She is a member of the Marketing Network, and is currently the chair.

TERRY COWHAM graduated in geography at Nottingham University before working in computing in the steel industry. He went on to teach computing in Cambridgeshire and at Blackpool and Fylde College. He moved to Manchester in 1984 and is now senior vice principal at Manchester College of Arts and Technology.

MAGGIE FARRAR worked in the London Boroughs of Newham and Greenwich before moving to Hackney. She is currently acting deputy head at Haggerston School with an interest in curriculum development.

DEREK GLOVER taught in Nottinghamshire, Harrow and Wiltshire before 'serving' 18 years as head of Burford School and Community College, Oxfordshire. In 1990 he took early retirement and now works with The Open University and as a research fellow at Keele and Leicester Universities.

SUE GODSMARK has been a practising Key Stage 1 teacher in Essex schools throughout her teaching career and is currently responsible for an infant department in a primary school. She has been studying with The Open University for the past six years.

NIGEL HARRISSON worked as a micro-analyst with Bristol University before embarking on a teaching career. He subsequently taught in Bristol for 10 years, before training as an educational psychologist at Exeter University. He currently works for Wiltshire psychological services in Swindon, Wilts.

ROSALIND LEVAČIĆ is a senior lecturer in the Centre for Educational Policy and Management at The Open University. She has written extensively on financial and resource management and on the impact of local management of schools.

ERIC MEADOWS is currently head of Westdene Primary School in East Sussex. His headship experience extends over 20 years and includes first and middle schools. He is also a course tutor in educational management for The Open University.

SUE MITCHELL has worked for Leicestershire Education Authority as a teacher for a number of years. She conducted a survey and study of IT systems and the local management of schools as part of an MSc course at Loughborough University. She is currently head of biology at Earl Shilton Community College in Leicestershire.

MICHAEL MURPHY entered teaching after a period in industry. He is a senior lecturer in corporate strategy and marketing at Nottingham Business School, Nottingham Trent University. He was previously course leader for in-service education.

KEITH NORRIS spent nine years in industry before embarking on a career in education. He has worked in a number of higher education and further education institutions. During this time he has conducted a number of research projects on the selection and recruitment of staff. Keith is currently the deputy principal of operations at Doncaster College.

DAVID OWEN has worked in the East End of London for 15 years. For 10 years he taught maths and physics and for the last five years he has been a deputy headteacher at Haggerston School in the London Borough of Hackney. His current interests are in the leadership and management aspects of schools under local management.

SUE RICHARDS taught for six years in Nigeria before settling in London where she has worked for nearly two decades in various comprehensive schools. She is currently head of languages and senior teacher in charge of staff development in a mixed comprehensive school in south-east London.

JENNY SHACKLETON entered further education in 1973 following five years as a mature student in HE. She worked in a college, training centre and LEA before joining Wirral Metropolitan College as its principal in 1987. Jenny has collaborated with relevant national organizations throughout her career, and has been a member of the National Commission on Education since 1991. This case study has been written by Jenny in conjunction with her colleagues Rhiannon Evans and Maureen Hanley.

LYNNE SLOCOMBE is an editor in the School of Education and has worked at The Open University for 18 years. She has been a parent-governor of a first school for two years.

RUTH WARREN has been head of department in two religious education departments and is currently working as equal opportunities development officer for Grampian Region TVEI. She is also setting up an equal opportunities consultancy business.

RICHARD WEEKS has worked in the London Borough of Hounslow for 18 years. He was deputy head of Heston Community School prior to moving to Isleworth and Syon School for Boys in 1993. He was co-author of *Your pastoral care* published by NEP in 1988. His MBA (Ed) at Nottingham University focused on strategic planning for schools.

PHIL WILD has worked on computerized administration systems from the time of the first microcomputers going into schools, both as a teacher and as a consultant for commercial organizations. He is currently a lecturer in education and IT co-ordinator at Loughborough University, with research interests spanning all aspects of the effective use of computers in the school curriculum, administration and management.

PHILIP WOODS is a research fellow in the Open University's Centre for Educational Policy and Management and is principal investigator on the Parental and School Choice Interaction (PASCI) Study. This research project is investigating how schools and parents are reacting to the more competitive environment and to the enhanced emphasis on parental choice. Prior to working for The Open University, he worked in the area of home–school links.

ACKNOWLEDGEMENTS

CHAPTER 7, S. Mitchell and P. Wild, A Task Analysis of a Computerized System to Support Administration in Schools, *Educational Management and Administration*. VOL 21, NO. 1, pp 53–61, is reprinted here by permission of BEMAS.

Introduction

MEGAN CRAWFORD

The book has been developed as part of an Open University course, E828, 'Educational Management in Action', which offers the opportunity to undertake investigations in educational management in schools and colleges. The course enables students to develop the skills needed to investigate key management issues in their own and other educational institutions, to reflect upon their own practice and that of others, and to contribute to improving the quality of education provided. It examines reflective practice, and the part this can play in professional development. Raising levels of personal awareness is not an easy task. As Osterman and Kottkamp (1993) state:

> To gain a new level of insight into personal behaviour, the reflective practitioner assumes a dual stance, being on one hand, the actor in a drama, and on the other hand, the critic who sits in the audience watching and analysing the entire performance. To achieve this perspective, individuals must come to an understanding of their own behaviour; they must develop a conscious awareness of their own actions and effects and the ideas or theories-in-use that shape their action strategies.
>
> (OSTERMAN and KOTTKAMP, 1993, p. 19)

This book contains practitioner investigations, most of them specially commissioned, and all of them examples of educational management in action. The book embraces diversity, both in people and in the viewpoints they have taken for their investigations. The selection is intended to give you some insights into how an investigation can enhance institutional development.

The companion book to this one, *Improving Educational Management Through Research and Consultancy* (Bennett *et al.*) addresses the range of issues that need to be considered when writing investigations of this sort, and would be useful to consult if you decide to undertake such a role in your college or school.

The chapters in this book provide examples of some of the many ways of investigating schools and colleges. The investigations can be grouped generally into four types: the work of an external consultant, brought in to analyse a set of issues and make recommendations for improvement; investigations by an internal consultant on issues identified by the institution; research by a 'disinterested' researcher in the sense that they want to find out what is happening in a certain situation, but are not personally involved in it; and finally the 'interested' researcher who is involved in what is being studied. However, as you read this book, you may like to consider the different stances taken by the various writers, and consider whether any of them actually fits neatly into the case study types that I have outlined above. In Chapter 13, for example, Derek Glover's position of critical friend may not fit neatly into the defined perspectives. The investigative methods are also varied. Writers use interview data, questionnaire responses, documentary evidence, diaries, and observations of meetings. All of the authors look at the appropriateness of their methods to the study, and discuss both their difficulties and successes in data collection.

The students who undertake research in educational management using this book will be people in schools and colleges with only a short time available to undertake their investigation, and limited knowledge, as they start, of how to go about investigating their area of interest. Five chapters in this book were written by previous Open University students (Chapters 2, 4, 12, 14 and 16) and are included not only on their own merit, but also to show what is possible, given the constraints outlined above. 'The Photocopy Lady' by Trevor Burton (Chapter 12) is an example of this type of project. It not only involves support staff (an under-researched setting in educational management), but is small scale and concentrates on the role of Mrs Knowles, a reprographics supervisor in a city technology college. The investigation itself is of use in several ways: both to the researcher and to the institution itself in terms of staff development issues for Mrs Knowles and the other support staff.

The book is divided into five key management areas, based on the Management Charter Initiative categories:

PART ONE: Managing the pupil/student experience
PART TWO: Managing resources
PART THREE: Managing people
PART FOUR: Managing external relations
PART FIVE: Strategic management.

The investigations in Part One are varied both in their approaches to managing the pupil/student experience, and, in particular, their sector of education. Implementing curriculum change is discussed from both the secondary and the primary perspective in separate chapters by Sue Richards and Sue Godsmark. Both chapters look at rational planning models, and flexible planning in practice. Problems encountered in those school settings were very different to those experienced by Graham Attwell in his work focused on the modularization of the entire provision at a five-site tertiary college in Wales. His chapter gives a lively account of the difficulties experienced in managing multiple change in such a large institution. Another aspect of the pupil's experience is examined by Nigel Harrisson, that of pastoral support in a primary school. Harrisson, as an educational psychologist, based his investigation on a school that was well known to him. He had identified it as showing good practice, and wanted to investigate what produced this in the school's daily life. Lastly in this part, the value-added approach to exam results is discussed through a case study of Leon Secondary School. Rosalind Levačić looks at how valued-added data can contribute to school effectiveness, and looks in detail at how Leon manage their data. She also gives some useful information to help overcome some of the problems that arise when handling data.

The focus of Part Two is resources of various kinds. Michael Murphy was involved in research that came about from issues involved in competitive tendering arrangements for primary schools. He looks at how two primary schools approached the issue, and how it influenced management practice. Phil Mitchell and Sue Wild's research into the use of computerized systems in schools deals with how such systems can be used by staff most effectively. They look at the barriers that occur to the use of such systems, and suggest ways that these could be overcome. The 'interested' researcher perspective is highlighted clearly in Owen and Farrar's study of flexible learning at Haggerston High School, where both were senior teachers involved in the idea of 'curriculum-led' resourcing. The chapter charts their research into how the flexible learning approach tied into resource allocation decisions at the school. In a large college, Shackleton *et al.* investigate how a change in the college's management has led them to be resource led. The investigations look at the benefits and problems that this approach has shown in practice.

In Part Three we consider how another institutional resource, people, is managed. At a large college in Suffolk, Keith Norris looks at how staff selection can be made as fair as possible for all concerned, by conducting a case study of the college's staff selection process over a specific period. From this research, he is able to make specific suggestions for selection in practice. Lynne Slocombe uses a personal experience as a parent-governor to inform her case study into the redundancy process in two primary schools. The ethical dilemmas that she faced make this a chapter of particular interest. Trevor Burton investigates the work carried out by a reprographics supervisor, and discovers that her job is more varied than he had imagined. Using his study, he makes recommendations for her training. Derek Glover worked at Swan Mill School as an external consultant. In his chapter he considers how the appraisal process was implemented, and how it felt to the participants. Ruth Warren's case study of Mr Stewart, the assistant headteacher in a large Scottish secondary school, examines the ambiguities of role, and staff perception of it, and offers the reader from England and Wales an insight into the Scottish system.

For Part Four, Philip Woods offers a commentary on the Scottish Office Education Department ethos indicators project. He considers, in particular, the research tools used in the work that was carried out. Lesley Brooman investigates the management purposes in initiating and establishing links between a high school and a business park. She uses a variety of research tools including interviews, meeting observation and documentary analysis. Jeanne Coburn's research at a college in Leicester investigates whether the image the college gives to school-leavers is helping or hindering recruitment. She is very much an 'interested' researcher, being the head of the marketing faculty within the college.

Finally, in Part Five, three case studies look at strategic management in primary, secondary, and further education. Richards Weeks reflects on the way changes in education are leading senior managers in secondary schools towards more market-oriented strategic planning. As a deputy headteacher, he wanted to investigate how his school took parents' views into account. Eric Meadow's case study of a primary school explores the implications of more parental choice for the school. He looks at the many and varied issues that were debated as the school struggled to maintain its numbers in the face of keen local competition. In the incorporated further education sector, Terry Cowham focuses on the development requirements of Supertec College.

SUMMARY

This book, then, represents examples of the kind of investigations which you might be able to carry out, and demonstrates that it is not an impossible task. If you are able to examine practice in a structured way, improvements in that practice can be made on the basis of sound evidence. None of our authors would suggest that the process is an easy one, but the richness of life in schools and colleges today means that there is no lack of subjects for investigation!

This book will give you some insights into the practice of educational management as it is carried out in schools and colleges all over Britain. But as well as describing the breadth of practice in various educational institutions, the authors seek to understand and reflect on what is happening. Each study is unique, but reading the examples of educational management in action in this book should help you see some of the possibilities that exist for you within your own place of work.

REFERENCE

Osterman, K. and Kottkamp, R. (1993) *Reflective practice for educators*. Corwin Press.

PART ONE

*Managing the
Pupil/Student Experience*

CHAPTER 1

Curriculum Change in French

SUE RICHARDS

ABSTRACT

This project documents the implementation of the National Curriculum requirements for French in an inner-city comprehensive school. As head of faculty, with
responsibility for the languages curriculum, I initiated the change. I acted largely
as an internal consultant, mediating and interpreting between different team
members without having an overt casting vote or using executive authority. It is
proposed that the relevant curriculum change model is a dynamic one given the
constant changes in education at the present time.

INTRODUCTION

Consultants are defined by Cockman *et al.* (1992) as 'People who find themselves
having to influence other people, or advise them about possible courses of action
to improve the effectiveness of any aspect of their operations, without any formal
authority over them or choosing not to use what authority they have' (p. 3).
Internal consultants are there not by invitation but because they are imposed by
circumstances or higher authority. In such circumstances it is important to define
both the identity of the clients and their needs. As an internal consultant I
deliberately tried to create a self-sufficient team rather than exercising my position
as head of faculty to impose innovation. Such imposition has been shown in the
past to be ineffective (Fullan, 1989; Buswell, 1988; Becher, 1989).

Bennis *et al.* (1985) present three strategy models for effective change. They
define these as empirical–rational, normative–re-educative and power-coercive. In
my project the approach was normative–re-educative, involving a new attitude to
power and change within the basic faculty unit. Whilst a power-coercive strategy
would have been simplest given the demands placed upon the department,
research literature (Fullan, 1989; Rudduck, 1989; Johnston, 1989) suggests
successful change depends on teacher involvement. Also teachers are remarkably
resistant to change in classroom practice when it is imposed from above. Buswell
(1988) shows how an attempt by a new headteacher to introduce a new curriculum

had little concrete effect on some staff who continued to teach as they had before. She defines three responses to imposed change or 'deskilling'. These are: acquiescence, which means that the new scheme fits the teacher's needs; ambivalence, where new materials are seen as good but teachers remain to be convinced of their effectiveness; and modification and resistance, where the requirements of the scheme are loosely fulfilled but the manner of implementing them is modified.

Ownership of and commitment to change has been shown to be the key to successful implementation (Alexander, 1986). Where change is demanded of people and they see no benefit to themselves their response will be at best half-hearted. Becher (1989) refers to the 'implementation gap' in introducing the National Curriculum in schools. His work illustrates the apparent adoption by teachers of innovations which fail because of passive resistance or lack of commitment by the individual teacher. An additional barrier to the implementation of change in education is the time factor. Innovation has to dovetail with teaching demands and be seen to be advantageous rather than overburdening (Fullan, 1989).

Becher and Kogan (1992) offer a model for change in educational institutions which takes account of various levels of organization and different modes of activity. The normative mode relates to the monitoring and maintenance of values and the operational mode relates to what people actually do or are required to do. Each mode has an internal and external aspect. The internal factors are those integral to education itself and the external are those factors which impinge from outside the system.

In my project the stimulus for change was the obligation to incorporate National Curriculum requirements into our foreign language teaching. This provided the impetus for a thoroughgoing review of our practice. To this extent the Department for Education (DFE) rather than the local education authority (LEA) may be seen as the central authority. The basic unit is represented by the faculty made up of eight individual teachers. Curriculum innovation needed to take account of the external aspects of professional standards, the norms and values of the society in which the changes were set as well as internal aspects at all levels, but principally at individual and faculty level. Teachers held a dual role as members of the faculty unit and as individual professionals with their own careers and personal needs. In order for innovation to succeed it was important for both these roles to be considered. The faculty had also to satisfy its own subject specialist needs and operate within the constraints of the existing school curriculum. Thus at the normative level there is interaction between all external modes while that between cells 5 and 6 is the most important. In the operational modes, the key interactions are between cells 9, 10, 13 and 14 (see Figure 1.1).

The aim of the changes in planning the curriculum was to harmonize the contradictions between these modes and aspects. The changes could only succeed in the long term if there was a high degree of congruence between normative and operational modes.

The faculty was fairly well regarded in terms of examination results and

Becher and Kogan		Individual	Basic unit	Institution	Central authority
Project		Teacher	Faculty	School	D of E
Normative	External	I	2	3	4
	Internal	*5	*6	7	8
Operational	External	*9	*10	11	12
	Internal	*13	*14	15	16

FIGURE I.I The elements of the Becher and Kogan model (adapted for this project). The numbers identify the cells. Interactions between these cells (*) are identified as important for this project. The term 'basic unit' is employed to cover the wide range of subgroupings of a school, college or university to which the individual might relate.

practice within the school by local colleges of education and by the community. However, faculty members had been working from a loose scheme of work which only required that a certain number of topics were covered within a given year. The manner in which they were taught and teaching styles were up to the individual teacher. I used the opportunity afforded by the National Curriculum to attempt to evolve a cohesive faculty teaching strategy which would survive even if individual faculty members changed. Beyond requiring assurance that the National Curriculum requirements were being fulfilled there was no input either at whole-school or at borough level. The languages adviser and inspector for the borough left the service immediately before my project started and were therefore not involved in it.

NEEDS ANALYSIS

I decided, given the research data already mentioned, and after consultation with the two deputy heads of languages to involve all teachers of French in Year 7 in the management of the changes required for the National Curriculum. This meant over half of the faculty would be involved. To overcome the restraints of time for planning, preliminary work on National Curriculum requirements was done by a small group of three. The style of all three members of the group differed. One was an 'administrator manager' with an interest in flexible learning programmes while another favoured a heavily structured approach incorporating systematic testing. The third was an enthusiastic classroom teacher for whom communication was the priority.

They thought their different styles would reflect the diversity to be found in most departments. In addition to time spent in individual research, four half-day sessions were spent in negotiating and mapping out an approach to the curriculum change. The rest of the faculty were as varied in personality and approach as the three and a structure needed to be found which would enable individual teaching styles to survive within a much tighter agreed framework than before. A curriculum change model (Figure 1.2) which loosely followed that of the Further Education Unit (FEU) (1989) was adopted.

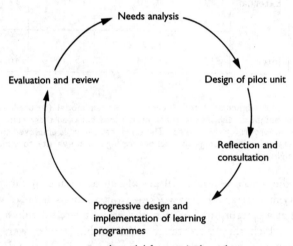

FIGURE 1.2   A model for curriculum change.

In order to facilitate effective change it has been suggested that a clear view of needs should be ascertained before any work is done on implementation. The needs analysis was in part done for us, in that we had set requirements which had to be met. On to these we had to graft a planning structure for our scheme of work which would enable the requirements to be set out clearly and allow space for future development. Having done this, the design of a pilot unit allows for reflection and for modifications to be made to the original scheme before the full programme is designed. In this case it enabled the staff involved to present their proposals to the wider group of teachers and obtain further feedback. Any innovation then needs evaluation and review before it becomes accepted practice. Here the evaluation took place at the end of the first year of implementation and a review is ongoing, in the second year, as a different team works with the materials.

At the end of this first period staff had also been canvassed concerning their expectations and fears about the National Curriculum. A first topic area (personal identification) with a subtopic (classroom language) had been identified. The canvassing was done on a formal level at regular faculty meetings where National Curriculum documents were studied, and at an informal level where I was acting as internal consultant. An acceptant mode of consultancy was used with openings such as 'How do you feel about teaching the National Curriculum next year?' with subjective data being gathered in this way. It became clear that staff had few fears about the language content of the curriculum but were feeling overwhelmed by the apparent multiplicity and confusions of programmes of study statements, levels of attainment and the lack of advice on assessment and recording. They all without exception welcomed the idea of a collective approach where we would not only lessen the workload by joint preparation of materials but would also bear a collective responsibility for the curriculum. Regular input from Post Graduate Certificate of Education (PGCE) students had meant that staff were aware of the most recent trends in language teaching and had adopted a number of new strategies. This did not lessen anxiety about the increased workload which the National Curriculum might bring, nor did it lessen a feeling of unease that, working without guidance as we were, we might have misunderstood some aspect of it. It was stressed at these preliminary discussions that a collaborative approach to planning and teaching would at least ease, if not greatly lessen, the total workload, whilst enquiries of other schools indicated that we were not alone in our fears. Individual discussion with staff and clarifying of worries as well as encouragement to value their competencies was a vital part of the internal consultancy at this stage. Becher and Kogan (1992) suggest that coercive change is inherently unstable if it conflicts with internal norms and will not translate from normative to operational. Manipulative change depends on offering an incentive for compliance. In this case there was no material reward on offer beyond the possibility of a lightened preparation load through teamwork and a feeling of empowerment and participation in the curriculum change. Normative change depends upon time for a period of adjustment and this was not available in this case. In order to make the changes palatable and operational each individual and the faculty as a whole had to be convinced of their practicability.

DESIGN OF THE PILOT UNIT

The first steps of the group of three involved thorough reading of the National Curriculum, a one-day course for one of the deputies and a re-evaluation of our existing French course (Tricolore). The whole faculty had already agreed before the exercise began that this course was outmoded and should be replaced if possible when the National Curriculum was implemented. This feeling was confirmed in the canvassing exercise. Faculty meetings discussing the perceived requirements for the course stressed use of the target language and a more stimulating and creative approach.

The three postholders researched materials and came up with a draft scheme for the first unit with suggestions for a basic course book. After various models and several trials of documenting schemes of work, an outline planning sheet was agreed which seemed to cover the set requirements and to be coherent as a guide to the teaching scheme. Classroom language was presented as a priority unit, so that target language use in lessons might be effective, but this was felt to be too dry to be presented on its own, so the personal identification material was introduced in parallel.

As this point the scheme was presented to the rest of the faculty and discussed. Amendments were suggested, the final course text chosen and the amendments implemented where agreement was reached. From the outset, consensus or at least a majority view was accepted as the basis for change or adoption. Whilst friction obviously occurred and would recur, the emphasis throughout was on developing a scheme of work which would endure for a number of years. Although the faculty had shared worksheets successfully in the past, the change meant the use of an agreed core of materials and a set corpus of vocabulary and grammar. Beyond this the individual teacher had some freedom in what else was introduced within the agreed time limits set for each topic. Target activities which were to be used as a basis for assessment were also agreed. Very little mediation was needed at this stage, since staff still felt that they had retained a certain amount of autonomy. They all tried to be positive even in rejection and modification.

This framework and the need for consensus or near consensus meant that although as head of faculty I had initiated the change process, my role thereafter was one of consultant and facilitator. As one individual in a developing and changing department I did not have a casting vote or overall control of the process. The contribution that I could make was that of an experienced teacher in the team, but all suggestions or mediations were subject to the decisions of the remaining members of the faculty.

Staff were aware that there was not enough information available nor enough time to plan an entire year's work in advance. We decided to develop one or two units at a time and to aim to complete six in the first year, following roughly the same topic areas as had been used in previous courses. It proved necessary to amend this programme in the first year of operation to include only five topics.

PROGRESSIVE DESIGN AND IMPLEMENTATION

As soon as the Year 7 team was known for the next year, further meetings were held and detailed planning took place. Staff were keen to participate in planning and decision-making. Initially meetings took place at weekly intervals, a proposal suggested by myself as internal consultant and agreed by the team, so that no great amount of work and effort was rejected or modified. Staff were concerned to co-operate for their own benefit as much as for the others and at no stage in this period did discussion become acrimonious. As internal consultant I acted as a sounding-board for ideas between meetings using acceptant or catalytic modes of consultation as appropriate. I encouraged rethinking or modifications before it came to whole-group presentations, while the first deputy in the faculty provided technical expertise on information technology (IT) and assessment issues. The first unit was in place ready for the beginning of the autumn term and the group kept about half a term ahead all the way through the year. By the summer term the work for the first term of Year 8 had been planned. Regular review and planning meetings were held, at which problems in implementation or timing were highlighted. At first the team had to resist a desire to 'cover' a topic or area of experience thoroughly, forgetting the level of the pupils and the possibilities in the National Curriculum for 'revisiting' topics. As the year progressed a house style for presentation had evolved, but the subsequent review of materials shows that, under pressure of work, all of us deviated from it at some point.

Assessment was a major area of difficulty as little or no guidance had been received. Materials introduced at a training day attended by all the faculty proved invaluable here. Modes of assessment were piloted and a range of assessment tasks were established. The mode of consultancy I adopted was mostly acceptant. I listened to staff worries and helped them to formulate ideas about the kind of assessment tasks they themselves wanted.

EVALUATION AND REVIEW

A basic disagreement was about the nature of assessment and testing. One member of the faculty sees assessment, particularly of speaking, as a testing situation and cannot be persuaded otherwise. The rest of the faculty agreed that assessment of speaking can take place by listening in in classroom situations. After lengthy discussion we decided that as long as the required assessment was done, the manner in which it was carried out could be left to the individual teacher. The alternative would have been a directive which might well have been ignored in the individual classroom situation anyway. Throughout, the group recognized individual personalities and teaching styles so that the scheme remained flexible. The fact that each individual teacher was contributing to the modules facilitated this. Assessment still remains the main area of uncertainty, but by the end of the summer term we had all developed one or two assessment tasks that had been approved by the group. By the end of the first year a substantial scheme of work and assessment had been devised.

We now had to consider the extension into Year 8. Throughout the year, other staff in the faculty had been kept informed of progress. In the summer term the remaining faculty staff were drawn in and two teams evolved, one refining and modifying the Year 7 scheme whilst the other piloted Year 8. Timetabling was planned so that the remaining members of the faculty were brought into Year 7 teaching. We were able to convert the vacant allowance post into a job-share post. From this a co-ordinator for Year 7 and one for Year 8 were appointed. Their task was to manage the paperwork created by the two teaching teams and to ensure that modules were planned ahead. They were to manage rather than lead the teams. This meant that my deputy and I were able to step back and function as team members rather than change agents or internal consultants.

At the end of the year, a full faculty meeting reviewed progress. We felt that the scheme of work could be streamlined and modified to make it more effective. The new Year 7 team took on the task of progressively reviewing the scheme and devising further assessment tasks, particularly for the early modules. They now meet regularly three or four times a term and have only needed to refer to me once as head of faculty to arbitrate a dispute about an overambitious assessment task. This was negotiated and a compromise reached by splitting the task into two. The Year 8 team, who were for the most part progressing from Year 7, continued as a group in the same pattern as before.

EMBEDDING THE CHANGE INTO NORMAL PRACTICE

Part way into the second year of the process, the Year 7 team is functioning effectively and recourse to the internal consultant is rare. The Year 8 team is beginning to take for granted the planning and implementation and there are signs that some mediation is necessary. Teachers are starting to feel that they are losing track of their goals for the topics. I see my role as internal consultant continuing within this group to mediate in the changing situations which occur. My job here is to monitor the situation and ensure that the collaboration is encouraged to continue.

The power-coercive method of change would probably have led to a ready-made course with assessments. This has been done by a number of other local schools. We feel, however, that the teamwork and participation involved in the change structure we adopted have led to a course which suits both National Curriculum requirements and our situation. It has also led to greater collaboration in other areas of language teaching. Two teachers of Italian have developed a scheme of work for Italian similar to the Year 7 scheme for French. In the German department staff are spontaneously devising assessment tasks and new materials to share. There is much more openness and sharing of materials between staff teaching the same year group. Staff teaching Year 10 French have now expressed dissatisfaction with the organization of their course and are proposing a major reorganization of their scheme of work. Pupils too have enjoyed a more creative and varied curriculum than when one teacher alone provided their stimulus.

CHANGE AND THE INTERNAL CONSULTANT

Apart from periodic difficulties with developing assessment strategies and over-enthusiastic attempts to include the whole GCSE syllabus in Year 7, this change process appears to be running successfully. It was, however, initially dependent on a group of committed staff who remained in post over the period. Once the scheme of work becomes the status quo and staff move on ways need to be found to maintain an interactive dynamic. This will be tested when the deputy head of faculty leaves and a temporary replacement takes over some classes.

Management by internal consultancy is time consuming and changes what is demanded of a head of faculty. The external functions of budget responsibility and reporting back to school management remain the same, but more time must be spent listening to staff and less directing their activities. A major requirement, however, is that staff are willing to work together and can see the benefits of teamwork. Co-operation has been helped in this case by the level ground from which we all started to implement the changes to our curriculum. Had one of the staff involved possessed specialized knowledge, it might have been much more difficult. One of the job specifications for our new vacancy is the willingness and interest in working collaboratively with other teachers. This has now become a fundamental requirement of the faculty.

The need to move curriculum innovation up the school is giving this development momentum. The danger is that incomplete changes will become the status quo and then be neglected and discredited. As circumstances change constant review will be necessary so that ownership remains with all staff. Becher and Kogan (1992) refer to change as an organic process and implementation of change as evolution. The transition from normative to operational mode necessitates constant adjustment between plan and implementation and the maintenance of a dynamic equilibrium. Pressman and Wildavsky (1973) maintain that

> many, perhaps most, constraints remain hidden in the planning stage, and are only discovered in the implementation process. . . . The solution space undergoes continuous transformations, shrinking in one direction, expanding in another. Consequently, the implementer's left hand must be probing constantly the feasibility boundary, while his right hand tries to assemble the various program components.
>
> (PRESSMAN and WILDAVSKY, *1973, p. 180*)

This curriculum change model is a dynamic one, undergoing constant review as it is implemented and affected by the interaction of the various modes and levels involved. The role of the internal consultant here is to monitor and advise rather than to instruct and coerce. Fullan (1989) suggests that successful change becomes embedded in regular practice and institutionalized but whilst this might be true of features like target language use and the format adopted for schemes of work, the constant revisions of requirements by central government are liable to leave the implementation as a dynamic one for the time being. Whilst, as an internal consultant, a certain amount of disengagement has been possible, there still remains the possibility of having to be called in again to advise on new changes and modifications.

REFERENCES

Alexander, L. D. (1986) Successfully implementing strategic decisions, in B. Mayon-White (Ed.) *Planning and managing change*. London: Paul Chapman.

Becher, T. (1989) The National Curriculum and the implementation gap, in M. Preedy (Ed.) *Approaches to curriculum management*. Milton Keynes: Open University Press.

Becher, T. and Kogan, M. (1992) *Process and structure in higher education*. London: Routledge.

Bennis, W. G., Benne, K. D. and Chin, R. (1985) *The planning of change*. New York: Holt Rinehart Winston.

Buswell, C. (1988) Pedagogic change and social change, in J. Ozga (Ed.) *Schoolwork. Approaches to the labour process of teaching*. Milton Keynes: Open University Press.

Cockman, P., Evans, B. and Reynolds, P. (1992) *Client-centred consulting: a practical guide for internal advisers and trainers*. Maidenhead: McGraw-Hill.

Fullan, M. (1989) Managing curriculum change, in M. Preedy (Ed.) *Approaches to curriculum development*. Milton Keynes: Open University Press.

Further Education Unit (1989) Towards a framework for curriculum entitlement, in M. Preedy (Ed.) *Approaches to curriculum management*. Milton Keynes: Open University Press.

Johnston, S. (1989) Towards an understanding of the values issue in curriculum decision making, in B. Moon, P. Murphy and J. Raynor (Eds) *Policies for the curriculum*. London: Hodder & Stoughton.

Pressman, J. and Wildavsky, A. (1973) *Implementation*. Berkeley: University of California Press.

Rudduck, J. (1989) Curriculum change: management or meaning, in B. Moon, P. Murphy and J. Raynor (Eds) *Policies for the curriculum*. London: Hodder & Stoughton.

CHAPTER 2

Evaluating History at Key Stage 1

SUE GODSMARK

ABSTRACT

This project investigates the management of the implementation of National
Curriculum history at Key Stage 1 in a primary school. It uses documentary and
interview evidence. The report concludes that little evidence of classical rational
planning was found prior to implementation and that pressure to implement other
subjects, the failure to provide sufficient information concerning the National
Curriculum and a lack of trust in traditional planning models were influential
factors. Some evidence was, however, found of more flexible planning strategies.
The report makes short-term curriculum recommendations concerning history
and long-term recommendations about flexibility and efficiency in the planning
process.

INTRODUCTION

My project involves an investigation into the management of the implementation
of history as a National Curriculum subject. The implementation of such
externally mandated curriculum change represents a new form of curriculum
management for schools in which the classic model of identifying needs,
negotiating and constructing solutions and, finally, implementing change appears
less than adequate. I looked at one particular implementation attempt in the light
of more general models of implementation and planning as they apply to such
change.

The statutory introduction of National Curriculum history can be precisely
documented. The Education (National Curriculum) (Attainment Targets and
Programmes of Study in History) (England) Order 1991 came into force for Key
Stage 1 (KS1) on 1 August 1991. The voluntary standard assessment task (SAT)
packs, which were intended to give guidance to teachers in the formation of their
teacher assessment, arrived in schools in the spring term of 1993 so adding to the
definition and interpretation of the attainment targets. Therefore the last months
of the academic year 1993 saw the completion of the formal introduction of

National Curriculum history at KS1. In this project I use 'introduction' to denote the establishment of the National Curriculum's compulsory framework and 'implementation' to denote the establishment of that framework as part of a working curriculum policy within the school.

The implementation process took place against a background of compulsory change in other areas of curriculum, financial and organizational restructuring. In 1991 the implementation of English, science and mathematics was barely complete and, in addition, science and mathematics had just been extensively revised in terms of attainment targets. National Curriculum geography was also being introduced. An additional and important factor was the movement from historic to per capita funding under local management of schools (LMS) which added significantly to the problems of financial management and to the general pressures felt by schools.

At the time of writing, I was responsible for a six-class KS1 unit (five- to seven-year-olds) within a 12-class primary school. In the early months of 1992 staff who were waiting for the arrival of the voluntary SATs expressed reservations about the progress of the implementation of the National Curriculum in history at KS1. They were concerned that an externally constructed measure might reveal inadequacies in our curriculum provision. They associated this with what they perceived as the low priority given to its implementation in contrast to the core subjects which had a higher level of preparation and planning. It therefore seemed profitable to examine the management of the process of implementation in order firstly to improve the delivery of the history curriculum and secondly, and of perhaps greater long-term importance, to review implementation as a management process so that we could prepare for future changes and modifications. My project then addressed the following questions about the management of the implementation process:

1. What processes were involved in the implementation of one particular example of externally mandated change?
2. How were the processes understood and interpreted by the participants?
3. Are there any implications for planning such implementation procedures in the future?

LITERATURE

Many writers who review the effects of a centrally determined curriculum (Marsh, 1992; Simons, 1988) suggest that there is no scope for teacher initiative or involvement in planning. Teachers become mere technicians. Several writers then consider whether there are any legitimate or useful management decisions to be made in the field of National Curriculum implementation. Simons (1988) concluded that teachers were destined to become merely the implementers of the curriculum.

Others, however, maintain that there is still a professional role to be managed.

Kirk (1991) claimed that the National Curriculum framework was not logically incompatible with pupil-centred learning and the professional autonomy of teachers. Fowler (1990) claimed that the Education Reform Act (1988) excluded any references to such factors as time allocations, teaching methods and internal school organization and so gave considerable freedom to the management of implementation. Simons points out that the government cannot maintain a state monopoly without the active collaboration of professional educators, and Becher (1989) quotes Pressman and Wildavsky's (1973) work on the implementation gap between policy as formulated and policy as practised. Without an active management strategy that fosters such collaboration there will always be a gap between public expressions of policy and the day-to-day educational practice of individuals. If there are decisions to be made then management of implementation remains a practical necessity.

Marsh suggests the implementation task is to find out how to use the new curriculum. This can be described as taking ownership. Marsh notes the common problems of overload associated with taking such ownership:

- too little time for teachers to learn new skills and practices;
- too many competing demands;
- failure to take into account the site-specific differences among schools.

He also notes various styles of leadership and considers their influence upon change:

- The Responder makes decisions in response to immediate issues.
- The Manager does not typically initiate change but will support it if given a high priority by others.
- The Initiator will seize the lead and make things happen.

Different models are offered by other writers but many consider the National Curriculum to play a part in decreasing the 'leading professional' role of heads so turning 'Initiators' into 'Managers' and 'Responders'.

In terms of implementation management, writers give whole-school planning a high priority. Day *et al.* (1990) point out that it is vitally important for the staff to create agreement about the purposes of the school. They maintain that the need to produce National Curriculum development plans, in the light of such an agreement, has firmly established planning as a key process in the educational management of schools. Campbell and Southworth (1990) note that the National Curriculum places a heavy burden of curriculum implementation on primary schools and points towards a collegial approach to management. They associate collegiality or 'the culture of collaboration' with a high degree of shared purpose and a sense of collective responsibility for work. They also note that research studies associate it with school effectiveness and successful implementation of change. The HMI Report *The implementation of the National Curriculum in primary schools* (1990) recorded that the introduction of the National Curriculum was having a positive influence on curriculum planning especially in the core subjects.

All this implies a classical, highly rationalistic planning model such as that outlined by Wallace (1992). It consists of sequential steps. These are: establishing agreement upon fundamental values; clarifying goals; identifying a range of possible strategies to achieve them; analysing all relevant factors; predicting the outcome of each strategy; and finally making the best possible decision. It is assumed that all goals are clear and consistent and all factors known.

Fullan (1992) and Wallace (1992) both point out problems associated with relying upon this model. Wallace claims that such models work less well in today's more turbulent and unpredictable educational climate. Many schools, he claims, face massive planning tasks because of the sheer scale of national innovation. In addition, the uncertainty caused by changes to the form, scope and timing of particular innovations compounds the problems.

Becher and Kogan (1980) maintain that even in normal circumstances implementation is necessarily a local task and must attend to local idiosyncrasies. Wallace claims that most decision-making is more pragmatically concerned with finding a satisfactory alternative which will improve the current state of affairs. Negotiation and consensus building then form an essential part of the normal pattern. In addition Fullan claims that the fit between any new initiative and the needs of a school must be established but it may not be clearly defined until implementation is under way. Louis and Miles (1990) maintain that successful schools adapt their plans incrementally so improving the eventual fit between the change and the conditions in the school.

Wallace noted that either strategic planning or experimental activity might come first. Planning to build coherence might follow from action to implement innovations. He went on to outline a flexible planning model which he considers to be a dialectical process. Extensive planning exercises specifying action well into the future may be interspersed with rapid informal planning activities in response to unanticipated events.

From the above review I concluded that empirical evidence might be sought in respect of the following questions:

1. How were attempts to plan implementation perceived by the participants and can these perceptions be understood in terms of the classical – rational model that Wallace reviews or his flexible planning model?
2. Is there any evidence of the type of difficulties that mitigate against rational planning models?
3. Is there any evidence of Wallace's 'flexible planning' model?

METHODS

This investigation relates to the experiences of one small school. It may not be applicable to other situations and in fact may be bound up with the idiosyncrasies and limitations of this one institution. However, as Becher and Kogan (1980) point out, implementation is a local task and local idiosyncrasies and limitations are what schools have in common. I collected evidence in a number of ways.

Firstly, I looked for documentary evidence of decision-making at the beginning of the two-year period or of those decisions being put into practice. I considered the minutes of staff meetings, long-term planning or policy statements, and topic and general teaching plans for the autumn and spring terms.

The quantity of written evidence was very small but it seemed essential to search. One of the dangers of investigating a familiar institution is to assume that you know what evidence exists and to fail to make the inquiries that would have been made by an outside researcher. The written evidence or lack of it also provided areas for comment for the interviewees.

The principal form of evidence for this study consisted of interviews with the participants. I was given the opportunity to explain the purpose of the interview at a staff meeting and everyone who was subsequently approached agreed to be interviewed. Individual confidentiality was promised to staff and it was agreed that the school would not be named. In addition the head would be named only in terms of post and the staff would be identified by pseudonyms. I interviewed the head, the four members of staff currently teaching at KS1 and two who were involved with the early implementation process but who were then currently teaching at Key Stage 2. The interviews were semi-structured and all interviewees were given the opportunity to comment on all of the questions. The interviews varied in length because some interviewees were involved in a greater number of issues and at greater depth. The average length was 45 minutes. Although the number of interviews was small it was comprehensive in that it was possible to speak to every member of staff who had been involved in teaching history at KS1 for the whole of the two-year period.

I chose semi-structured interviews because:

- It was possible to interview all the participants involved in the implementation process. A questionnaire would not have had the advantage of reaching more people and it would have resulted in loss of information.
- The interviewees were asked to engage in a considerable feat of memory. The standard answer to questions such as 'Can you remember what initial decisions were made?' was 'no', but when prompted with supplementary questions many could then recall independently other circumstances that had been forgotten initially.
- In addition it was not an issue at the forefront of people's minds. Respondents were in some cases formulating opinions not merely reporting them. The opportunity to probe for meaning and to reflect back impressions of what had been said was extremely valuable and it would have been lost if a questionnaire had been used.
- Facial expression and tone of voice were also part of the response pattern. In an interview situation it was possible to follow up and explore any such impressions and particularly to test any indication of the strength of opinions.

- The interview structure also allowed me to cross-check memories of factual detail and impressions and perceptions of events that took place over a considerable period of time. Recollections did, in fact, show a high degree of agreement and consistency.

ANALYSIS

An analysis of the documentary evidence revealed little specific structured decision-making prior to implementing the National Curriculum in history. The period in question predated the regular minuting of staff meetings and so those records were not available. However, staff interviewed remembered the implementation of history being discussed at a staff meeting.

Some documents did, however, suggest a tradition of classical rational planning. There was a policy document relating to history although this was in place before the National Curriculum and threw no light on the implementation process. Two long-term planning documents were drawn up by KS1 and KS2 staff in the months preceding the implementation of history. These set out those areas of the National Curriculum, including history, to be covered in each term. The topic and general teaching plans for autumn and spring were obviously constructed from the two-year planning cycle and both contained historical elements. Staff commented upon the drawing up of the document and their interpretation of it in the interviews.

Decisions are, however, sometimes made without a written record being kept. Interview evidence might have revealed this but responses ranged from a very frank, 'We must have done something but I can't remember what' to what appears to be a fairly accurate recollection by the head: 'I know that we talked it through. It was the time when both departments were producing a two-year cycle of topics and most people at KS1 seemed to feel that history would fit in.'

If few decisions were made it becomes important not only to ask why but how the participants interpreted the situation and finally whether 'doing very little' was a management strategy in itself. No member of staff had any significant suggestions for decisions or strategies that should have been adopted and those which I suggested as possibilities were mostly rejected. The making of a detailed whole-school plan, arranging a staff training exercise to investigate our current teaching methods, and extending our resources were all rejected by a majority of staff. The reason given was similar in many cases.

A common reason given was that although 'it' might have been a good idea there was insufficient time. This was particularly related to the pressure to implement other subjects. This supports Marsh's view of the problems of implementation and Wallace's account of curriculum overload. As the head said, 'There was so much pressure to do everything at once, as soon as you'd got the core subjects you got history and geography and now PE, art and music. These things were coming so thick and fast.'

Two teachers were keen to point out that it wasn't a criticism of the concept of a

National Curriculum: 'It's a brilliant idea as far as I'm concerned but I would have liked a three- or five-year gap between the core subjects and history and geography – to get them running properly.' This was a reflection perhaps of Kirk's more optimistic view.

Most teachers thought that history had a low priority at KS1 and three of them would not have taught history at the depth required by the National Curriculum by choice. Most were interested in teaching history and said that its low priority was due to the pressure to teach other subjects. This suggested at least an informal prioritization in the face of problems of implementation and overload (Marsh, 1992; Wallace, 1992).

Most respondents noted that there was insufficient information in the National Curriculum documents on which to base plans and decisions. Wallace again noted lack of information as a limitation upon classical/rational planning. All inter-viewees said that the documents contained sufficient information to enable minimum compliance with the law but that the programmes of study and attainment targets gave no indication of the depth required at each level. These were provided by the voluntary SATs packs but they were only available to schools at the end of the implementation period. Most people commented that if it is possible to determine the depth required now then it was possible two years ago which is when the packs should have been available: 'We didn't know two years ago – knowing the content area isn't the same as knowing how much detail or depth is required.' It might be argued that determining depth was irrelevant but, as the head pointed out, the correct balance between depth and breadth is necessary to fulfil the programme of study in the time available.

Without an indication of that point of balance most respondents rejected the suggestion that a critical examination of our teaching methods would have been a useful strategy. Most teachers claimed to have accepted the usefulness of an integrated topic approach two years ago in a fairly unquestioning way: 'I don't think we questioned it.' In general the requirements of National Curriculum history teaching were seen to be an unknown quantity two years ago and therefore an appropriate teaching method would have been difficult to determine. The two-year implementation period was seen by several teachers as one of experimenta-tion and learning: 'We've had to learn about the suitability of our teaching method as we went along – that some of our methods don't work well in National Curriculum terms and will have to change.'

Fullan (1992) claims that educational change is a learning experience and Wallace (1992) states: 'That strategic planning or experimental activity may precede each other.'

There was some evidence that a reliance upon policies was replaced by a reliance upon people. Commenting upon the continued acceptance of the topic approach it was suggested that staff could be trusted to cover the National Curriculum requirements: 'We're all professional' and 'Our topics were planned very carefully. We've always done it that way.' All staff mentioned the tradition of termly KS1 planning sessions where short-term plans were made for the coming term. Such co-operative planning may in fact have helped to define the delivery and purpose of the National Curriculum. Fullan claims that 'Implementation makes further policy; it does not simply put predefined policy into practice.'

Some staff would have liked to have seen closer monitoring of the usefulness of the teaching that was being carried out: 'Yes, I don't mean someone looking over your shoulder all the time but just for us – to see where we were going.' Others felt that the KS1 co-operative planning and review meetings had been a form of monitoring and support during the process of implementation. They reflected that during those meetings, and less formally over coffee, they had shared experiences and given and accepted advice in a way that constituted a very effective monitoring process and which helped to establish an informal common policy. 'We were working on a trial and error basis, planning and reviewing our work helped a lot.'

In contrast to Day *et al.* (1990) and the HMI Report (1990), where whole-school planning was advocated, there was a unanimous lack of faith in the formal planning process as an automatic answer to the problems of implementation. This may have been influenced by the problems of 'overload' exacerbated by lack of time and information outlined by Wallace (1992). At its mildest, opinion was represented by the comment 'You need to have a good insight into the subject first, then you can look at a policy' and the most forceful was a long statement by the head:

> I think we've learned from past experience – we've spent a long time producing our own documents reflecting the National Curriculum and then it's been changed – people are now more careful – it's no use planning in detail unless things are going to be there in two or five years' time – plans must be worth the time expended on them. You must have minimum plans but the rest is experimentation and learning.

If the minimum plans are the framework of the National Curriculum and the aims outlined in the history policy document, then the head is reflecting Fullan's message, 'Have a plan but learn by doing.'

Models of effective leadership are generally associated with a belief in formal planning. In terms of Marsh's leadership styles the head would no doubt claim that Initiators and Managers seem constrained by circumstances to be Responders. However, Wallace's 'flexible' planning model seems to imply a legitimate need for the use of all three of Marsh's styles. There is some evidence that refraining from formal planning may have been a management strategy from the head's point of view: 'If people had been told at the beginning that they had to change the way they teach they wouldn't have understood that decision. They had to learn that some of their methods didn't work in National Curriculum terms.' Whether this represents a contemporary attitude or a retrospective justification is difficult to say. However, no member of staff attributed such a motive to the head.

The degree to which all the participants saw the management of the curriculum in collegial terms surprised me. Not only did the head and staff voice similar opinions, but whenever a failure of the system was discussed responsibility was always shared in terms of 'we'. No teacher at any point blamed the head for the fact that decisions were not taken: 'It was our responsibility if they [the decisions] weren't taken.' No member of staff recalled any difference of opinion about what should have been done. Perhaps Day *et al.*'s 'agreement about purposes' and a measure of Campbell and Southworth's 'culture of collaboration', which implies both a high degree of shared purpose and a sense of collective responsibility for work, allowed co-operative planning and review meetings to become flexible planning structures that formed implementation policy. The staff, however, still saw 'planning' as the construction of formal planning documents and noted their absence. No one suggested that effective if informal policy formation might have been in progress throughout the implementation period.

What were the effects of such limited pre-implementation planning? The teacher of Year 2 children points out that the teacher assessment is producing satisfactory levels of attainment measured by the voluntary SATs. All the staff interviewed and the head are convinced the school is meeting its legal requirement and our most recent member of staff claims to understand how history is planned and taught at KS1. Another effect may be some almost unanimous opinions held by the staff. They felt that now was the time to write a whole-school policy so as to 'consolidate and make good use of experience' and now is the time for a staff training exercise 'now that we know what the problems are'. It is also the time to review resources because 'we have the experience to know what to buy'.

There was certainly evidence that opinion had changed in response to the implementation process. A greater range of teaching methods were being applied more flexibly: 'I'd go for mini-topic, history days, fixed lessons, anything that worked – a mixed approach – but I wouldn't expect to cover it all in one topic.' Some staff felt that the National Curriculum would ensure continuity and progression but others felt that it was in our hands and now was the time to plan for it: 'It's a bit hit and miss at the moment but it will be better next year when we know where we are going.'

CONCLUSIONS

- There was little evidence of overt planning for the implementation of National Curriculum history in a classical rational sense but there was considerable evidence of strategies developed from short-term planning mechanisms. A more flexible approach to planning was strongly defended by the staff who claimed that it promoted a period of experimentation and learning.
- The head saw this, in part, as a deliberate policy to allow staff the opportunity to come to terms with the need to change.
- Pressure to implement other subjects, insufficient knowledge provided concerning National Curriculum attainment targets, and trust in detailed curriculum planning were all factors which influenced the situation.
- A lack of detailed advanced curriculum planning seems to have had some beneficial effects in this instance. The staff appear to have both the experience and the will to construct more formal policy statements. However, the whole

process appears to have been heavily dependent on experienced classroom teachers with a tradition of co-operative working in a self-monitoring process.

RECOMMENDATIONS

- In the short term the staff should capitalize upon the situation. Staff have experience of teaching history and other subjects in a National Curriculum framework and are looking for effective and flexible ways to teach. Now would appear to be the time to formulate a whole-school policy.
- In a future implementation situation, especially if staff change, it would seem unwise to rely again upon such a minimalist approach to planning. The very minimum additional requirement would be a more formal monitoring system during the period of change to facilitate Wallace's dialectical process between 'specifying action well into the future and rapid informal planning activities'.
- In the longer term the school should review its whole approach and attitude to planning. Instead of investing many hours producing documents that are designed to remain fixed for a period of years, policies might come in modular form and reflect the different levels of planning and the balance between the need for change and stability. They might contain overall aims and objectives that will presumably change very little, teaching methods that will change more slowly and subject content that can change as National Curriculum documents change. Policy documents and plans might be kept on word-processing disc and small modifications added as appropriate.
- Most of the participants in this study including myself would have to recommend to the government that they leave longer time intervals between the introduction or change of subjects to encourage more effective implementation. This would, however, express our hope rather than our expectation.

POSTSCRIPT

I would like to acknowledge the time and help given by the head and staff of the subject primary school in answering the interview questions, and to thank Essex County Library staff who were not only anxious to help but endlessly efficient.

REFERENCES

Becher, T. (1989) The National Curriculum and the implementation gap, in M. Preedy (Ed.) *Approaches to curriculum management.* Milton Keynes: Open University.

Becher, T. and Kogan, M. (1980) *Process and structure in higher education.* Heinemann: London.

Campbell, R. J. and Southworth, G. (1990) Rethinking collegiality: teachers' views. Paper presented to the annual meeting of the American Research Association, Boston.

Day, C., Whitaker, D. and Johnston, D. (1990) *Managing primary schools in the 1990s.* London: Paul Chapman.

Fowler, W. S. (1990) *Implementing the National Curriculum*. London: Kogan Page.

Fullan, M. (1992) Causes/processes of implementation and continuation, in N. Bennett *et al.* (Ed.) *Managing change in education*. Milton Keynes/London: Open University/Paul Chapman.

HMI (Her Majesty's Inspectorate) (1990) *The implementation of the National Curriculum in primary Schools*. London: HMSO.

Goodlad, J. I. (1975) *The dynamics of educational change*. New York: McGraw-Hill.

Kirk, G. (1991) The growth of central influence in the curriculum, in R. Moore and J. Ozga (Eds) *Curriculum policy*. Oxford: Pergamon Press.

Louis, K. S. and Miles, M. B. (1990) *Improving the urban high school*. New York: Teachers College Press.

Marsh, C. V. (1992) *Key concepts for understanding the National Curriculum*. London: Falmer Press.

Pressman, J. and Wildavsky, A. (1973) *Implementation*. Berkeley: University of California Press.

Simons, H. (1988) Teacher professionalism and the National Curriculum, in D. Lawton and C. Chitty (Eds) *The National Curriculum*. London: Kogan Page.

Wallace, M. (1992) Flexible planning: a key to the management of multiple innovations in N. Bennett *et al.* (Eds) *Managing change in education*. Milton Keynes/London: Open University/Paul Chapman.

CHAPTER 3

Curriculum Development:
The Case of Gwent Tertiary College

GRAHAM ATTWELL

ABSTRACT

This chapter describes a major curriculum and staff development project currently being undertaken at Gwent Tertiary College in South Wales.

The project, to develop units and introduce a fully modularized curriculum across the college, is based on a theoretical framework published by the Further Education Unit in *A basis for credit*. The threefold aim is to enhance the participation of learners, the attainment of learners, and the quality of provision, through a credit framework based on defining and crediting learning outcomes. The project is funded by Gwent Training and Enterprise Council and has attained endorsement by the Welsh Office Education Department.

The chapter outlines the difficulties faced by an ambitious project of this nature and looks at the barriers to change within the further education sector. It suggests that it is vital that classroom staff are given ownership and control over curriculum reform and that curriculum development receives the active support of management at every level of the college. It concludes that curriculum and staff development activities need to be integrated and only through a full programme of curriculum support activity can staff be won to support radical change and innovation.

NOTE ON METHODS

In 1992 Gwent Tertiary College began an ambitious programme of curriculum reform, reorganizing the total college curriculum into a modular structure. As the project director, I explore the problems and achievements of the project after some 18 months.

It is essentially a descriptive case study (Yin, 1984) of a reflective and retrospective nature (Osterman and Kottkamp, 1993). It rests on my experience of having been 'inside' the innovation from the beginning, and having to prepare documents such as position papers, formal proposals, bids for external funding and proposals for the organization and administration of the scheme, which have generated a sound documentary base for the review. In addition, there are minutes of team meetings of the unit involved in promoting the innovation – the Training Shop – and my recollections of the informal contact between project members. As an active trainer and staff developer, I have also been in contact with the college staff involved in putting the innovation into practice.

However, there are a number of limitations. In particular, it was not possible to 'triangulate' the discussion by having Training Shop colleagues read and comment on the accuracy of the report and my interpretation of events, nor could I sample the opinions of other college staff specifically concerning the innovation. Nevertheless, I have attempted to be sensitive to the frustrations and irritations within the college, and a significant part of the discussion focuses on problems encountered and how they might be overcome.

INTRODUCTION

Gwent Tertiary College is the product of a merger in September 1992 between two tertiary colleges, in Cross Keys and Pontypool, and two traditional further education (FE) colleges situated in Newport and Ebbw Vale. The local agriculture college at Usk had already been merged with Pontypool College. The college covers a distance north to south of about 35 miles, has around 20,000 enrolled students, some 8,000 full-time equivalent (fte) students and 1,000 staff. The merger, promoted and organized by the local education authority (LEA) and the college principals was designed to forestall some of the worst effects of competition engendered by incorporation through the Further and Higher Education Act (1992). With the merger being announced at the end of the summer holidays the college suddenly had a completely new management and organization structure; in fact many of the staff and students did not even know it had taken place. For the coming year the management were to be preoccupied with changes resulting from the merger and incorporation so curriculum development and innovation was low on their agenda.

A BACKGROUND TO MODULARIZATION

In September 1991 the Welsh Joint Education Committee (WJEC) launched phase 1 of its modularization project. The project was funded by the Welsh Office through a Department of Employment fund for development projects in colleges of further education. In Wales the LEAs, who then still controlled post-16 education, decided to pool their money through a central agency. Five colleges were involved in the work, with central administration and consultancy provided by the WJEC. The project was inspired by the Scottish Vocational Education Council (SCOTVEC) modular system and hoped to address some of the problems colleges were facing introducing National Vocational Qualifications (NVQs) as well as the demand for more flexible provision for adults in further education. The scope of the work was limited. Small-scale demonstration projects were located in different college units and departments. From the outset there was a strong emphasis on staff development with regular workshops for college project co-ordinators.

The following February 1992 the Further Education Unit (FEU) published the seminal paper *A basis for credit*. The document was to become the basis for the development work in Gwent and in Wales as a whole. In a foreword FEU chief officer, Geoff Stanton, summarized the central tenets underpinning the idea of a credit framework. 'This paper', he said, 'describes the benefits which could be gained by producing a post-16 credit accumulation and transfer (CAT) framework, which encompasses all levels and types of qualification; from Key Stage 4 of the National Curriculum through to the [higher education] HE masters/professional qualifications'. *A basis for credit* introduces 'the concept of an "open system" and the potential this has for allowing the system to grow from the bottom up, in a voluntary manner over time' and 'argues the case for qualifications within this framework to be based upon coherent sets of outcomes, to be described as units'. The FEU emphasized that *A basis for credit* was intended as a discussion paper. Geoff Stanton drew attention to the risks he foresaw: 'The reward to be gained is so great that enthusiasts may build up too many hopes and schemes on what turn out to be faulty foundations. . . . Existing preconceptions, ideologies and vested interests may cause mundane, technical or terminological problems to be much exaggerated.'

Despite his reservations, *A basis for credit* became the blueprint for developments in Wales within the context of modularizing the curriculum. Following the merger of the Training, Education and Enterprise Department (TEED) with the Education Department in Wales, a Welsh Office working party endorsed the credit framework and set a target of 1996/7 for all Welsh colleges to implement a fully modular curriculum.

In Gwent the LEA submitted a bid on behalf of the new tertiary college to the Training and Enterprise Council (TEC) for funding to participate in the modularization project's development. The project application had three foci:

• To take existing courses and deconstruct the curriculum to produce modules.
• To develop the college infrastructure to support a modular curriculum.
• To provide a wide-ranging programme of staff development to introduce a credit framework and modular curriculum.

A BASIS FOR CREDIT

The central theoretical underpinning of *A basis for credit* was that all learning could be brought into a common framework. This could be achieved by describing the outcomes, the level and the assessment criteria of any particular piece of learning. By then ascribing a notional learning time to that activity a credit value could be arrived at, facilitating the comparison and transfer of learning between different qualifications. Students would be able to construct programmes of learning across the academic and vocational divide and could accumulate credits towards final qualification goals. Such a credit framework could operate through all phases of education, including school, further and higher education.

While *A basis for credit* provided a theoretical base, it was left to the Welsh colleges to develop a practical application for the work. One of the most difficult tasks proved to be the development and definition of the module descriptor. Much time was expended in defining outcomes and assessment criteria. At first every college wrote its own module descriptor. In Gwent, as in many other Welsh colleges, this included both units of assessment (details of outcomes and notional time) and modules of delivery (how the unit was to be assessed and how and where it was to be assessed). The need for an external quality assurance process forced colleges in Wales to agree on a common descriptor in September 1993. It was agreed to separate out units of assessment from modules of delivery. Units, based on a common format, were to be subject to external quality assurance, while modules, the means by which a unitized curriculum could be delivered in an individual institution, remained the property of the colleges.

The unit descriptor has five parts:

1. title;
2. learning outcomes;
3. assessment criteria;
4. level;
5. credit rating.

The statement of 'learning outcomes' was seen as allowing the modules to cover a wide variety of learning, from specific skills and competences to forms of subject knowledge and concept development. It thus allows NVQs, GNVQs, general interest programmes and A-level courses to be presented within this framework. The assessment criteria had to be clear enough to allow a judgement to be made on the level and volume of work involved and thence the credit value of any module delivering the unit.

Credit value is determined by allocating notional learning time to groups of learning outcomes (1 credit = 30 notional hours). Level is decoded with regard to a hierarchy of level descriptors, designed to provide an approximate equivalence to existing national qualifications: NVQs, GNVQs and GCSEs and A-levels.

Module descriptors describe the actual delivery of the learning, defining the units included, the assessment methods and the methods of learning. The first major task the Gwent project faced was to redefine the heterogeneous post-16 curriculum in terms of a unit-based modular framework.

WHY DO IT AT ALL?

At this point it is worth considering the motives of the different agencies, and in particular the motivation for Gwent Tertiary College and for the local TEC in getting involved in such a project. The different colleges in Gwent already had a reputation for involving themselves in curriculum and staff development projects. Furthermore the former Newport College's modularization project had been personally run by principal Gareth Nichols who was now director of corporate affairs elect for the newly merged college. An added drive came from director of education Geoffrey Drought, a member of the TEC board and an original member of the team which had set up SCOTVEC. In this way much of the motivation came from the interest and enthusiasm of a few key individuals. There were other motivations too. Curriculum and staff development projects, particularly ones like this, are a risk. On the one hand there is the opportunity to try out new ideas, to invest in technology and provide new and exciting opportunities for staff. The financial assistance and the opportunities that provides are also an incentive not to be underestimated. On the other hand, institutions playing a leading developmental role have to make all the mistakes and carry their staff through sometimes frustrating periods as ideas develop and change. As the largest college in Wales, Gwent was prepared to adopt a proactive strategy and to live with the risks that brings.

STRATEGIC DRIVING FORCES

There were further macro and strategic reasons underpinning the motivation for change. For a number of years there has been growing concern over the relatively poor education and training figures emanating from England and Wales in comparison to other European countries. Areas highlighted for attention are participation, especially 17- and 18-year-olds, and attainment. More recently education and training underachievement has come to be linked to poor economic performance. Commentators have pointed to the relatively low numbers of technicians being trained in England and Wales compared with France and Europe. Scotland has significantly higher participation and attainment rates (McPherson *et al.*, 1990; Weir, 1988). In 1993 the government reacted to reports from the Confederation of British Industry (CBI) and other bodies by announcing the national education and training targets. Expansion of universities and higher education was to be curtailed with resources switched to the newly independent further education sector. College funding, now switched to the funding councils, was to be in part dependent on the achievement of ambitious targets for expansion in student numbers. However, there was not to be a commensurate increase in overall funding levels to provide for the projected increase in student numbers.

In such a climate college managements have started to look at the credit framework proposal as a way of reorganizing the curriculum to provide increased opportunities for a wider student body. Flexibility will allow students more choice of subject combinations and wider access to the curriculum. A modular curriculum could in principle provide the chance for students to enrol at any time in the academic year and to access learning opportunities at the times when they are free. The provision of a curriculum split into discrete parts might be attractive to employers who could take up the parts of a course they perceived as relevant to their particular needs. College managers thought that the credit framework and a modular curriculum could be more cost-effective in the use of resources especially, through allowing 'common' curriculum subjects, like maths and communications, to be taught together.

There is, therefore, a conjuncture of different interests in curriculum change and motivation. For managers modularization might offer the chance to expand student numbers through the more cost-efficient organization of resources. For those interested in student provision and access, the credit framework and modularization offer a wider choice for individuals.

THE FLEXIBLE COLLEGE

The concept of a flexible college is not new. Partly in response to increasing numbers of adults entering further education and partly as a reaction to the decline of the apprenticeship system, a number of reports and projects in the 1980s proposed changes to the curriculum and organization of post-16 provision to provide access and flexibility. While it has become generally accepted that colleges need to become more flexible in their approach to the provision of education and training the reality of the situation has failed to live up to the ideal. Many of the projects were small scale and failed to continue when external funding expired. Even large and well-funded and publicized initiatives like the Open College failed to make a significant impact on traditional patterns of learning and teaching. The complexity of post-16 provision in England and Wales, with differing qualification routes, different controlling bodies, different sets of standards, different taxonomies of level and different methods of assessment and award, confounded the intentions of reformers. The constituent institutions of Gwent Tertiary College have participated in many initiatives intended to bring about such change. Various projects have looked at quality in further education, access for non-traditional groups, outreach provision, open learning centres, the accreditation of prior learning, support for women returners, foreign exchange visits and enterprise training, to name but a few. Some have been successful, others less so; all have failed to produce a fundamental change in the ethos, curriculum and infrastructure of the college. The credit framework and modularization project was intended from the outset to produce this sort of change.

STAFFING THE WORK

With the approval of project funding I was appointed project director. With the impending demise of the LEA in post-16 education a college base appeared the best avenue to forward this work. Jenny Hughes, the LEA officer, and I had drawn up and presented to Gwent Tertiary College management, plans for a new curriculum and staff development unit, to be called the Training Shop. The Training Shop was to be a new kind of development unit, taking on and managing European projects, undertaking curriculum development work for the college as a whole, and providing a staff development service for colleges throughout the country as well as in Gwent. In part the plan was conceived as a response to the demise of the old-type advisory services, who with heavy overheads and statutory duties could no longer fund and support the brokerage model of curriculum and staff development in which the advisers identified a need and brought in outsiders to run courses. The Training Shop would have a small central staff of curriculum and staff development specialists, low overheads and a floating staff of full- and part-timers seconded from other sections in the college. The seconded staff would act as internal consultants within Gwent to facilitate and promote curriculum and staff development. In a period when opportunities for promotion were few a period working with the Training Shop could provide a chance for professional development and to gain new and wider experience. However, the problem of developing the multiple skills required for this sort of work has had to be acknowledged and addressed.

The modularization project was set up under the Training Shop banner, operating from borrowed office space in a TVEI unit based in a primary school in Cwmbran. The Training Shop supported the work of the project providing the wider expertise and consultancy in curriculum and staff development that classroom-based staff lack. Training Shop staff provided support and training for the project development workers. Through the provision of a central curriculum and staff development unit the Training Shop was able to provide far greater resources and infrastructure to support the work than college development staff can normally draw upon. Initially six part-time staff were appointed on secondment from different college campuses to take part in phase 1 of the project from November 1992 to April 1993 and a further four joined the project in June 1993.

WHAT THE PROJECT HAS DONE

The first major focus of activity for the development staff has been the deconstruction of the existing curriculum to produce units and modules. The work has been undertaken by teams of staff drawn from every campus of the college in each curriculum area. Workshops in which the task of analysing and rewriting each syllabus were organized by the development staff who usually took the initiative in starting up an activity, and selected the staff to be involved in conjunction with the 'unit manager' responsible for that subject area within a particular campus. From the outset great emphasis has been placed on ensuring that ownership of the new curriculum lies with classroom practitioners. The strategy adopted was one in which the workshop members were encouraged increasingly to take full responsibility for the work done, with the project officer increasingly taking a supporting role. Many of the workshops have involved school and community education staff and where possible employers have also been consulted. The project staff have produced guidelines on how to carry out the work and a common staff development programme has been written. In late 1993 an internal quality panel was established to approve units prior to their submission to South East Wales Access Consortium for external approval. Inevitably the redefining of units and modules and the establishment of an external quality process has resulted in major revisions of work already undertaken, leading to some resentment from classroom staff. The project staff had to mollify this resentment as best they could, often by directing the resentment outside the college to 'them'.

The next focus for the project has been to develop a modular framework to deliver the newly unitized curriculum. Progression routes have been defined along with advice on how much time should be spent in classroom teaching and how much may be learnt through workshops and supported self-study. The development of model timetables for modular awards has proved taxing for staff.

In some curriculum areas this work has proved relatively simple; BTEC awards already specify outcomes and are to some extent modular in structure. For A-level practitioners, however, many of the concepts are completely new. The A-level curriculum has previously been defined by the end assessment process, the outcomes of which can best be gauged by a study of past papers. The task of defining the learning for students has often proved contentious and challenging. In other areas like community education and special needs there has traditionally been no written curriculum. Staff in these areas have responded enthusiastically to the tasks set by the project, motivated in part by the prospect of a unitized curriculum becoming eligible for funding through the Further Education Funding Council (FEFC).

The reconstruction of units and modules to provide learning programmes for students reflects these curriculum divisions. Despite the radical intentions of *A basis for credit* it has been recognized that in the initial phase most students will choose modules which can provide them with traditional qualifications. Nevertheless new programmes of learning have been produced in areas where there are no existing national qualifications, such as special needs, or in areas where there have been recent technological developments, like information technology.

Considerable emphasis has been placed on the identification and production of learning materials to support a modular curriculum. Project funding made it possible to organize workshops to write teaching and learning materials with technical assistance provided by the Training Shop's publication unit. Once again, this work has been done by the teachers themselves, with the development staff providing facilities, resources and expertise.

A major consideration for the project management has been support for the development staff. The tasks and competences involved in project management and development are very different from classroom teaching. Hence the professional development of the project staff has been seen as an integral objective for the project. Despite considerable time pressures on development staff, the project has held regular half-day meetings to allow for the sharing of experience and to provide an opportunity for the development of the concepts and ideas associated with the credit framework. The team meetings have been supplemented by termly residential workshops focusing on staff development skills and latterly on the process of writing reports and articles. Additionally staff have been encouraged to collaborate with practitioners from other colleges in Wales and to take part in external conferences and seminars.

A second major focus for the project has been the development of the college infrastructure. It became very obvious in the early months of the work that the present college organization could not support a modular curriculum. This view was reinforced by an examination of the difficulties faced by HE institutions which had recently introduced modular learning programmes.

Present management information systems are based on providing information on courses for funding bodies and are totally incapable of tracking students through a modular curriculum. With funding from the Welsh Office the project has produced a full functional specification for a computerized tracking system. This work has been undertaken in conjunction with other Welsh colleges with the intention of developing software through a consortium of Welsh education institutions.

Another concern has been the provision of information for students. Post-16 education provides a very broad and heterogeneous choice of learning programmes for students from a wide range of backgrounds and abilities; modular learning programmes might be confusing to students, careers advisers and staff alike. Project staff, working with outside consultants, have developed a multimedia computerized information system to facilitate student counselling and choice. Similarly it has been recognized that counselling and guidance systems for students need to be reviewed and revised and this has provided a major focus for work in 1994.

The third major area for activity has been staff development. The rash of curriculum reform and the pace of change in further education over the last decade have led to what has been described as 'initiative fatigue' in classroom practitioners. It is easy for staff to be cynical towards what may seem like just another new scheme which will disappear as fast as it appeared. Hence great emphasis has been placed on staff development, to inform staff of the objectives and activities of the project and involve them in the determination of the change process. All the project staff have been trained in delivering staff development and materials produced to help them run workshops and seminars. Particular attention has been paid to staff development for curriculum managers throughout the college.

WHAT HAS BEEN ACHIEVED

By April 1994 532 units had been submitted to South East Wales Access Consortium for unit approval. In many curriculum areas materials have been produced, assessment materials drawn up and model timetables produced.

Four pilots of the modular structure were launched in the autumn of 1993. Programmes involving over 100 students in special needs and in community education have proved extremely successful with college credits being awarded to students. All the college access programmes adopted a modular common skills core allowing flexibility and choice for students, individual learning programmes, workshop delivery and the rapid development of new subject areas. Modular access programmes are being further developed and amended and in September 1994 the first credit-based awards will be introduced. Modular A-levels in business studies and law have proved less successful. Introduced without sufficient prior staff development and without the necessary support from the project staff, A-level teachers continued to follow the traditional curriculum though formally adopting a modular structure. The introduction of General National Vocational Qualifications has provided a further opportunity to pilot modular curriculum structures. While the support of the project in providing materials, timetables, and assessment documentation has proved invaluable it is too early to evaluate the overall success of the work.

Almost every full-time member of staff has now attended modularization seminars and workshops. Regular updating events are held for college management. Nevertheless more work is needed especially if the project is to develop its full potential in changing the teaching and learning methods in the classroom. At present, campus management are aware of the scheme, but have yet to develop the knowledge of it that some course teams have established.

Finally a start has been made in developing a new infrastructure for the college which will not only support a modular curriculum but will provide flexibility and access to learning for every section of the community within Gwent.

The major achievement so far, in the view of the project management, has been to make the curriculum central to the college's planning and development process. Curriculum development, staff development and planning of the college infrastructure have become interlinked and interdependent through a central focus on modularization.

BARRIERS TO CHANGE

Inevitably a project of this kind will encounter considerable barriers, both internal and external to the college. Some of these problems were anticipated in advance and ways of overcoming them were planned, others became apparent in the course of the project and changes had to be made to deal with them. One overriding problem is the short-term perspective which informs so much curriculum change within the further education sector. Funding is made available at short notice and there is an expectation that visible outcomes will be produced in the immediate future. Planning and preparation are sacrificed in the scramble to deliver measurable outcomes. A more thorough and rigorous planning process would allow barriers to change to be properly approached and also provide more cost-effective and efficient delivery.

The biggest barrier to change is the conservatism of staff within the college itself. Many have invested considerable time and effort in developing the existing curriculum and in accumulating teaching and learning materials to deliver their courses. Any change to the status quo promises only more work for them. More radical programmes of change have implicit threats for their professional life and practice. Many of Gwent Tertiary College's staff have been in post for a considerable period of time. Teacher training has been traditionally focused on didactic classroom teaching; new methods of learning, experiential learning or workshop delivery are viewed with suspicion and sometimes hostility. Attitudes are aggravated by two further factors: firstly the difficult industrial relations climate engendered by recent government attempts to reform long-standing contractual relations and practices, and secondly a widespread scepticism towards the many changes emanating from central governmental agencies in the last 10 years. Teachers and lecturers have come to feel their own professionalism is being questioned and their work and role undervalued. Project development officers were frequently asked 'What's in it for us?'

Project officers recognized that they had to launch a 'hearts and minds' staff development programme following the principles identified by writers on change such as Fullan (1992) and Huberman and Miles (1984). I have spoken at dozens of meetings on every campus of the college. This is not seen as a finite activity; as the project develops staff need to be kept up to date with both the ideas and philosophy which underpin the credit framework and the ensuing changes in the college work. The project management also established the principle that staff would be paid to undertake development work. Workshops took place in normal college hours with project funding being used to pay for lecturer cover. The project has paid for the development and publication of teaching and learning materials as well as the development of a new multimedia electronic prospectus to help staff in providing counselling and guidance for prospective students.

Often project work is seen by staff as an élite activity, divorced from the day-to-day world of the 'chalk face'. Every effort has been made to involve as many staff as possible in the development work and promote a feeling of ownership amongst the college staff. Nevertheless this process is not without its difficulties. The key internal change has been that the work has become more systematic and tightly focused on particular areas of the curriculum rather than remaining on an *ad hoc* basis dependent on individual enthusiasm. Other changes have been imposed from outside as organizations and colleges have become involved in the credit framework development. This has meant staff have had to go back over their work and make substantial revisions; inevitably there has been resentment at this process.

If the support and involvement of college staff is one key component for implementing change, a second requirement is for college managers to actively support the project. In just the same way as project development work can be seen as separate from the everyday work of college staff it is also often peripheral to the concerns of college managers. The modularization project team have been conscious of this problem from the very start of the work. Brian Robinson, campus principal for Pontypool, was given overall responsibility for liaison and reporting from the project with the college senior management team. As the project set up working groups to tackle individual areas of the work the college assistant principals were given responsibility for working with the different teams. The application for funding set out an allocation of managers' time as part of the college's commitment to the resourcing of the project work. Even so there is a further stage to turn paper commitment to active involvement and support. Part of the challenge has been to convince senior managers that the project really can achieve its objectives and should form a legitimate and important part of their work. Progress is uneven as different members of the management team have different views and ideas which determine their personal priorities.

College middle-managers have faced contradictions between the demands of day-to-day crisis management and the longer-term demands of curriculum development. Such a conflict is particularly acute in a college which has recently undergone major reorganization and with major external changes imposed by incorporation and new funding methodologies. Curriculum development activities only add to an already considerable workload. Much effort has been expended in trying to ensure college middle-managers are kept fully informed of the project's objectives and work. A further focus has been to integrate modularization within the middle-management training course. In this way, 20 middle-managers each year are introduced to the issues involved in planning, developing and managing modular curriculum structures and provision.

The selection and training of development officers is key to the project. The task of project development work and of leading change is a very different one to day-to-day classroom activity. There is no recognized training course in further education for curriculum development staff and at the outset of the project only myself and one other member of the development staff had any experience of delivering staff development. The need to train development staff and the time taken for them to gain experience is a barrier to the speed in developing the project. In itself this is not a major problem; however, it is seriously compounded by pressure from funding bodies to prove measurable outcomes.

In addition project officers have to prove their credibility in front of possibly the most demanding audience comprised of their own peer group. The project management has developed a system of support for development officers through organizing workshops for training the trainers, producing staff development materials and through a mentor system.

MANAGING CHANGE

The management of change is a complex process. While the project was in its initial stages and the boundaries of work were easy to discern then it was possible to control the areas of activity centrally. As the work impinged on more and more of the college curriculum and increasing numbers of teaching and management staff became involved it was increasingly hard to maintain such control. This was compounded by lack of communication in a large geographically dispersed college with new and untested management structures.

Control of the quality of the development work proved increasingly difficult as project management became more devolved. Even more problematic was the task of reporting on the outcomes of the work. Funding bodies, in particular the TEC and the Welsh Office, were quite understandably concerned that they were getting value for money. Quite apart from the problem of measuring change it has often been difficult to separate areas of project development and outcomes from other activity taking place in the college. In this respect the project management have found themselves in a contradictory position. The more successful they have been in embedding change within the everyday activities of the college, the harder it has become to manage and control the process of change and to measure and quantify the outcomes of the project.

SOME EARLY CONCLUSIONS

I have reported on some of the lessons and processes from a curriculum project which is still only in its initial phases. Project managers have always emphasized that they believe it will take a minimum of four to five years to implement the fundamental curriculum reform implicit in the project's aims and objectives and probably longer before many of the changes become transparently observable and quantifiable. The difficulties of measuring change using presently acceptable evaluation tools is one of the key lessons of early development. Project managers face the challenge of not only embedding the outcomes of change within the college but of gaining acceptance for the dynamic of change itself within the day-to-day activity and life of the college.

The process of change is complex: while this study has focused on one institution there are many external pressures and influences which impinge on college development. In overcoming these barriers the role of change agents is key. Despite the centrality of such key agents insufficient attention has been paid in the past to training and developing staff to undertake this process. Thus the project faces a twin challenge in developing and implementing new curriculum processes while at the same time developing the instruments and agents able to carry out such fundamental change.

REFERENCES

Fullan, M. (1992) *The new meaning of educational change*. London: Cassell.

Further Education Unit (1992) *A basis for credit*. London: FEU.

Huberman, A. M. and Miles, M. B. (1984) *Innovation up close*. New York: Plenum.

McPherson, A., Raffe, D. and Robertson, C. (1990) *Highers and higher education*. Edinburgh: Association of University Teachers.

Osterman, K. F. and Kottkamp, R. B. (1993) *Reflective practice for educators*. Newbury Park: Corwin.

Weir, A. D. (1988) *Education and vocation 14–18*. Edinburgh: Scottish Academic Press.

Yin, R. K. (1984) *Case study research: design and methods*. Newbury Park: Sage.

CHAPTER 4

Managing an Aspect of Pastoral Care in a Primary School

NIGEL HARRISSON

ABSTRACT

This project took place in one primary school and is an interpretative single case study approach to one aspect of pastoral care, namely the management of behaviour. Evidence was obtained via in-depth and semi-structured interviewing as well as through non-participant observation and documentation. The outcome of the project indicates that the school has a generally well-developed and positive philosophy and practice regarding behaviour. This has been developed through strong management, exemplary leadership and the sharing of values amongst the whole school community. Suggestions are made which may enhance the school's good practice.

INTRODUCTION

The research endeavoured to investigate those management issues, processes and styles which might be influential in a whole-school approach to behaviour. From the literature survey it was clear that the methodology should attempt to investigate any underlying value system, as well as overt structures and procedures. The investigation aimed to: (i) identify existing approaches to the management of behaviour, (ii) critically examine those approaches, and (iii) suggest how existing policy and practice might be enhanced.

Several management issues were identified and investigated and, in turn, provided a framework for analysis. These revolved around the nature and effectiveness of:

• the development of philosophy, policy and practice;
• support and communications;
• consensus of approach;
• the balance between academic and pastoral curricula;

- the balance between encouraging positive behaviour and discouraging unwanted behaviour; and
- staff roles and responsibilities.

Westlea is a five to eleven primary school situated on a relatively new private housing estate. The headteacher has been at the school since July 1987. The ages of the school population are shown in Table 4.1.

TABLE 4.1
Population of Westlea School in January 1993

AGE	TOTAL NO.
4+	44
5+	69
6+	66
7+	53
8+	52
9+	51
10+	39
Total	374
Special unit	17

Westlea is well known to me, since I have been the school's educational psychologist since September 1991. It has a 'feels-good' reputation for managing, amongst other things, behaviour. On entering the school one notices exciting display materials and purposeful classrooms with an open and positive atmosphere which is well respected by both parents and professionals alike. The headteacher maintains a high profile and actively promotes the school within the community.

The selection of Westlea was influenced by a desire to investigate, systematically, the school's 'feels-good' reputation in an attempt to isolate any management factors contributing to its apparent success in this pastoral area. It was felt that an investigation into positive aspects of management practice would be as worthy of study as one which focused on an area of concern.

The relationship between myself and the school is an unique aspect of the study (and raises issues which are addressed in the methodology section). My usual role is that of a client-centred consultant, that is, a 'catalytic' role, which aims to enable the client – class teacher, headteacher or staff group – to maintain ownership of problems and not to force preconceived solutions upon them. It was felt that the skills involved in consultancy would prove invaluable in the research project. The prime purpose of the research was to gain an insight into the

management process, and not to explicitly influence practice although, undoubtedly, recommendations would be made if only to consolidate good practice.

Such a research project is well suited to the role of an external adviser/
consultant who can only advise and has no power to act.

LITERATURE REVIEW

Most studies into behaviour management have been carried out within secondary
schools. However, there is no reason to assume that many of the principles
identified as underlying good practice cannot be observed within good primary
practice.

The Elton Report (DES, 1989) was the culmination of a study into school
discipline. The Elton Committee concluded that major incidents of indiscipline
were rare. However, the committee highlighted 'minor' indiscipline which they
saw as preventing the educational process happening efficiently. A major influence
in improving this situation was seen as effective school management.

The committee recommended that headteachers and governors should ensure
that rules regarding behaviour were derived from the principles underlying
behaviour policies and were consistent with them. In essence, the role of
management was emphasized in developing clearly understood behavioural
policies, consulting widely within the school community and giving due regard
to pupil self-esteem.

HMI (DES, 1987) also identified several factors which, they suggest, influence
behaviour and discipline within schools. These include:

- leadership;
- achievement and success from challenging teaching;
- active involvement of pupils in their own learning;
- consensus of essential values and consistency of approach;
- good relationships between teachers and pupils which are grounded in the ethos
  of the school;
- high expectations;
- nurturing of pupils' growing maturity and self-esteem.

Both the Elton Committee and HMI suggest that discipline is most effective where
the school's leadership sets a good example: where there are clear aims and high
expectations, and a commitment to staff support and professional development.
Buckley (1985) further suggests that an effective headteacher provides a sense of
direction and engenders a feeling of confidence.

Tomlinson (1992) suggests that effective management depends upon the social
and educational values, goals, expectations and aspirations held by those in
positions of power within the organization. Such values are generally derived from
those in positions of power. These, together with micropolitical considerations,
determine the organization's approach to quality and accountability, as well as

influencing judgements and decision-making. Importantly those values also determine the extent to which the style of management is biased towards the 'mechanistic', that is dependent upon systems or procedures, or 'organic', that is emphasizing the dynamic, interactive aspects of the organization. However, as Best *et al.* (1983) point out, the power of the head is not absolute as it is dependent upon the acceptance of the head's authority: only through the compliance of the staff can a goal become fully realizable.

Docking (1989) further suggests that any approach to managing behaviour must also take account of pupil perceptions. Thus pupils are less likely to feel alienated if they are given opportunities which enable them to feel empowered and significant participants. Any behavioural policy or approach, it is argued, must be directed at all pupils, not just those who are deviant.

The literature reviewed emphasizes the positive elements of effective management. If this is accepted then, conversely, one can argue that ineffective management is likely to be due to their absence or the presence of various negative attributes. This might be characterized by the imposition of rules which were not derived from, or consistent with, the principles within the behaviour policy; little consultation or regard for the perceptions and values of others; little emphasis on staff development in relation to behaviour management; or a behaviour policy and practice aimed only at those who are deviant.

Just as effective management can create a positive spiral of high expectations and commitment to shared values, so ineffective management may result in unclear aims and/or low expectations; an unclear and essentially disparate value system; non-commitment of staff to 'shared' organizational values; or the non-compliance of staff and/or pupils.

It is evident that management has a distinct role in encouraging desirable behaviour. Undoubtedly a relatively objective and impersonal management role, which might involve the development and evaluation of procedures, for example the development of the structure of a pastoral/guidance system, is important. Good pupil behaviour is also heavily dependent upon the values and leadership style which are held by influential people within the organization and demonstrated in their own behaviour.

METHODOLOGY

Some constraints

Many types of research, both outside and within education, embrace the concept of 'sponsor' which tends to imply the provision of funding. However, a sponsor is, effectively, any individual, body or institution initiating the research. Researchers will be aware of the values, expectations and financial constraints implicit in such sponsorship. In turn, this may influence research in many subtle ways, for example via the researchers own belief and value system in relation to the topic, such as smoking, and potentially enables bias to enter the research at various stages. In extreme cases research findings may not be published if they disagree with the sponsor's values or have significant resource implications. It is not intended to imply that sponsored research is implicitly flawed, but to argue that by openly declaring sponsorship one allows the reader to make a choice as to whether to accept the information given as a whole, and places the research in its wider social context.

This current study has no effective sponsor; however, I am aware of the values, expectations and time constraints placed on this study by my 'line management'.

Many studies also acknowledge the concept of 'audience' and the implicit constraints it imposes. My unique relationship with the school provides many benefits but was also likely to introduce bias. As a regular visitor to the school, and being labelled a 'psychologist', I could affect the actions and reactions of participants. In addition, I had to continue working with the school after the project and therefore the awareness of the school as an audience has been paramount.

Perhaps the most imposing constraint was the desire to meet Open University deadlines which led to the necessity to limit data collection to a small, but hopefully representative, cohort.

The 'feels-good' reputation of the school and a desire to focus on positive aspects of behaviour management might have led to the research taking place through 'rose-coloured spectacles'. However, via the literature survey, I became aware of the potentially negative aspects of ineffective management and the interview schedules reflected these points.

Research style

Yin (1984) examines various case study research and design methods including single case study, multi case study and exploratory approaches. In this study it was felt particularly appropriate to adopt an interpretative single, holistic, case study approach of the revelatory type, which would permit the researcher to penetrate aspects of the regime not always readily accessible via other methodology relying on large numbers. As Preedy (1984) points out, such an approach allows the researcher to access the unique perceptions of individuals, examine informal as well as formal aspects of the organization and investigate the influence of micropolitics upon the institution.

The case study approach embraced a variety of techniques, as well as evidence from different sources, leading to an exponentially increasing pile of evidence which needed to be managed effectively.

The pre-specification of categories, relating to the analytical framework, was seen as a necessary precursor to the analysis. The approach allowed for theoretical sampling and analytic induction (Open University, 1987), and attempted to embrace the whole context in which the phenomenon occurred. The presentation of the outcomes of case study, for example narrative, vignette or analysis, was seen as comprehensive and having potential for reaching a wide audience.

An important aspect of the approach adopted was progressive focusing (Open

University, 1987; Nisbet and Watt, 1984) where research becomes more focused and systematic from the general 'milieu' towards particular aspects. Such techniques involve the researcher as a 'filter'. Certain aspects might be focused upon because they are of personal interest. Attempts were made to overcome these problems. Firstly, I declared my personal stance; secondly, by the use of analytical induction when analysing data; and finally by the use of a critical friend to aid reflection.

Documentation

It was envisaged that a source of data would be school policy or guidelines on behaviour, but no direct documentation existed. The philosophy of the school, however, was reflected in its professional development interview document.

Interviews

These were the major data collection instruments. A cross-section of the school community was interviewed including:

- the headteacher;
- the special-needs co-ordinator (Senco);
- two teachers (together);
- three educational support assistants (ESA) (together);
- four pupils (together).

It was also envisaged that at least one parent would be interviewed. However, due to time constraints and difficulties of selection, this aspect was abandoned.

The selection of interviewees, that is pupils, teachers and ESAs, was undertaken by the Senco based on availability for interview and not, I am assured, due to any particular allegiance to school philosophy. The pupils were selected on my specifications, that is Year 5 or 6 pupils, mixed ability and gender.

The interviews were carried out in a comfortable 'small classroom', except that with the headteacher which took place in his office. The interviews were taped, with permission, and transcribed as a whole.

The principal format was a semi-structured interview. This entailed a carefully worded interview schedule where a degree of latitude was incorporated, via the use of an initial question followed by probes. However, some aspects, especially involving the headteacher, were felt to be more befitting to in-depth interviews. Wragg (1984) suggests that considerable skill is required in undertaking in-depth interviews, and further suggests that practitioners such as psychotherapists have such skills. As a qualified psychologist and skilled counsellor I felt justified in using this technique. This involved a general focus on the area of study, yet did not restrict the respondent to a predetermined agenda. By judicious use of reflection and active listening, for example the observation of the respondents' non-verbal as well as verbal responses, the repondents' perceptions were developed (Gordon, 1974).

The interview schedules were devised with reference to the identified management issues. A series of prompts were placed in the margin to aid further questioning. This provided a framework for data collection and ensured that relevant areas were covered. Consultation over the schedule design took place with my 'critical friend'.

Non-participant observation

Two classrooms were observed using a simple observational schedule that I had devised to distinguish between positive, negative and neutral interactions between staff and pupils. This took the form of 'incident' sampling – each time the teacher interacted positively, negatively or indifferently (that is the observer being unable to assign to the positive or negative category) a box was ticked. Pre-specification of what constituted a positive interaction (smile, wink, verbal praise, etc.) or negative interaction (scowl, frown, verbal rebuke, etc.) provided an *aide-mémoire*.

Validity and reliability

Wiseman (1985) points out that in a qualitative study one is trying to make valid sense of the data by reconstructing the social world of the participants. It seems sensible, therefore, that a particular methodology is valid if it allows one to enquire effectively into the subject's views of the world and effectively recreate them. Checks were made on the data at the draft report stage by inviting the headteacher and staff to comment on possible 'misconceptions' that may have occurred during analysis. No adverse comments were received. Pressure of deadlines prevented the sharing of the analysis of individual interviews; however, in retrospect, this may have enhanced the validity of the research.

Similarly, reliability refers to consistency between independent measures of the same phenomenon. In this study triangulation is used, that is the collection of data from different sources and methods, to aid reliability.

ANALYSIS

One important aspect of interpretive case study analysis is the emphasis on linking the researcher's own analytical concepts with the terms in which the subjects themselves understand their situations and actions. It is from this general perspective that this analysis took place, albeit under similar constraints to those previously mentioned.

The interviews were transcribed, coded and allocated to a specific category by physically cutting up the transcript. The aim of the analysis was to 'reconstruct' the views of the participants which related to specific aspects of the management of the whole-school approach to behaviour.

What follows is a 'portrait' (Nisbet and Watt, 1984) of the management of behaviour at Westlea School. An attempt has been made to be non-judgemental in the analysis stage. The research produced a wealth of evidence which is difficult to represent fully. It is hoped the following analysis, which runs the danger of being a 'caricature', will provide the reader with a basic understanding of how the school functions in this area.

The development of philosophy, policy and practice

All respondents reported similar views that the headteacher is a major influential figure and there is evidence to suggest that it was through his influence that the approach developed:

> I think the philosophy very much now is part of the school, though I think to begin with it certainly stemmed from [the head].
>
> *(Senco)*

> [the headteacher] is a tremendous driving force behind what we do in this school.
>
> *(teacher 1)*

The head acknowledges that this influence is due to his clear personal philosophy and reflects that his position may be 'too central':

> They [the staff] know what I want this school to be and I do worry about that sometimes. I do worry about how big an imprint I sometimes have made on this school.
>
> *(head)*

Ancillary staff and pupils also felt that the head was the principal influence on the school's approach: 'everyone looks up to [head]; he works hard to get what he wants and we all agree with it' (ESA). One pupil suggested that if the head ever left, 'It would be chaos!' (pupil).

The adult respondents put forward similar views that the integrated and caring approach to special needs was also a significant influence on behaviour. The pupils did not volunteer this as an explanation.

> [Special needs] are crucial. The fact that other children know children who are different and need understanding, need tolerance and patience . . . definitely adds to the quality of the children's lives in the school and makes a difference to behaviour.
>
> *(Senco)*

> It's good having others with special needs in school because they see they all have to
> get on together.
>
> *(ESA)*

The school's philosophy was consistently represented as promoting positive and caring relationships which were built on clear expectations:

> the school does try to be quite clear to children about what sorts of behaviours are
> not acceptable.
>
> *(ESA)*

> [the head] talks to us in assemblies and things about caring for each other and what
> we can't do.
>
> *(pupil)*

Support and communications

The communication of the school's approach and philosophy appears to be implicit. The ethos of the school is such that long-established staff provide models as to how children's behaviour can be effectively managed. Behavioural issues were observed to be openly discussed as and when they arose: 'I would say there is a positive dialogue about behaviour as an issue all the time' (head). The teacher respondents valued the annual professional development interview with the head, which was felt to reinforce the school's philosophy: 'there is a sheet with a list of things that this school believes a teacher should be and it has things like encouraging success and all such things' (teacher 2). The document referred to lists the 'characteristics' which the school believes makes a 'first-class teacher'; these include:

- Tries to ensure that every child has an experience of success.
- Gives responsibility not only to children who can discharge it but also to children whose development needs this experience.

> *(Westlea professional development document)*

Staff meetings on particular issues are held as they arise, as are training days, for example on self-esteem. Teaching staff interviewed felt that they would value further in-house professional development.

> I think it would be a good thing to check on as a staff maybe than rather go off on
> courses.
>
> *(teacher 1)*

> so that we could make sure . . . that we are still all barking up the same tree.
>
> *(teacher 2)*

The school has made successful attempts to involve the non-teaching staff in its philosophy: 'we have done in-service work with support assistants constantly. . . . We have done our own thing with the dinner ladies as well' (head).

There is no formal written policy, and the communication and evaluation of the approach is seen as an ongoing process. Clear messages regarding the values held by the school, such as looking after each other and the right of everyone to enjoy school, are given to pupils on reception and are reinforced via assemblies, and as incidents arise. Newly qualified teachers are given induction which encompasses the school's philosophy of positive encouragement. All parents are strongly encouraged to attend 'pre-entry' workshops that cover such issues as behavioural expectations. (I have been involved in these workshops, in a consultant role, and would suggest that it is rare for prospective parents not to attend these sessions.)

Consensus of approach

There is evidence that the headteacher and staff attempt to promote a consistent approach via a shared value system. This has been the focus of school development.

> we have got consistency now across the staff . . . we have had to work at it so it's not entirely luck.
>
> *(head)*

> I think we all expect roughly the same from the children. . . . We know generally how each other is going to react to a problem.
>
> *(teacher 2)*

The adult respondents related behaviour to what would appear to be shared beliefs in happiness and caring for others.

> in this school everything focuses on the needs of individual children . . . there's a definite family feel to it.
>
> *(ESA)*

> life and its happiness in this school is theirs too [the child's] and caring about themselves caring about others.
>
> *(head)*

These underlying principles of behaviour tended to be the focus of its management:

> we just say hang on a minute, what was that about caring about other people.
>
> *(head)*

we're told to care about other people's feelings . . . it's a good idea really . . . other people have feelings as well.

(pupil)

Other pupils appeared to hold the view that there were several specific rules: 'No bullying. No kicking. No punching' (pupil).

Teaching staff are encouraged to raise issues regarding the effectiveness of the approach at any time. ESAs have regular meetings with the headteacher where any issues are addressed: 'we meet every week with [the head and Senco] and we can talk about how we can deal with any problems we have' (ESA).

Balance between academic and pastoral/guidance curricula

There are no formalized links between the pastoral and academic curricula. Links are 'engineered' where appropriate and such techniques as circle time, where youngsters are given the opportunity to share and learn from their own experiences in order to help develop greater self-awareness and self-confidence, are employed where issues arise (Ballard, 1982): 'we certainly don't have any plan . . . the fourth years have sex education . . . [circle time is] only used by class teachers in class situations as it crops up' (teacher 2).

The headteacher appears to be seen by both staff and youngsters as a major figure in discipline matters: 'He [pupil] was working in [the head's] office today, all day . . . In the end I do use [the head]' (teacher 1). Whereas the Senco is viewed more in a 'pastoral' role:

if you're upset then [Senco] will talk to you to find out what's wrong.

(pupil)

if I've got a behaviour problem, and I'm not sure what to do then I tend to come and ask [Senco]. . . . It's through her that I've learnt, over the years, these ideas about stars [etc]. I've occasionally used her as somebody to provide the reward. . . . They all tend to like her a lot.

(teacher 2)

The 'stars' referred to have been used as a reward by giving them to pupils immediately following the performance of a desired behaviour, for example remaining on task for a longer period.

Roles and responsibilities

Day-to-day pastoral aims appear to be focused on caring and positive relationships. Longer-term aims focus on academic, emotional and social development. Roles and responsibilities, along with pastoral aims, appear to be implicit within the basic philosophical stance of the school: '[We aim] to help the child develop and relate to other children and to their work and to adults, to make them more comfortable to themselves' (Senco).

In general, staff see parents at regular parent evenings, or on request. Issues arising from staff – parent interviews are fed back to the headteacher on a weekly basis, via the Senco. However, the teachers indicated some uncertainty about specific roles: 'we've never been given a [pastoral] role as such . . . there's nothing formally set up. . . . Are we told that we should [invite parents in] or is it something we just do?' (teacher 2).

The ESAs interviewed were generally clear about their roles and were positive about the philosophy of the school. They felt well supported by other members of staff:

> I think we're all made to feel part of the school . . . we're here to try to help the teachers do what's best for the children.
>
> *(ESA)*

> We generally know what the teacher wants and we just fit in with things. After all they're the ones in charge. But most of them work in the same way so you know where you are.
>
> *(ESA)*

Encouraging positive behaviour

The vast majority of observed interactions were positive (65 per cent) or neutral (25 per cent) as opposed to negative (10 per cent). Positive behaviour was observed to be rewarded, mainly, by verbal praise. A widely observed technique was 'catch-them-being-good'. The school does not have a system of formal extrinsic rewards, much to the disappointment of one pupil who suggested '[we] could have a cup of hot chocolate with [the head]' (pupil) as a reward for good work or behaviour. The headteacher suggested that social rewards, such as smiles, should be sufficient motivators and the logical consequences of desirable behaviour.

Although there are no set procedures, unwanted behaviour is reported to be dealt with promptly and tackled, when appropriate, as a whole-class/school 'debate'. As incidents arise, such as bullying, the class teacher encourages a whole-class discussion on the incident, as soon as possible after the event. The discussion usually focuses on the incident in relation to principles such as care and respect for others. If such incidents are considered as having implications for a larger group or the whole school then the debate would be introduced into assembly times. The school has not experienced a major breach of discipline for several years: 'we try to see poor behaviour as something troubling a child inside . . . we work on trying to understand what's wrong so we can help sort it out . . . we wouldn't reject a child out of hand' (Senco). One teacher accepted that 'keeping to the philosophy is not always easy. Sometimes I have to shout "For goodness sake!"' (teacher 1).

Behaviour modification, that is a systematic way of discouraging unwanted behaviours and encouraging desired behaviours via the manipulation of stimuli, rewards and punishments such as star-charts, has been tried with particular youngsters (Herbert, 1987). However, staff felt 'it's difficult to keep it going over a period of time' (teacher 1).

The teachers appeared to have a limited confidence in dealing with behaviour before referring to the head. The head suggests that '[teachers] often feel that some of the discipline issues are too big for them to handle and my message has had to be we all handle whatever situation comes up' (head) and is aware of his pivotal role.

Respondents felt that parents were frequently involved when the school experienced difficulties with unwanted behaviours: 'in some cases we also include parents in on this from quite an early stage' (Senco).

Finally some confusion appeared to exist regarding the school's 'policy' on informing/contacting parents:

> it would be useful to have a staff meeting to talk through . . . [to] establish quite clearly in all our minds . . . regarding such things as informing parents, and what we should and shouldn't inform parents about . . . parents might prefer a clearer understanding of what the situation is . . . differences between one teacher and another.
>
> (*teacher 2*)

The philosophy and practice of the school appears 'enshrined' in the ethos and ethics of the school community. As such, it would be in normal circumstances spurious to try to isolate 'factors' which contribute or otherwise to aspects of the school's behaviour management. For the purposes of this report, attempts have been made to isolate features which merit attention; however, such features should not be seen in isolation. In the same way, bricks and mortar make a house, but it takes something special to make it a home!

The management of behaviour at Westlea School can be seen to have its roots in a shared value system, which revolves around caring and respect for others. The school benefits from the headteacher's dynamic leadership which is based on personal commitment. In order to sustain such a value system the headteacher demonstrates an awareness of the values associated with the common goal, that is a 'vision' of what desirable behaviour entails, and the ability to interpret it for others. There is consensus to these values and staff accept and welcome the head's style. Despite, or because of, the head's management style, minor concerns exist regarding the level of confidence some teachers may have in dealing with certain aspects of unwanted behaviour, in the absence of the head.

Pupils are generally willingly compliant and the approach can be viewed as 'whole-school' and not aimed just at those who are deviant. Clear and consistent expectations are laid down, to both pupils and parents, on entry into school and are reinforced and reaffirmed throughout their school career.

The presence of children experiencing a range of special needs is influential in the school's approach. The positive view held by most respondents, that 'ordinary' youngsters have a lot to learn by being educated alongside 'special' pupils, seems an integral part of the school's philosophy.

Staff are encouraged to engage in continuous open dialogue and mutual support 'as issues arise' which undoubtedly facilitates a consistency of approach.

The commitment to staff support and development has been an area of success, particularly in relation to ancillary staff. The ESAs were generally clear about their roles and responsibilities and viewed the teachers as good role models for developing their own behaviour management skills. Both the Elton Committee and HMI saw staff development as essential.

On the surface there appear to be few links between the pastoral and academic curricula, that is planned personal and social education lessons or circle time. However, implicit links do exist, for instance a whole-school emphasis is placed on encouraging success, measured against one's own abilities, and protecting and developing self-esteem.

The micropolitical dimensions of the school appear to revolve around the headteacher, who is seen as the driving force. Whilst the head's approach is generally welcomed, there appear to be some concerns, also expressed by the head himself, that teaching staff may become over-reliant upon his 'presence' which in turn may hinder their own development. The role and approach of the Senco also appears supportive of the head's philosophy. No other specific member of staff was mentioned as especially influential within the organization. There appears to be supportive, yet well-defined and accepted boundaries between the head, teaching staff and ESAs.

Tomlinson (1992) also suggests that organizational values determine the extent to which the bias is towards the organic or mechanistic. Clearly Westlea's approach favours the organic. The reliance on formal systems and procedures appears to be minimal, in contrast to the emphasis on relationships, and staff are aware that positive relationships encourage desirable behaviour.

CONCLUSIONS AND SUGGESTIONS

Westlea's approach to behaviour management is based on a consensus to a shared value system supported by the personal commitment and leadership style of the headteacher. Such a consensus is repeatedly reaffirmed 'as issues arise' as well as via more formal staff support and development. Many of the procedures and approaches emanate from, and are implicit in, the school's philosophy.

The headteacher's central position may, on occasions, lead to a lack of confidence, by teaching staff, in dealing with some procedures, for example regarding parental contact or unwanted behaviours.

The absence of a written behavioural policy makes it difficult to determine a 'baseline' from which developments can be monitored and evaluated. The approach appears to be derived from underlying principles which tend to be expressed in general terms, for example 'a caring approach based on mutual respect'. There may be times when these aims need to be expressed as objectives. It could be argued that policy documents often gather dust once written and that the absence of such a document provides the opportunity continuously to develop, monitor and evaluate practice. In practice this can be demanding in terms of time and energy, although this was not seen as an issue for teaching staff. Consideration should be given to developing a written behavioural policy. This process, in itself, should reaffirm and consolidate good practice and make explicit the values and principles that underlie the management of the whole-school approach to behaviour.

Teaching staff interviewed felt they would benefit from further development in managing behaviour and would welcome opportunities to discuss and share ideas. Behavioural management is a skill which is acquired over a period of time via practice, reflection and adaptation. Consideration might be given to developing a 'support forum' where staff could share experiences in a safe environment.

Consideration might also be given to clarification of the pastoral roles of teaching staff, particularly in relation to parental contact, as well as developing the pastoral curriculum which might include such techniques as circle time.

These suggestions should not be seen as implied criticisms of what is, in essence, exceptionally good practice.

Since reporting the findings of this project, the staff at Westlea have begun work on a written policy document.

ACKNOWLEDGEMENTS

I am indebted to the headteacher, staff and pupils at Westlea School, West Swindon, Wiltshire, for their open and friendly acceptance of this project and the frankness with which they were willing to discuss the issues raised. Special thanks are due to Maureen Heaven for typing this report and to Wiltshire Library and Museum Service for their prompt and efficient service.

REFERENCES

Ballard, J. (1982) *Circlebook: a leader handbook for conducting circletime, a curriculum of affect*. New York: Irvington.

Best, R., Ribbins, P., Jarvis, C. and Oddy, D. (1983) *Education and care*. London: Heinemann.

Buckley, J. (1985) *The training of secondary school heads in Western Europe*. Windsor, Berks: NFER Nelson.

DES (Department of Education and Science) (1987) *Behaviour and discipline in schools. Education observed 5* (HMI Report). London: DES.

DES (1989) *Discipline in schools* (report of the Committee of Inquiry chaired by Lord Elton). London: HMSO.

Docking, J. (1989) Elton's four questions: some general considerations, in N. Jones (Ed.) *School management and pupil behaviour*. Lewes: Falmer.

Gordon, T. (1974) *T.E.T.: teacher effectiveness training.* New York: David McKay Company, Inc.

Herbert, M. (1987) *Behavioural treatment of children with problems. A practice manual.* London: Academic Press.

Nisbet, J. and Watt, J. (1984) Case study, in J. Bell, T. Bush, A. Fox, J. Goodey and S. Goulding (Eds) *Conducting small scale investigations in educational management.* Milton Keynes/London: Open University/Paul Chapman.

Open University (1987) *Research methods in education and social sciences* (Course D304). Milton Keynes: Open University Press.

Preedy, M. (1984) The management of pastoral provision: progress monitoring at Ashbourne school, in S. Goulding, J. Bell, T. Bush, A. Fox and J. Goodey (Eds) *Case studies in educational management.* Milton Keynes/London: Open University/Paul Chapman.

Tomlinson, D. J. (1992) Performance management of schools, *Local Government Policy Making,* Vol. 19, no. 2, Oct, pp. 50–5.

Wiseman, J. P. (1985) The research web, in J. Bryner and K. M. Stribley (Eds) *Social research principles and procedure.* Harlow: Open University/Longman.

Wragg, E. C. (1984) Conducting and analysing interviews, in J. Bell, T. Bush, A. Fox, J. Goodey and S. Goulding (Eds) *Conducting small scale investigations in educational management.* Milton Keynes/London: Open University/Paul Chapman.

Yin, R. K. (1984) *Case-study research and design methods.* Newbury Park, Ca: Sage.

CHAPTER 5

Improving Student Achievement by Using Value-Added Examination Performance Indicators

ROSALIND LEVAČIĆ

ABSTRACT

The chapter starts with a basic introduction to the measurement of value added, citing a number of recent examples. It examines how a school can develop its own value-added performance indicators. Two sets of issues are dealt with – the technical issues of collecting, analysing and presenting the required numerical data, and the management issues relating to how value-added performance indicators are used to assess and improve student, department and teacher performance. These issues are explored by means of a case study. The technical appendix provides a guide to the computer analysis of value-added examination results.

INTRODUCTION

One of the more robust statistical relationships to emerge from educational research is that individuals' educational achievements in terms of examination results and income-earning capacity are strongly related to their cognitive ability (as measured in standardized tests) and their parents' social background. In the 1960s and 1970s it was widely thought from the Coleman Report (a massive study published in the USA in 1966) that students' educational attainments were due to their social background and prior ability and were not influenced by the school they attended. Since then research has established that schools do make a difference though it is not nearly as large as the effects of social background and prior ability. This has been established through major studies of groups of schools (Rutter et al., 1979; Mortimore et al., 1988; Smith and Tomlinson, 1989) and statistical analysis of all schools in a local education authority (LEA) (e.g. Gray et al., 1990; Jesson and Gray, 1991, 1993; Hedger, 1992; Wilms, 1992; McPherson, 1992).

Therefore raw examination results, which take no account of students' social background and ability, are totally unreliable as a measure of school or college performance. While this has been known for many years, the publication of raw examination results in so-called 'national league tables' in England and Wales has awakened much greater interest in obtaining 'value-added' measures of examination performance. Value-added measures take account of the effect on examination results of pupils' social background, ability and other factors, such as gender – over which the school has no control except through overt or covert selection – and so enable the amount contributed by the school to be estimated.

There are a number of reasons why a college or school can benefit from having a value-added indicator of examination performance.

- Only such a measure shows whether the results are as good as can be expected, or are better or worse than expected, given the prior attainment, social background and other student characteristics which are externally determined. A value-added indicator which shows performance to be satisfactory or better enables schools and colleges, particularly those with below-average raw exam results, to demonstrate to the outside world and to themselves that they are doing well.
- Value-added measures can indicate differential performance in the different curriculum areas which cruder comparisons using, say, average the GCSE score over all subjects, cannot do as effectively.
- Value-added measures are performance indicators which can be used internally in conjunction with other information in securing improved performance from students and teachers.

ROLE OF INVESTIGATOR

In this investigation I took on the role of a consultant to a school considering the introduction of a centralized information system whereby the academic progress of its students would be related to their educational attainment on entry. The school had for a number of years tested its intake pupils in maths, reading comprehension and non-verbal reasoning in order to use the information for initial setting arrangements and for identifying pupils with learning difficulties. No use had up till then been made of the information for estimating value-added examination results.

The investigation has two distinct aspects, which I have labelled 'technical' and 'managerial'.

Technical issues

To assess the operational feasibility of a school obtaining its own value-added measures of student performance by investigating the following questions:

- What value-added indicators can be estimated from the data a school currently possesses?
- What kinds of comparisons can be made in order to assess performance?
- How can the data be assembled together so as to undertake computer analysis?

Management considerations

To report on the management issues surrounding the use of such value-added indicators within a school as a system for securing improved performance.

As value added is an example of a performance indicator (PI), the widely advocated characteristics which PIs in general should possess provide a benchmark against which to make recommendations about the implementation of a value-added indicator system. Distilling from a number of sources (DES, 1989; Hulme, 1989; Hargreaves and Hopkins, 1991, pp. 140–1; Rodgers and Badham, 1992, pp. 12–24; Aspinwall *et al.*, 1992, pp. 139–68), the recommendations for performance indicators are that they should:

- be consistent with the goals of the organization and contribute to their achievement;
- provide a basis for making useful comparisons over time, with similar organizations or between units within the organization;
- be acceptable and credible to people within the organization as well as to those outside it;
- be as simple and as few as possible;
- be used as indicators of performance not as final judgements and absolute measures of performance;
- stimulate appropriate questions about the nature of the performance and the factors that contribute to different standards of performance;
- be used therefore for self-evaluation from which emerge ideas for actions to improve performance;
- be acceptable in terms of the costs of operating the PI system relative to its benefits.

METHODS EMPLOYED IN THE INVESTIGATION

Evidence was gathered from two schools: Willowbrook School, which was considering developing value-added indicators, and Leon School which had developed its own system over the last three years. Different methods of data gathering and analysis were employed for the two aspects of the investigation. For the investigation of technical feasibility the main instruments were formal and informal interviews to obtain information about the availability of data, the current uses to which they were put and the workload involved in analysing them.

Access to data at both schools was obtained and a statistical analysis performed in order to assess the feasibility of producing value-added indicators using a spreadsheet program, in this case Microsoft Excel.

In order to explore the management issues involved in implementing a value-added indicator system, a small-scale case study of Leon School was undertaken. This set out to investigate how value-added indicators are measured at Leon and how the system is used within the school. Data were gained mainly through interviews supplemented by the study of school documents. Interviews were conducted with the headteacher, Bruce Abbott, five teachers and five students to explore issues concerned with how the value-added indicator system is used in monitoring student, department and teacher performance and how it is perceived to contribute to raising student achievement. It must be made quite clear at the outset that the purpose of the case study is to explore general issues concerned with the ways in which a value-added indicator system can be used as an internal management device through discussion with teachers and students who have experience of such a system. It is not a case study of the impact of value-added indicators at Leon School since this would have required a much larger-scale study.

THE MEASUREMENT OF VALUE ADDED

The concept of value added refers to the amount the individual school contributes to students' educational outcomes once allowance has been made for the effects of social background, prior attainment, gender and any other factors which are not directly controlled by the school. As the concept is used here, value added is restricted to the assessment of educational outcomes which can be quantitatively measured. Of course, schools and colleges contribute 'added value' to students' acquisition of skills, knowledge, understanding and behaviour which are vitally important but cannot be quantified. To focus on quantifiable indicators of educational performance is not to deny the importance of the non-quantifiable. The two are interlinked, as school and college concerns with the pastoral and cultural sides of their activities often testify.

In order to obtain comparative estimates of school effectiveness in terms of value added, data have to be gathered on a common basis from a relatively large group of schools (at least 40) and analysed statistically. A number of authorities have been undertaking such research, often using academic consultants. One of the earliest was Fife (Wilms, 1992). In England, Shropshire (Hedger, 1992) and Nottinghamshire (Jesson *et al.*, 1992; Jesson and Gray, 1993) are two authorities which have funded value-added research and have published the results, thus providing valuable examples of practice.

To obtain statistically valid value-added indicators one must have quantitative data on individual pupil characteristics, in particular gender and prior attainment and/or social background. School averages are not sufficient (Goldstein, 1987). Shropshire, for example, has LEA-wide pupil-level data on reading comprehension (verbal reasoning) taken at 10-plus. Nottinghamshire, which did not have LEA-wide testing, asked schools to provide information for a 20 per cent random sample of pupils on free school meals entitlement and on three broad categories of parental occupation (manual, clerical and professional). The pupil background variables, such as a measure of educational attainment on entry to secondary school (prior attainment), social status, gender and ethnicity are called the *explanatory variables*. They are used to explain students' examination performance which is measured quantitatively by giving an A grade 7 points, a B grade 6 points, a C grade 5 points and so on. (Unclassified results and non-appearance at the exam score 0.) Each student's numerical grades for all subjects entered are then totalled to arrive at an overall total GCSE performance. This can be turned into an average GCSE subject score by dividing through by the number of subjects taken. In this example the GCSE exam score is the *dependent variable*, since it depends on the explanatory variables.

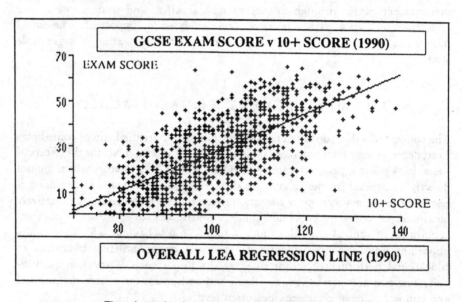

FIGURE 5.1   The relationship between examination results and prior educational attainment. Source: Hedger, K. and Raleigh, M. (1992) GCSE examination results: improvement of: route I, *The Curriculum Journal*, Vol. 3, no. I, p. 54.

One way to see the relationship between prior attainment and GCSE performance is to plot the two variables on a scatter diagram as in Figure 5.1 which displays data from Shropshire. The total GCSE exam score is measured on the vertical axis and the score on the verbal reasoning test taken at 10-plus is measured along the horizontal axis. The statistical relationship between the dependent variable (in this case the GCSE exam score) and the explanatory variable (in this case verbal reasoning at 10-plus) is estimated by calculating the line of best fit, which can be seen as the diagonal straight line in Figure 5.1. If the correlation between GCSE exam score and NVR at 10-plus were perfect (i.e. 1) then all the points would lie on the line of best fit. (The procedure for calculating the line of best fit is called statistical regression.) A straight line such as that in Figure 5.1 is plotted using an equation which has been estimated from the data. The equation specifies how far up the vertical axis the line starts (this is the constant in the equation) and it specifies the slope of the line. The general form of the equation for the relationship between GCSE exam score and prior attainment is:

GCSE exam score = constant + coefficient × prior attainment test score
$$= a + b \times (prior\ attainment\ score)$$

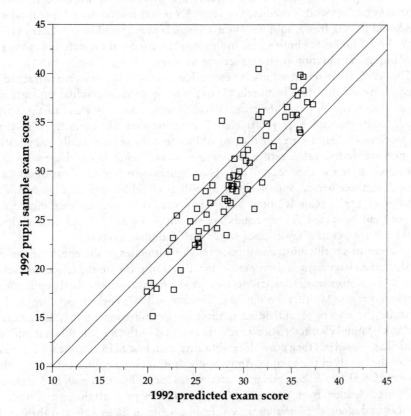

FIGURE 5.2 School average examination score versus predicted examination score. Source: Jesson, D. and Gray, J. (1993) *GCSE performance in Nottingham-shire 1992: further perspectives* Nottingham City Council.

If more than one explanatory variable is involved, as when gender, ethnic origins and free school meal entitlement (as a measure of social disadvantage) are included as explanations of GCSE results, then more terms are added to the equation above. For example the Nottinghamshire study used as explanatory variables for GCSE scores parental occupation category, gender, and free school meal entitlement (FSM) in the estimated equation reproduced below.

Examination score = 24.5 points (if student is female, manual and has no FSM)
              + 10.6 points (with 'intermediate' parental occupation)
              + 19.5 points (with 'professional' parental occupation)
              − 3.9 (if student is male)
              − 7.1 (if student received free school meals).

This equation predicts that a student will score 24.5 points at GCSE if she is female, has parents in manual occupations and is not entitled to free school meals. A girl with parents in clerical-type (intermediate) occupations will score 35.1 points rising to 44 points if her parents are professional workers. A boy of whatever background is predicted to score 3.9 points less from each occupational base, and having free school meals on average is anticipated to reduce the GCSE score by 7.1 points for both sexes. In this way the effects of the different factors in explaining examination performance are allowed for.

However, these relationships are estimates and there is some error attached to them. It would therefore be unreliable to pronounce that individual students had under- or overachieved if their exam scores were relatively close to the scores predicted by the explanatory variables. The further away the exam score lies from its predicted value, the greater the probability that the student really has negative or positive added value rather than the observed score being due to random variation. It is for this reason that Nottinghamshire published its results for schools in three bands: schools doing as well as could be predicted (51 out of 67 schools in 1992), schools doing better than predicted, and another nine doing worse than predicted. These bands are shown in Figure 5.2. All schools lying within the upper and lower lines were 'performing as expected'.

In order to get the most statistically reliable estimates of the effects of student characteristics on examination performance and to estimate the effects of individual schools on exam grades, it is necessary to have data on individual pupils not on school averages. Multilevel modelling (Goldstein, 1987) is the procedure used to estimate the effects of individual schools on examination results, after taking account of pupil characteristics which are external to the school. When multilevel modelling is used it is then possible to obtain a line of best fit for each school, not just for all the pupils in the sample. An example of estimating a different relationship between GCSE exam score and prior attainment for each school in an LEA is shown in Figure 5.3, taken from Jesson and Gray (1991). The prior attainment of students is measured along the horizontal axis (from a score of 91 to 111) and the overall exam score up the vertical axis. Each school in the LEA is represented by its own line. If you take any prior attainment score, say 101, and move vertically up to the regression line, you can read off from the vertical axis the predicted examination score. In this example the lines fan out, showing that different schools have different sloped lines. Another feature of this example is that none of the lines cross. The evidence is therefore that *in this sample* schools with the higher regression lines are more effective in value-added terms across the middle-ability range and, because the lines fan out, that the differences in effectiveness between schools are greater for more able students than the less able.

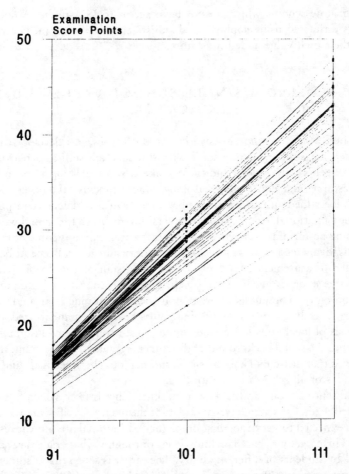

FIGURE 5.3 Differential school effectiveness: student examination performance in relation to prior attainment differentiated by school. Source: Jesson, D. and Gray, J. (1991) Slant on slopes: using multilevel models to investigate differential school effectiveness and its impact on pupils' examination results, *School Effectiveness and School Improvement*, Vol. 2, no. 3, p. 240.

An important conclusion for quantitative school effectiveness research is that a crude ranking of schools in terms of a measure of effectiveness is highly unreliable. This is because small differences in effectiveness are not usually statistically significant. Also schools can be differentially effective for different kinds of pupils which cannot be shown by a simple ranking of schools.

Value-added research has in the past been used mainly to test the hypothesis that schools do make a difference to pupil performance and in some cases to establish the factors associated with effective schools. However, it is only when schools use value-added indicators of their own student performance that the indicators become part of an internal management information system which has the potential for improving student achievement. My chief concern here is to investigate how schools which do not have access to LEA-funded value-added indicators estimated using sophisticated statistical techniques can, nevertheless, develop their own value-added indicators.

DEVELOPING A SINGLE SCHOOL VALUE-ADDED INDICATOR

Leon School, a 12–18 comprehensive in Milton Keynes, has developed its own value-added measure and now uses it with students and staff as a performance indicator. Leon's value-added indicator makes use of existing tests in maths, verbal reasoning and non-verbal reasoning which students take on entry to the school. Value-added measurement was begun in 1990 as a 'defensive response' to the coming of national 'examination league tables' in which the school would not appear to be performing well since its catchment area contains some of the more socially disadvantaged estates in the locality. The headteacher, Bruce Abbott, sees value-added measurement as a way of improving staff morale by showing that they and the students are achieving well, given the educational attainment of students on entry. The pupils' average non-verbal reasoning is around 100, but their average reading score is about nine points below the standardized average. On the basis of local knowledge, one would judge Leon's examination results to be good once the social background of the students is taken into account: the 1992 data showed that the school had the smallest differential between male and female GCSE grades of all schools in the locality.

In the absence of comparable data from other schools from which to estimate value added, Leon has set an internal target for the overall GCSE score which each student is expected to get depending on his/her educational attainment test score on entry. This target was based on knowledge of roughly what grades are achieved nationally by students of different ability. The target is set so that a student with an entry test score of 130 is expected to get the equivalent of 10 Cs at GCSE, or a score of 50; a pupil with an entry score of 70 is expected to get 1 grade G or a score of 1. A straight line is drawn on a graph joining the two points. From this the expected overall examination score for each student, given his/her prior attainment, is determined. The actual overall GCSE examination score each pupil achieves is then plotted on a graph which is reproduced in Figure 5.4. Positive value added for the school as a whole is calculated as the percentage of students appearing above the line. In 1993 80 per cent of Year 11 achieved positive added value for the GCSEs as a whole. However, all individual subject targets are more ambitious since a target of grade C in every subject for students with 120–130 on their entry test would set expectations too low. These students are expected to achieve grade B in individual subjects, while students who score 70–80 on entry are expected to achieve a grade G in each subject. There is therefore a standard way of establishing target grades for each student based on their verbal reasoning score on entry. However, students who entered the school late are currently missed out of the system as they have no verbal reasoning scores on record.

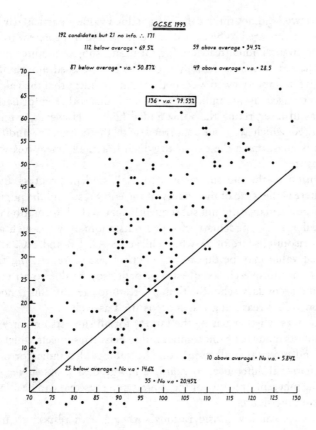

FIGURE 5.4 **Value-added graph used.**

All the added-value calculations have been undertaken manually, which has limited the amount of calculation that can be done and hence the amount of experimentation with the data. So, for example, only one of the three tests, the verbal reasoning, is used in setting the added-value target, though some internal analysis indicated a good correlation with the other tests. The headteacher spends two days a year on the calculations, including a day spent with the head of Year 11 analysing the results when they come in. The head's work in setting up the system and undertaking the value-added calculations for the overall GCSE results, as well as the value-added indicators for departments and teachers, is widely acknowledged.

The value-added system is used not just to analyse GCSE results and to learn from them: it is also used to monitor students' progress through the school by comparing their end of year and mock GCSE examination scores to the target value predicted from their initial test score. It is up to heads of year and form tutors to undertake overall internal exam performance calculations for their own students. Heads of department and subject teachers are responsible for the extent to which they derive and use value-added indicators for internal examinations.

The staff interviewed did not think calculating added value a particularly onerous task, though there appeared to be considerable variation in the extent to which it was undertaken by individual teachers for form and subject monitoring.

How the indicator system is actually used will be discussed more fully in the next section. The staff interviewed were in the main confident that the value-added percentages were used as an indicator only and that other information was brought to bear in interpreting the value-added figures. However, a number of points were raised which were all concerned with the construct validity of the indicator: that is questioning the extent to which it actually measures what it is desired to measure.

First, in relation to the measurement of overall student progress and hence added value, there is the issue of the quality of the entry tests and the pupil scores. Some students' performance did not subsequently match the information from the tests. In particular a few students performed outstandingly well, such as a boy with a verbal reasoning score of 98 who achieved 8 As, 1 B and 1 C. Such high measured added value may be due to rogue entry test scores arising from the random results on multiple-choice questions, or it may be due to an intelligent child coming into secondary school with a low reading age. But this is not picked up unless a non-verbal reasoning test score is used as well.

Another issue was whether basing the targets for all subjects on entry reading comprehension tests made for valid comparability between subjects which differed in the mental and physical skills required. The value-added indicator makes no allowance for national differences in examination grades across subjects due to differences in the inherent difficulty of the subject and these have to be allowed for when interpreting the figures.

Further construct validity considerations surfaced with respect to using the value-added percentages as an indicator of teacher performance. For instance in a few subjects classes are shared by teachers and so the contribution of each cannot be disentangled except by comparison over many classes. While some teachers thought that top sets produced better value-added percentages than bottom sets, the headteacher had found no evidence of this across the school as whole. Though the 70–80 entry test students were expected to get one G grade overall, the target of a grade G in each subject meant that this would not be achieved by some or most subjects. One reason why value-added might be lower in bottom sets is that they contain pupils with behavioural problems who do not have the lowest entry test scores. A couple of disaffected pupils in class could alter class dynamics and adversely affect the quality of learning. These problems with low value-added in bottom sets could be due to the way a department sets students.

Given these concerns over the construct validity of the value-added indicator, it is particularly important that the resulting figures are used as *performance indicators*, to be interpreted sensitively, drawing on other contextual information, and used to stimulate questions about the factors influencing student, department and teacher performance. As one teacher interviewed commented, 'I don't think anybody is seriously offended here because it is used sensibly. I could see problems if the results were taken as hard evidence with little interpretation.'

USING A VALUE-ADDED PERFORMANCE INDICATOR WITHIN SCHOOL

Leon uses its value-added system as a performance indicator in order to motivate students and staff and thereby secure improvement. The ways in which it is used correspond to the criteria for effective PIs set out earlier. It focuses attention on both good and poor performance so that questions are asked, further information sought, reasons for any confirmed differential performance deduced, and ideas on how to improve performance discovered, shared, put into practice and evaluated. The value-added indicator system has been developed over the last three years. Initially data were gathered by the head and analysed to see what kind of information they would reveal. It is only in the last 18 months or so when the value of the information obtained was confirmed that the head introduced the system to the staff. As already noted, there appears to be some variation in individual teacher practice, as is to be expected when an innovation is becoming institutionalized. The three distinct areas of monitoring – student, department and teacher – are now considered in turn.

Student achievement

The value-added indicator is used by heads of department and subject teachers to alert themselves to underachievement well before the GCSE exams so that the student's attention and that of the parents can be drawn to the problem, reasons sought and specific measures taken, such as spending more time on course work, improving writing skills or learning how to revise for exams. One department regularly reviews individual student performance. Another is planning extra after-school lessons for students indicated as underachieving in the trial GCSE exams.

An important feature of the value-added indicator is that students who are obtaining E, F and G grades in their work can be shown to themselves and their parents to be making good progress, given the level they were at when they entered the school, and thus encouraged to achieve some GCSEs. The indicator is also increasingly used by form tutors in Years 10 and 11. Year 11 tutors interview all students who are expected to get five or more A to C grades. Students are shown the graphs and thus are roughly aware of their initial entry score. A crucial issue is whether the system motivates students. Most of the teachers interviewed thought it did in many, but not all cases. Some difference of opinion remains as to whether low-ability students are motivated by achieving positive value-added or are demotivated by having 'low expectations' in terms of raw exam results indicated to them. From the students interviewed, it would appear that those who had low entry scores and had done well were pleased and motivated, higher-ability underachieving students were usually, though not always, motivated to do better, while it was felt that the below-average underachievers remained un-interested.

Departments

Since value-added measures can vary quite considerably from year to year, the longer the time period over which value-added comparisons in school or departmental performance have been recorded, the greater the reliance that can be placed on data showing persistent trends. At the time of the study Leon had accumulated three years of value-added GCSE performance by subject, which is collated by the headteacher and passed on to heads of department. Departments differ as to whether they share the teacher PIs openly or not, though it was thought impossible to keep such information hidden since it would emerge through gossip. Departments respond to the value-added indicator whether they have above- or below-average PIs. In one department with above-average value-added:

> the graphs were passed around at our first meeting in September. One staff member had 80 per cent with a mixed-ability group and the other staff members had 57 per cent. We asked how we could improve the performance of those who don't reach the right levels. We think we can do it through course work and INSET.

The value-added indicator puts pressure on heads of department with poorer performances across the department as a whole than they can justify when other factors are taken into account to seek changes, such as ways of improving teaching in the department.

Value-added as an indicator of teacher performance

Though it is not used in appraisal, value-added as an indicator of teacher performance is the most contentious aspect of the system. It was made clear by the teachers interviewed that the PI is used to ask questions about performance, not to make hasty summative judgements. It is only used to compare performance within a department where like can be compared with like, and not across departments. The system can motivate individual teachers if they respond to the PI by engaging in self-evaluation. As one teacher put it:

> For teachers who have a lower percentage of value-added, it ought to be pulling them up sharp to ask 'Why haven't I achieved?' Sometimes it's a difficult group with whom you don't relate. But this shouldn't happen over a period of years. Those who are consistently underachieving need to ask what is wrong with their teaching.

Heads of department may ask teachers to explain a low PI score and the headteacher also has a word with such teachers. The main emphasis is on asking teachers to explain a low PI either in terms of specific factors, like a few difficult pupils in the class, or in terms of required improvements in practice. The head, head of department, or a senior teacher, all offer support to individual teachers, such as advice on getting better informed on GCSE marking standards or on lesson planning. Some departments are more reluctant than others to use value added as a source of information on teacher performance on the grounds that it is an unreliable measure, demotivates teachers with low PIs, and is divisive when PIs differ within a department. In such an atmosphere it is argued that teamwork would be undermined. Other more reliable and less divisive information on teacher performance, such as knowledge of subject, relationships with students, amount of preparation and marking are available to heads of department. In general terms this is an argument for input and process PIs rather than output ones. The head's view is that these process indicators of good teacher performance are required for a good value-added indicator, and that the latter has the advantage of being less dependent on subjective judgement.

One strength of the value-added indicator is felt to be that teachers with lower-ability sets cannot dismiss the low grades as inevitable and are given an incentive to improve grades. However, given the view held by some that value added is more difficult to achieve with lower-ability sets, departmental setting policy and the allocation of sets to teachers are clearly issues upon which the PI system focuses attention. Equity and staff morale could conflict with the efficient allocation of teachers to teaching groups if one teacher, say, is effective with top sets but poor with low-ability sets. In some circumstances there could be a conflict between a departmental policy of ability setting to improve exam results and one of all mixed-ability sets to avoid differential teacher PIs.

COMPUTER SOFTWARE IN THE PRODUCTION OF VALUE-ADDED INDICATORS

As stated at the beginning of this report, one of my objectives was to assess the feasibility of using information technology to analyse value added in schools. The main problem was to assemble in one place (or computer file) data which were held in different computer systems, and to perform simple statistical analysis on these data and present the results graphically. This task proved quite feasible and is reported in more detail in the technical appendix. The type of graphs which can be used to present the value-added information are shown in Figures 5.5 and 5.6. Figure 5.5 is the computer-generated version of the manual value-added graph shown in Figure 5.4. The solid black line is the target line which Leon set. The dotted line is the line of best fit estimated from Leon's Year 11 students' verbal reasoning scores in Year 8 and their average GCSE score. As explained earlier, a student who gains more than the target grade in a subject is deemed to have positive value added. Figure 5.6 shows the number of students with positive value added in each GCSE subject as a percentage of the total number of students who took that subject. There are clearly considerable differences in subjects' percentage value added but these indicators need to be carefully interpreted using further contextual information. For instance the two subjects with 100 per cent value added are minority languages and the subject with the smallest value added is a low-achieving set.

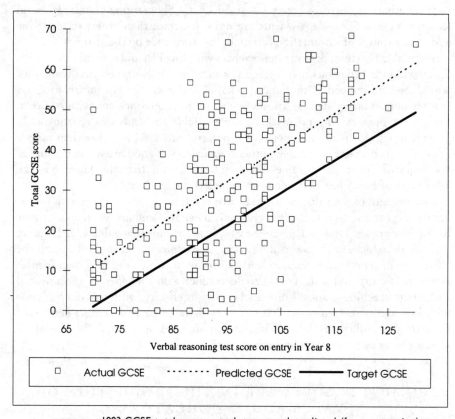

FIGURE 5.5 1993 GCSE total score: actual, target and predicted (from regression). Overall target is set so that a student with VRQ on entry of 70 is expected to get one grade G and with a VRQ of 130 is expected to get 10 grade Cs (a score of 50). Predicted grade is based on values from a regression equation ($a = -49.3$, $b = 0.859$).

CONCLUSIONS AND RECOMMENDATIONS

A value-added performance indicator is consistent with school aims for developing each student's potential as far as possible since it focuses on individual achievement and this can be obtained at every ability level. Clearly care has to be taken with how the indicator is used with students and parents.

A workable value-added system can be created with a few, simple PIs, such as the difference between actual exam score and that set as a target or target range based on prior attainment scores.

The value-added indicator system provides a useful basis for making comparisons between departments and for the school over time. Several years' data are required before conclusions can be reliably drawn and value-added measures have to be supplemented by other contextual information. It is particularly important that added-value teacher PIs are used sensitively. However, while a static target

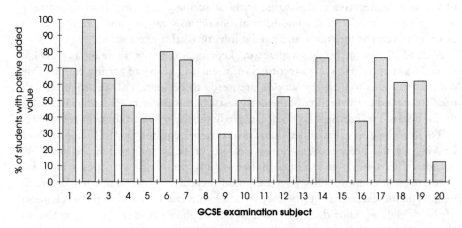

FIGURE 5.6 Percentage added value by subject: GCSE 1993. (Added value is by comparison to school target. Test 130 = B: test 70 = G.)

ensures the goalposts do not move, it may breed complacency as national results get better year by year. The availability of comparative data from other schools would considerably strengthen a school's value-added system.

A value-added PI system can be made acceptable and credible to people within the school. Outside credibility would be considerably enchanced by comparability with data from other schools. Doubts about the construct validity of the value-added indicator reinforce the need for sensitive interpretation. A computerized system would enable some of these doubts to be tested out.

The Leon case provides an example of a value-added PI being used as generally recommended – as a pointer to asking questions about performance, to encouraging teachers to focus attention on pupils' individual learning needs, to indicate areas of good practice, to encourage shared ideas and supportive professional development. It must be recognized that not all teachers will see PIs in such a positive light but that acceptability is likely to be diffused through most staff over time provided the system is used sensibly and sensitively. In particular, it is important to put the prime emphasis, as at Leon, on the value-added measure as an indicator of student achievement and not as a system of departmental or teacher monitoring.

A value-added PI system need not be costly to operate and can be done manually. Computerization is feasible as the data already held in schools' computer systems can be extracted to a spreadsheet for statistical analysis and graphical presentation of a type not possible with manual methods. However, this does require some investment of time by someone, such as a maths teacher, who is already quite competent at using spreadsheets. Once the initial investment of time has been made, the production of descriptive and analytical statistics becomes much more routine and speedier. Computerization would reduce duplication of effort since all teachers could be provided with a print-out of their teaching and form group added-value indicators. Students could be shown numerical estimates of positive or negative added value without seeing their entry level attainment score relative to others. Also additional simulations can be done on alternative prior achievement measures and predictions of final outcomes.

A good PI system needs good record keeping. As many students as possible should have entry test scores recorded for them and a way of getting comparable data on students joining the school late needs to be found. More attention will need to be paid to the quality of the entry tests. In this respect regression analysis is useful because it indicates how good a predictor the prior attainment test(s) are.

To introduce a value-added indicator system requires the full support and backing of the headteacher. Governors are unlikely to make much progress without this. Clearly it is not a matter of just producing statistics which are pored over in committee by governors and members of the senior management team. The indicators have to be used by staff with students and in self-evaluation of their teaching. Staff therefore need to be convinced that the indicator has an important role to play in motivating students, alerting staff to individual student needs, and contributing to the search for improved practice. This requires a credible indicator which is sensitively interpreted using other contextual information. It will take two or three years to establish a set of added-value performance indicators which begin to reveal consistent patterns. The senior management team have a vital role to play in ensuring that a value-added indicator system becomes embedded in the self-evaluations conducted at school, departmental and individual teacher level. At the end of the day a value-added indicator system is just one element in the management arrangements for achieving an effective school: used appropriately it should support and contribute to all the other elements of effectiveness.

ACKNOWLEDGEMENTS

I wish to thank Bruce Abbott and members of staff of Leon School for all their help with the case study.

REFERENCES

Aspinwall, K., Simkins, T., Wilkinson, J. F. and McAuley, J. (1992) *Managing evaluation in education*. London: Routledge.

Coleman, J. S. (1966) *Equality of educational opportunity*. Washington, DC: Department of Health, Education and Welfare.

DES (Department of Education and Science) (1989) *School indicators for internal management: an aide-mémoire*. London: DES.

Goldstein, H. (1987) *Multi-level models in educational and social research*. Oxford University Press.

Gray, J., Jesson, D. and Sime, N. (1990) Estimating differences in the examination performances of secondary schools in six LEAs: a multi-level approach to school effectiveness, *Oxford Review of Education*, Vol. 16, no. 2, pp. 137–58.

Hargreaves, D. and Hopkins, D. (1991) *The empowered school*. London: Cassell.

Hedger, K. (1992) The analysis of GCSE examination results in Shropshire, *Management in Education*, Vol. 6, no. 1, pp. 29–33.

Hedger, K. and Raleigh, M. (1992) GCSE examination results: improvement of: route 1, *The Curriculum Journal*, Vol. 3, no. 1, pp. 53–62.

Hulme, G. (1989) Performance evaluation and performance indicators for schools, in R. Levačić (Ed.) *Financial management in education*. Milton Keynes: Open University Press.

Jesson, D. and Gray, J. (1991) Slant on slopes: using multi-level models to investigate differential school effectiveness and its impact on pupils' examination results, *School Effectiveness and School Improvement*, Vol. 2, no. 3.

Jesson, D. and Gray, J. (1993) *GCSE performance in Nottinghamshire 1992: further perspectives*. Nottingham City Council.

Jesson, D., Gray, J. and Tranmer, M. (1992) *GCSE performance in Nottinghamshire 1991: pupil and school factors*. Nottingham City Council.

McPherson, A. (1992) *Measuring added value in schools*. London: National Commission on Education.

Mortimore, P., Sammons, P., Stoll, L., Lewis, D., Ecob, R. (1988) *School matters: the junior years*. London; Paul Chapman.

Rutter, M., Maughan, B., Mortimore, P., Ouston, J. (1979) *Fifteen thousand hours*. London: Paul Chapman.

Rodgers, G. and Badham, L. (1992) *Evaluation in schools*. London: Routledge.

Smith, D. J. and Tomlinson, S. (1989) *The school effect*. London: Policy Studies Institute.

Wilms, D. (1992) *Monitoring school performance: a guide for educators*. London: Falmer Press.

TECHNICAL APPENDIX

The data needed for value-added indicators are largely, if not entirely, held in computer systems, with the School Information Management System (SIMS), which Leon uses, being the most ubiquitous. Student records on gender, date of birth, ethnic origin, entry test score and internal examination results are held in the STAR (student records) module of SIMS. Examination results are transmitted directly to schools in computer-readable format and held in the SIMS examinations module. For value-added analysis the data at present need to be extracted from SIMS (or another similar system) and combined in a spreadsheet for further analysis. Staff at both Leon and Willowbrook extracted these data (by printing them to disk from SIMS) and gave them to me on disk. Student names are not required so long as they are identified by matching their examination numbers and school record numbers.

Transferring examination and pupil record data from SIMS for use in Excel

The examination results (or any other data) when extracted from SIMS by using the print to disk command will be saved with a file extension 'prn'. (To read the file remember to ask for all *.* files in the open dialogue box in Excel.) When this is loaded into Excel it will look like this:

Summer Results   **Examination**

NAME LEVEL	RESULT	EXAMINATION TITLE
R.Khatun		
GCSE	C	ART AND DESIGN
GCSE	B	ENGLISH LITERATURE B
GCSE	A	ENGLISH B
GCSE	B	GERMAN CC + BW + HL + HR + HW
GCSE	C	HISTORY B
GCSE	B	MATHEMATICS
GCSE	B	PHYSICAL EDUCATION
GCSE	D	CDT (DES. & REAL.)
GCSE	C C	SCIENCE DOUBLE AWARD

In the transfer process the column formatting will have been lost and all the data entered into one column as shown above. To get the data back into the required columns use the DATA PARSE command in Excel. First select the entire first column containing all the data in the file and then apply DATA PARSE. In the dialogue box that then appears square brackets must be put around each digit that is a separate entry in a data field. It helps to have a hard copy of the SIMS data to see which figures have to go in separate columns. In the examination results data shown below four columns of data are required: the candidate's name, exam grade, subject and examination title. The first row with the candidate's name in it must be selected as the first parse line. In the example above this is:

[Khatun] [C] [Art and Design] [GCSE].

If the row above with the general headings is chosen then the surname will not appear.

After parsing, an entry such as the one below is created and the column headings can be labelled with an appropriate title (e.g. name, grade, subject title, exam).

Rukia KHATUN	C	ART AND DESIGN	GCSE
	B	ENGLISH LITERATURE B	GCSE
	A	ENGLISH B	GCSE
	B	GERMAN CC + BW + HL + HR + HW	GCSE
	C	HISTORY B	GCSE
	B	MATHEMATICS	GCSE
	B	PHYSICAL EDUCATION	GCSE
	D	CDT (DES. & REAL.)	GCSE
	C C	SCIENCE DOUBLE AWARD	GCSE

Every candidate's results will now be entered in columns and rows. Each candidate will have as many rows as she/he has examination subjects.

While this way of presenting the data is designed for printing off results to send to students, it is not in the form required for statistical analysis.

First of all the letter grades have to be replaced with the standard numerical coding: A = 7, B = 6, etc., with X, Y and U all equivalent to 0. To cope with the double science entries either convert each double letter grade into its own, different letter or adjust by hand.

In order to arrange the data in a matrix with each row containing all the examination results by subject of a single student, it is necessary to define a database in Excel for the fields 'name', 'grade' and 'subject title'. Before defining the database, fill down each student's name so that it appears in each row against the examination subject taken. Once the database has been defined, a cross-tabulation (available in Excel version 4) is undertaken with student names in the row headings, examination title in the column headings and grade in the cells.

When this is completed the total number of entries, passes and grades A–C can be counted and turned into percentages. Total and average subject scores for each student can also be calculated. (The EXAM module also provides a file with the total and average examination score and number of A–C passes which can be used instead for these variables.)

At this point the student background data with entry test results and gender, ethnicity and date of birth as additional variables can be copied into the same spreadsheet. These data will previously have been extracted from the SIMS STAR module using the print to disk command.

At this point it is necessary to ensure that the two sets of student names, derived from STAR and the EXAM module, match row by row. There are likely to be some examination candidates without entry test results. These have to be removed from the data used for value-added estimates. This can be done by sorting the whole data set by descending order of entry test result and removing all those without an entry test score. The data are now ready for analysis and presentation using all the statistical and graphical facilities of Excel.

Statistical analysis and presentation of results

With Excel one can graph the data in exactly the same way as Leon did. This is shown in Figure 5.5. The target line for the overall GCSE score given the VR test score in Year 8 was derived by solving the simultaneous equations which set the standards expected from VR score of 70 (1 grade G i.e. an overall score of 1) and 130 (10 Cs or an overall score of 50).[1]

[1]
$$1 = a + b70 \qquad (1)$$
$$50 = a + b130 \qquad (2)$$
Thus subtracting the first equation from the second:
$$49 = b60$$
thus
$$b = 49/60 = 0.817$$
Substituting 0.817 for b in (1) produces
$$a = 1 - (0.816 \times 70)$$
$$a = -56.16$$

Target GCSE total exam score $= -56.16 + 0.817 \times$ (VR test score)

However, value-added results are calculated directly by Excel and are only graphed as a means of presentation. To obtain the added value for each student their target score is subtracted from the actual GCSE score and the number of students with positive values calculated. An alternative measure would be to sum the size of the differences between actual score and target so that the size of the added value (positive or negative) is taken into account.

As well as the overall GCSE examination score, the value added by each subject can be calculated using targets for individual subjects, such as those set at Leon. These are 1 (grade G) for a student with a VR score of 70 and 6 (grade B) for a VR score of 130. This sets the equation relating target GCSE grade to VR:

Target GCSE grade $= -4.83 \times 0.083 \times$ (VR score)

By subtracting the target exam grade from the actual grade the value-added performance of each student in each subject was calculated, the number of students with positive value added calculated and reported as a percentage of the total number of entries for that subject. The results are shown graphically in Figure 5.6.

The data were also used to undertake statistical regression of the influence of prior attainment, gender, ethnic origin and age on GCSE examination scores. At Leon 40 per cent of the variability in the 1993 GCSE exam results was explained by the VR test score in Year 8. (This was restricted to the 176 candidates who had taken the entry tests.) None of the other variables was significant. The line of best fit for Leon is quite close to the target line for the individual subjects, though above the target line for the overall GCSE score. From the regressions of GCSE total and or average subject score on entry test results one can obtain estimates of the constant and the coefficient in the line of best fit equation. By using these values together with students' prior attainment test score their expected examination results can be calculated.

Comparative data from different schools illustrate how the statistical results can vary. For example Willowbrook's entry test (non-verbal reasoning) only explained 30 per cent of the variation in exam results but gender was significant, with boys performing considerably less well than girls for a given NVR score. These different results for the impact of gender suggest that further investigation of the effects of different prior attainment measures would be informative and that different school improvement strategies may be required when there is poorer performance by one gender than when this is not the case.

PART TWO

Managing Resources

CHAPTER 6

Compulsory Competitive Tendering in the Primary Sector

MICHAEL MURPHY

ABSTRACT

The main aim of this investigation is to inform primary school governors and managers to help them to decide how their school can best respond to the requirement to manage services, in particular those subject to compulsory competitive tendering (CCT) legislation.

A second aim is to raise awareness of the potential for operating the school as a business organization in order to support its core learning functions as effectively as possible.

INTRODUCTION

Schools have become more like business organizations in having responsibility for managing the physical environment that supports the core purpose of the business which, in the case of educational institutions, is learning outcomes. How to manage operational services, such as grounds and building maintenance, without detracting from the management of the core purpose of the school, is particularly problematic for small schools because the headteacher has few, if any, options for sharing or delegating managerial functions to others. Responsibility for operational services is just one aspect of the greater autonomy of schools in resource management which has increased the range of management issues facing head-teachers.

The Local Government and Land Act 1980 required local authorities to put out to compulsory competitive tendering (CCT) several service areas for which they had responsibility. The Local Government Act 1988 extended CCT to school services and a year later the implementation of the Education Reform Act 1988 began. This required local education authorities (LEAs) to delegate the bulk of their schools' expenditure as budgets to be managed at school level. By this time CCT was an established fact of life in local government and had changed the culture of most local authorities. Before 1980 councils delivered most services themselves and managed people rather than contracts. Their way of defining and managing work 'may have been flexible but only because specifications for the work were often vaguely worded . . . changes could be made easily, since management and the workforce were usually in the same department' (Audit Commission, 1993). The same report suggests that where some local authorities have been less successful in providing good-quality services this has usually stemmed 'from a failure to adequately involve the consumers of the service in the contract process'. Further, it states that in 'a well managed authority . . . the headteacher on behalf of the school, its students and their parents . . . plays an important part in the specification and monitoring of a contract'.

The relevant service areas where CCT currently affects schools are cleaning, grounds maintenance, school meals, and vehicle maintenance and repair.

Voluntary-aided and grant-maintained schools, where staff are employees of the governing body not the LEA, are outside the 1988 legislation. But where this is not the case, for example school meals staff, the CCT legislation applies. The 1988 Act gave local authority schools with delegated budgets three main options with respect to these services. They can:

- ask the LEA to make arrangements for the work to be done;
- set up a school-based direct service organization (DSO) and try to win the contract in competition with outside organizations;
- invite tenders for the work from external providers – which may or may not include the local authority's DSO.

The relative costs and benefits of these arrangements will vary with the size of the institution. Small schools were later exempt from the CCT requirements for cleaning and grounds maintenance. To qualify a school must have a fully delegated budget and employ no more than three full-time equivalent staff on ground maintenance and cleaning combined. Beginning in 1994 any school with no more than 111 hours per week being used for the combined tasks of cleaning and grounds maintenance will be exempt. Most primary schools are therefore exempt. These schools are free to appoint (and dismiss) staff engaged on cleaning or grounds maintenance tasks in the same way that they already do for teachers and other members of staff (Coopers & Lybrand, 1992). An exempt school which employs its own cleaners is therefore in effect managing its own DSO but does not have to put out the cleaning contract to competitive tendering. There is increasing evidence that many schools eligible to take advantage of the exemption which came into force in August 1992 are keen to do so. Whilst they certainly involve management time, school-based DSOs are becoming more common. Though large bulk contracts negotiated by LEAs are still the norm, increasingly schools are deciding to switch to individual LEA contracts so securing some flexibility while avoiding the management effort of running their own services.

METHODS

My role was that of an external consultant concerned with reviewing the issues and presenting recommendations which would assist the managers of a primary school in developing a strategic approach to managing CCT services. My concern is with the broader issues of how to manage CCT services in relation to the efficiency and effectiveness of the learning environment rather than with the details of any particular service agreement. The methods employed were familiarization with the relevant background literature and interviews conducted with the headteachers of two grant-maintained primary schools and with officers involved in managing LEA service contracts. Since the culture and history of CCT within a local authority may affect the quality of the communication channels between schools and authority, I felt that it would have been inappropriate for me to conduct interviews only with school personnel. Since grant-maintained primary schools have gone further than most in managing their own operational services, I selected two for investigation.

I conducted face-to-face interviews with the headteachers of Redhill and Borrow Wood primary schools in Derbyshire, and telephone interviews with key LEA personnel in Leicestershire, Nottinghamshire and Derbyshire. Redhill had 176 pupils and a full-time teaching staff of 6 plus the headteacher. It was due to become grant maintained on 1 January 1994, when an immediate increase in staffing by 0.1 was anticipated, and an additional teacher was due by September 1994. Borrow Wood which became grant maintained in April 1992, had 233 pupils and 8.4 teachers and the head. It has recently increased its staffing by two teaching days, one for special needs and one to release the deputy head from teaching duties. With almost two years' grant-maintained experience, Borrow Wood provided an interesting contrast to Redhill, about to enter the grant-maintained arena.

I felt that interviewing was appropriate since it allowed me to pursue particular aspects. I felt that a visit to the schools, bearing in mind their very busy circumstances, was preferable to issuing questionnaires. An open-ended set of questions was used and responses recorded in note form during the interviews. The purpose of undertaking parallel and small-scale case studies of the two schools was to obtain data from actual practice in similar organizational settings. I hoped that the data would provide evidence for testing out a 'management process model' which I explain more fully in the next section. This model sees 'operational support services' as being managed in order to secure efficiency and effectiveness in relation to the core purpose of the organization. Also, my investigation could assist in developing recommendations for practice in other similar settings.

The purpose of using the case study method for consultancy is, as Hope in Bennett *et al.* (1995) points out, different from that in academic research, which demands a greater depth. An academic researcher seeks to achieve representation of the full reality of a particular case, often by developing grounded theory (Easterby-Smith, Chapter 5, in Bennett *et al.*, 1995). The consultant will usually approach a case study with a predetermined frame of reference or model. The model is used to structure the information being sought in order to judge whether it provides a suitable framework for developing more generalizable recommendations for practice. Clearly there are questions of validity and reliability in relation to the data and how they are interpreted. However, the role of a consultant is to use judgement based on expertise, which may be specialist and technical, as well as reliant on consultancy skills (Cockman *et al.*, in Bennett *et al.*, 1994).

ISSUES

The 'management process model' referred to above relates inputs, processes and outcomes. A function of management is to select inputs and to process them in order to secure intended outcomes. In relation to schools the key issues are how to ensure that operational services are provided efficiently and effectively without taking managerial resources away from the school's core educational purpose. Ideally the contribution which the physical enviroment makes to learning should be maximized at minimal cost to staff time and energy. However, CCT may have offered schools more opportunity to control and monitor their own resources, but potentially to the detriment of the quality of the learning environment.

For small schools the management of CCT is particularly problematic. Unit costs in small schools are generally higher than in larger schools where economies of scale result in lower cost per pupil (Coopers & Lybrand, 1993). Larger schools also benefit from economies of scope, that is reductions in unit costs due to a larger number of managers being better able to cope with multiple tasks through specialization. The process issues and resultant time-consuming demands of managing a service subject to CCT need only to be listed to be appreciated. They are as follows:

- Identifying the school's needs.
- Specifying the contract. Doing this well is the key to securing value for money. The specification must set out clearly what is to be done by the contractor, what conditions the contractor has to meet, for example vetting staff for criminal records, and what the default procedures are.
- Inviting tenders.
- Choosing the successful tender.
- Monitoring that the contract is being complied with, raising non-compliance with the contractor, triggering default clauses and docking payments if the contractor defaults.
- Evaluating the service and contract in order to amend the contract if necessary when it comes up for renewal.

Managing efficiently and effectively is concerned with achieving outcomes through managing processes which relate inputs to the outcomes. Efficiency is defined either as achieving a predetermined amount of outcomes at minimum cost or maximizing outcomes for a given level of cost. Effectiveness is achieving desired outcomes. In the management process model inputs are taken through a set of managerial interventions in order to achieve a satisfactory set of outcomes. Both the inputs and the managerial processes are incidental necessities, since the organization is wholly focused on outcomes. To relate this model to schools, learning – indicated by such dimensions as knowledge, skills and attitudes – is taken as the desired outcome: the organization exists to service this desired outcome, whilst the rest of the organization's activities are an incidental expense en route to its outcomes. From this perspective the managerial process itself is a cost incurred in the service of the desired outcomes: teaching itself is cost incurred, as are other costs, in the production of outcomes. The organization is not finance led but is focused on outcomes. Teaching and management have no inherent virtue and can be defended only in terms of learning outcomes. Value for money is measured in terms of the quality and quantity of the outcomes and not in terms of input processes.

Throughout the 1980s, and increasingly since 1988, the drive for value for money has encouraged schools to develop a business orientation as the means through which to achieve a greater efficiency and effectiveness. This orientation has been helped along by a variety of contributors: from those who would emphasize managerial systems, or organizational restructuring, to behaviouralists emphasizing human resources in preference to systems. Whilst organizational theorists may emphasize different approaches to treatment and analysis of inputs, they share the view that a unit of input is not a fixed entity; it only represents a potential capable of being released. If the potential captured, so to speak, within the resource is managed appropriately it will provide more for the organization to use in its pursuit of outcomes. CCT ideally lends itself to this view of organizational input as potential rather than fixed entity. To see the organizations' inputs as potentials, rather than givens, requires imagination; to fully exploit the potentials requires managerial skills.

SCHOOL RESPONSES TO MANAGING CCT

Selecting and monitoring service contracts: DSOS and private suppliers

Redhill and Borrow Wood were selected for investigation as examples of independent management of operational services. Going grant maintained had encouraged both headteachers to join an informal consortia of schools in order to share experiences and to pass on information about the CCT process. The Borrow Wood head, however, felt that this kind of networking would decrease as service handling became an embedded process. Redhill had to learn quickly. As an exempt school it already ran its own cleaning, using the local authority's contract specifications supplied by the technical services department. Catering, as a more regulated area, proved more difficult. Again, the school was helped by its local authority and, from January 1994, began providing catering itself assisted by a consultancy contract with the local authority for the first year – described by the headteacher as 'hand-holding insurance'. Initially both schools relied on the local authority for advice and appraisal of existing contracts and specifications.

Gradually the schools had become more independent of the LEA. With spirited entrepreneurialism, Borrow Wood had begun to build up a bank of specifications from suppliers, the contents of which could be reshaped to suit future occasions. Borrow Wood also learnt to cost its own specifications prior to setting up meetings. This enabled the school to counter the hard-sell approach adopted by many suppliers. The schools learnt to bargain down and ask for quotations to be resubmitted. Redhill, for instance, soon discovered that by bargaining and by manipulating specifications, savings of up to 33 per cent were possible.

The CCT process released new opportunities for redrawing the caretakers' job descriptions to include opening up for lettings and general maintenance. Borrow Wood reduced their caretaker's cleaning responsibility to 25 per cent leaving the remaining 75 per cent for general maintenance work which reduced costs. For example, broken windows had previously incurred call-out costs, temporary boarding up, then a second round of visits by a glazier. Now Borrow Wood's caretaker boards up windows for temporary security at night and next day fits the glass.

In both schools the monitoring of service agreements was shared between the headteachers and various subgroups of their governing bodies. Teaching staff were not responsible for either introducing or monitoring contracts except through their membership of the school's governing body. These arrangements helped to keep contractor and client separate: the headteacher assumed the role of contractor, the governing body that of client. In this way Redhill's and Borrow Wood's cleaning, catering and grounds maintenance contracts were monitored by various working parties of governors. Contractor compliance was assured by either relevant line management (caretaker, headteacher), or through working groups of the governing body (for example, premises committee).

Contract renewal was simplified by the application of rules. Borrow Wood governors, for example, delegated to the headteacher the power of automatic contract renewal where the new price did not exceed 5 per cent of the previous price and where there was no major change to contract specifications. Where the new price was 6–10 per cent higher the contract was reviewed by the governing body's services committee, but the full governing body would preside over a service increase of 11 per cent or more. Even so, unless the original service specification was considered inadequate or inappropriate to new circumstance, the specification renewal was also automatic. In the case of Borrow Wood the resources consumed in the initial stages of shopping around were considered loss leaders, investments which were now paying dividends.

The structure of the governing bodies was of great importance in managing the contractual processes associated with CCT. Both headteachers felt fortunate in having on their governing body accountancy, legal, building and quantity surveying experience. Where there was a collective lack of expertise amongst the governors, headteacher and staff, both schools bought in consultancy advice. Governors' meetings had become more frequent – in the case of Redhill sometimes twice weekly.

The management process model in action

CCT has certainly helped to reduce unit costs in real terms, although the opportunity costs of additional administration during the first year when staff were coming to terms with new systems and new ways of working may have been high. However, the workload had diminished and stabilized at a level a little higher than pre-CCT. This was certainly true in the case of Borrow Wood. But the opportunity costs should be set against the potential gains. Certainly, Redhill and Borrow Wood could be said to be highly cost-conscious organizations, though not wholly finance led.

The Borrow Wood headteacher observed, given the amount of negotiating and bargaining that goes on in the school day due to CCT and service management, the school felt like a small business with the headteacher as managing director. The school could no longer be regarded, as it had once seemed to many, as 'a friendly charity'. Both headteachers saw the CCP process as bringing with it a change of culture and an extension of their role. Both were acutely aware of the demands CCT had made on management time and both expressed concern about the dangers of being drawn away from direct day-to-day involvement in teaching and learning. The management of CCT services together with the enlargement of other management functions had been a prime factor in their decision to give up classroom teaching duties. But both headteachers had found the financial resources, partly acquired through CCT savings, to release the deputy heads from some part of their teaching – a half day per week at Redhill and one day per week at Borrow Wood. As the headteachers assumed a greater resource management role so the deputies assumed the curriculum leadership of their schools.

LOCAL AUTHORITY PERSPECTIVES

The local authority departments most directly involved with CCT in schools included contract, financial, legal and technical services. The general feeling in the three authorities contacted was that the majority of schools had relied heavily upon the relevant department for advice and for the use of model contract specifications. The local authorities' own direct Service organizations had won approximately 85 per cent of school business (Redhill and Borrow Wood being exceptions). Various personnel from departments concerned with CCT expressed optimism about their business relationships with schools which, though not guaranteed, were likely to be secure, at least in the short to medium term. These personnel felt that the schools particularly appreciated their visits to help establish the terms, conditions and details under which contracts would be carried out. The LEAs thought that the client service units were trusted by schools. These units are responsible for monitoring, appeals and complaints and are quite separate in practice from the departments which controlled the DSOs.

In respect of CCT it was thought that schools particularly needed advice because of their tendency to:

- poorly define, and in some cases over-define, specifications;
- arrive at unenforceable contract conditions;
- set up inadequate tender evaluation procedures;
- fall prey to inefficient contract monitoring;
- become too bureaucratic and unrealistic in their contract administration.

RECOMMENDATIONS

Primary schools, as the case studies show, can develop along the lines suggested by the management process model whereby the task of management is to manage inputs and processes so that their potential is exploited for the benefit of the core purpose of learning. However, this conclusion rests on the perceptions of those involved, not on any direct empirical evidence of the effects of autonomous resource management on educational outcomes. However, given the potential that self-management of CCT (and other) operational services offers schools in terms of improved quality and/or lower cost of service, governing bodies and headteachers need to make strategic choices regarding how far independent management of these services is likely to benefit their school, given its specific characteristics. Whether to use LEA contracts, private suppliers or the school's own employees (DSO) is not an all or nothing choice since different forms of provision can be adopted for different services. In each case the benefits of the form of provision need to be weighed up against the likely costs. In general terms the attractions of private suppliers or school DSO are, firstly, improved quality through the school being able to specify its individual needs more precisely and deal directly with the service provider in monitoring the contract, and, secondly, the lower costs gained by shopping around and better control of the service. Against these advantages are the costs in time and energy of self-management of operational services compared to buying into an off-the-peg LEA contract, which may be cheaper if the LEA secures quantity discounts not available to a single school.

Table 6.1 shows how this analysis of costs and benefits can be systematically undertaken by considering each stage of the contracting process. Each task is listed in the first column: the cost and benefit implications of the three forms of provision are shown in the other columns. The advantages of a DSO or using the school's own employees (last column) are as follows.

TABLE 6.1
The Costs and Benefits of different Forms of Service Provision

CONTRACT MANAGEMENT TASK	USING LEA CONTRACTS	PRIVATE-SECTOR CONTRACTS	OWN EMPLOYEES
Identifying the school's needs	Less need or incentive to do this. How worthwhile spending time this way is depends on flexibility of contract choice	An essential preliminary to specifying a contract	On-the-spot continuous indentification
Specifying the contract	Can use LEA expertise	Can specify own individual requirements	No need to specify such a clear contract as it is negotiated directly and continuously
Inviting tenders	Done by LEA	Have to encourage bids	No need to bother if exempt
Choosing the successful tender	Done by LEA	Exercise own choice	Select own employees. More difficult to dismiss for unsatisfactory performance
Monitoring that the contract is being compiled with, raising non-compliance with the contractor, triggering default clauses and docking payments	Monitoring has still to be done by school but have to get LEA to secure contract compliance. Poorer quality may result from managing at a distance and lack of employee loyalty to school	School in direct control of contract compliance procedures. More direct lines of communication. Greater incentive for contractor to perform well for the individual school	Informal monitoring. Much less of it required if own employees are well motivated to provide a high-quality service
Evaluating the service and contract in order to amend the contract if necessary when it comes up for renewal	School still needs to evaluate the contract: may be limited scope for amending contract to suit individual needs	School needs to evaluate the contract: can amend it to suit its needs	Continual informal evaluation occurs. Continual adjustment of service possible. Resources must be devoted to human resource management.

- The school's needs, say for cleaning, can be continuously renegotiated with the cleaners.
- Given good working relationships, the contract does not need to be formally specified in every detail.
- Alternative tenders are not needed provided the school is exempt from CCT.
- The school can select its own cleaners rather than subcontract this out. Employees of the school are likely to be better motivated and more loyal than contract workers and thus produce better-quality work. There is much less need for formal monitoring as much more reliance can be placed on quality assurance by the employee. The costs of contract compliance are therefore less.
- Evaluation is done informally and continuously and the service flexibly adjusted to meet changes in perceived requirements.

The costs of employing the school's own staff include the following.

- A DSO is considerably more costly if the school is not exempt from CCT and so has to engage in the time-consuming process of drawing up formal tenders and inviting bids against the DSO. The costs include those of specifying a contract in detail and searching for the least-cost supplier for the quality of service sought.
- The costs of managing the labour force (which need to be compared to the costs of managing contracts). These include recruitment, training and pay-roll services.
- The inflexibility of having directly employed staff because of the costs placed on employers by employment legislation such as the difficulty and cost of dismissing poorly performing staff.

The best choice for each school depends on its own circumstances, in particular the areas of expertise of the governors and the amount of time they can devote to service management. This was an important factor in the case study schools. The headteacher's own views as to his/her role, in particular on how to reconcile the demands of instructional leadership with those of chief executive, are crucial. The size of the school also has an important bearing since a headteacher with class teaching responsibilities has less time to manage a wide range of operational services and will therefore prefer LEA contracts. The characteristics of the school community are also a key factor in whether labour services of the required quality can be hired. Primary schools in particular can enjoy the support of local people, often parents or those with a long association with the school, who will provide high-quality services. The quality of the LEA services will also be a decisive factor, since the poorer they are the more the school will be induced to seek alternatives.

CONCLUSION

If schools are to realize the potential benefits they need to adopt a strategic perspective to the management of operational services by systematically evaluating alternative approaches. Primary schools can help all staff to see organizational inputs (such as CCT) as resource potentials to be used with skill and imagination. Schools are becoming more aware of the environmental determinants which make them more business oriented. Managing internal processes without losing sight of the school's mission, and ensuring that these processes serve the curriculum and do not become ends in themselves, demands considerable managerial skill. By maximizing the potential of the resources at its disposal, the school is better able to defend its values and enrich the learning experiences of its pupils. Managed strategically, and with due care for ethical and professional values, the school as a business organization serves the core activities of teaching and learning. From this point of view the school as a business organization is merely a device and not an alien set of values in itself.

ACKNOWLEDGEMENTS

I would particularly like to thank Mr Reid of Redhill School and Mr Fearnehough of Borrow Wood School for giving so generously of their time, as did the staff working with CCT in the local authorities of Nottinghamshire, Derbyshire and Leicestershire. All errors of fact and interpretation are my responsibility.

REFERENCES

Audit Commission (1993) Right first (and next) time, Chapter 3 in *Realising the benefits of competition*. London: HMSO.

Bennett, N., Glatter, R. and Levačić, R. (Eds) (1994) *Improving Educational Management through Research and Consultancy*. London: Paul Chapman.

Coopers & Lybrand (1992) *Buying for quality: a practical guide for schools to purchasing services*. London: DFE Publications.

Coopers & Lybrand (1993) *Good management in small schools: a good practice guide for locally managed small schools*. London: DFE Publications.

CHAPTER 7

A Task Analysis of a Computerized System to Support Administration in Schools

SUE MITCHELL AND PHIL WILD

ABSTRACT

This [chapter] reports upon a task analysis study, which focused on the Local Resource Management package of the SIMS database. This revealed some interesting findings about the system and of users' reactions to it. Their evaluation was conducted in a small sample of secondary schools within one local education authority.

INTRODUCTION

The use of information technology (IT) systems to support local management of schools (LMS) is a natural aim within the growing technological environment of schools. Whether the implementation of IT is yet right is open to question. The Schools Information Management System (SIMS) software package is dominating the market at the moment. This package [. . .] includes modules covering most areas of school administration. [. . .] This wide use, however, means that 'getting it right' is extremely important. The implementation of IT systems to the benefit of industrial and commercial organizations in the way first envisaged has proved very difficult, with full success figures of 20–40 per cent being cited. In this chapter [. . .] some questions are raised as to the success of the present system in helping schools to 'manage' themselves.

The potential of IT systems is starting to be recognized by school managers. [. . .] The inability to realize the full potential with the main software is likely to cause frustration. There is evidence that this failure of present systems does exist as some schools are setting up their own spreadsheets of data taken from SIMS output to support the 'what if . . .' management decisions. A successful IT system would not require such double handling of data.

The experiences of industry have been well researched and evaluation methods [. . .] have been established which can help to ensure system success. Adaptation of these evaluation methods to the education context is a growing need. This chapter describes work in progress which is trying to contextualize the industry – based evaluation techniques. [. . .] Initial work based on such analysis seems to be showing that there is a potential system rejection due to its inflexibility.

BACKGROUND

[. . .] A survey by the Foundation for Information Technology in Local Government (FITLOG) (1988) identified the need to support the administrative and management aspects of LMS changes with computer network systems. This led to the Coopers and Lybrand Report (1988) which recommended that £25 million annually, over a four-year period, be made available to support and develop school and LEA administrative needs.

The present study was conducted in one LEA. Their strategy included the development of the Local Education Authority Management Information Systems Team (LEAMIS) whose brief is to phase the implementation of information technology into all the LEA schools over a four-year period. The implementation process involves a training programme to support users of the system. Our study was conducted two years into the project.

The computer system introduced into schools includes hardware and software utilized by the LEA to support administration. The LEA has adopted the SIMS software. This package includes word-processing, local resource management, pupil and staff database, exam records and results, timetabling and system manager facilities. The long-term plan hopes to establish network links between schools and the LEA for the two-way communication of data.

It is envisaged that there will be an increase in the interchange of data between schools and the LEA for administration. Currently the LEA has a monitoring role for the control of finance. The LEA sets a budget for the schools according to a formula and the schools spend the allocation according to their need under local management of schools. The LEA receives invoiced expenditure from schools, monitors spending and sends lists of expenditure back to schools for them to match with their computer records.

THE INVESTIGATION

Our interest was restricted to the Local Resource Management (LRM) package of the SIMS database. This is the finance management module, providing ordering, invoice, reconciliation and accounting facilities. A high-level task analysis was used to reveal details about the users, the structure of the SIMS LRM system and how the computerized accounting system meets user requirements. The technique for the task analysis included elements of Personalized Task Representation (Gregory, 1979) and Open Systems Task Analysis (Harker and Eason, 1979). A combination of these techniques gave a broad analysis and overview of the

users' tasks on the computer database and how these linked with the administration and management of the organization. The task analysis was subjective
through qualitative measures and some open-ended questions.

For this investigation the users of the system were broadly categorized into two
types: either direct or indirect users. The direct users are those people who operate
the computer system regularly in their work. They are not required to make
decisions on the data in the computer. The indirect users are those people in the
organization who do not use the computer regularly, if at all, but are required to
use the output from the computer to support their management decisions. They
are usually members of the school's senior management team.

The questions in the task analysis related to specific tasks within LRM.
Information was obtained about facilities for setting up the budget, ordering,
reconciling, overall financial summaries, petty cash and use of 'local cheque'.
Local cheque is a facility enabling schools to maintain orders and pay for goods on
the system independently of the LEA. Some open-ended questions were included
to allow respondents freedom to add comments about the system and its facilities.
Questions probing training, support and environmental working conditions were
also included.

The study was conducted in four schools; two were middle (11–14 years)
schools with approximately 600–700 pupils on roll, two were upper schools (14–
19 years) with 650 and 1,250 on roll respectively. One direct and one indirect user
were interviewed in each of the schools sampled. [. . .] Users were asked to state
their 'experience' with computers, 'frequency' of use, 'knowledge' of the database,
and their attitude and motivation to use the computer in their work (Mitchell,
1991).

RESULTS

The findings revealed that the direct users were all frequent users of the system,
using the system daily, whereas the indirect users were using the facilities monthly
or less. In one case the computer was not used at all by the indirect user. Computer
experience varied. All direct users considered themselves to be skilled users of the
system and were competent in using the areas of the database they required in their
daily work. Computer experience of the indirect users varied. Some were expert and
able to use a range of facilities with some competence, others described themselves
as novices as they were unable to use the computer to use or obtain information.
Indirect users were generally not as familiar with the facilities of the computer
database as direct users were. The direct users held the job title registrar or
administrative assistant and were described as having a good knowledge of the
system. The indirect users were, in large schools, vice-principals who had little
regular use of the system, teachers of computing, or a registrar who was also the
direct user of the computer system. The diversity of allocation for responsibility was
marked. Small schools with fewer administrative staff had a greater workload than
larger schools where a number of people shared the workload. In larger schools,

there were two or three indirect users and two or three direct users (Mitchell, 1991).

The questionnaire gave information about use of SIMS LRM by the users (Figure 7.1). The information showed that indirect users were involved with setting up the budget and the overall management of the system. Some indirect users did comment that although they had this responsibility, they had little time to familiarize themselves with the facilities, or potential of the system, because of their workload. Questions were also asked about the direct users' satisfaction with their working conditions. This revealed that three out of four users considered the 'stress' aspects of their work to be unsatisfactory. When probed about this, users commented that the pressure and pace of work had increased. They are expected to work at least as efficiently as they had with the previous manual system even when system problems are outside their control. The users under stress were also those who were dissatisfied with the environment conditions of noise, light and location. Half of the users interviewed were dissatisfied with these factors as some work stations were located in busy offices or, in one case, a large cupboard without ventilation apart from the door.

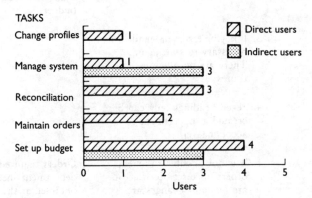

FIGURE 7.1   Direct and indirect users' tasks on SIMS LRM.

Problems perceived by direct users when using the LRM facilities are shown in Table 7.1. The main difficulty when setting up the system is the unacceptable time delay in receiving information about the budget from the LEA. Inconsistent coding between the SIMS database and the LEA mainframe results in time delays and difficulties in processing some information. Some routines in the order system are cumbersome to work through. For example, users are required to backtrack their way through the database to correct errors.

The task analysis resulted in the users' task sequences in SIMS LRM being represented as flow diagrams, which provided an overview of the jobs of the direct and indirect users to manage the delegated budget. The sequence of tasks closely matches the previous manual system. The diagrams (Figures 7.2 and 7.3) clarified how the information on the database could be used to support management decisions and how this information links with the LEA's budget monitoring and regulatory role.

TABLE 7.1
Summary of users' problems with SIMS LRM module

TASK	SIMS	ORGANIZATION
SET UP BUDGET	1. Delays to set up the budget occur because it is not possible to carry over a balance into the new financial year until reconciliation is complete	1. Budget allocation from the LEA is often delayed and 'dummy money' has to be entered to maintain the system
	2. There is insufficient information on the screen when viring between budget headings	2. The overall financial position is not clear at the beginning of the financial year if reconciliation is not complete. This affects decisions for allocation of the budget
	3. If keying errors are made it is necessary to start again. There are no quick escape routes	
	4. Seven headings only can be created at department account level	
ORDER SYSTEM	1. It is not possible to amend orders once set up. If errors are made or changes are required a new order has to be set up	1. Orders required by the departments need to be obtained at the correct time for processing
	2. SIMS will not permit a second invoice request when payment by the LEA is delayed	2. Departments are not all familiar with the order details required by SIMS
	3. SIMS does not record the invoice date, this is done manually. The system gives access to one user at this level	3. Schools often need to chase up delays in payment by the LEA. Some suppliers are refusing to trade because of this problem
	4. Only one order item per line is permitted which causes problems for detailed items	4. Limited access to users will cause organizational problems as the use increases

(continued over)

RECONCILIATION	1. The system is slow to process credit reconciliation	1. There are delays in receiving 'tabs' from LEA. This imposes serious constraints on the system
	2. SIMS automatically updates system by weeks, users have to access correct week of invoice manually to match the item to be checked	2. Codes and journals on the 'tabs' do not have clear meaning for users. There are often errors on the LEA 'tabs' which affect the accuracy of the accounts. Discrepancies may go undetected for some time before being realized
FINANCIAL SUMMARY	1. The audit trail does not give the previous figures obtained for comparative purposes	1. The financial print-outs are not user friendly for the indirect users. A clear graphical analysis would help the representation of the data. This facility is not available on SIMS
	2. Totals are not available at each level of access; these can only be obtained from the audit trail which is a lengthy procedure	2. It is not possible to remodel the financial analysis to suit user requirements. Some users are now obtaining spreadsheet software, for example 'Excel', to do this task
	3. Financial years run in isolation. It is not possible to compare details with previous years or carry forward financial information into future years	

The construction of the database and the links with the organization shown by the flow diagrams demonstrate the rigidity on the order of tasks. For example, meetings between the LEA, governors and senior management impose time constraints in setting up the budget on the system. The system will not operate unless this procedure is carried out (Figure 7.2). Users occasionally need to alter amounts allocated to the different budget headings, or move money (virement) between headings. The difficulty here is that it is not possible to move money sideways. Amounts that need to be altered are processed in a vertical direction. It is therefore necessary to go back to the top sequence 'set up budget' in order to modify the allocation at a lower level. This is time consuming and is further complicated by the changing financial position not showing on screen as changes are made. If this facility were present it would give users important information as

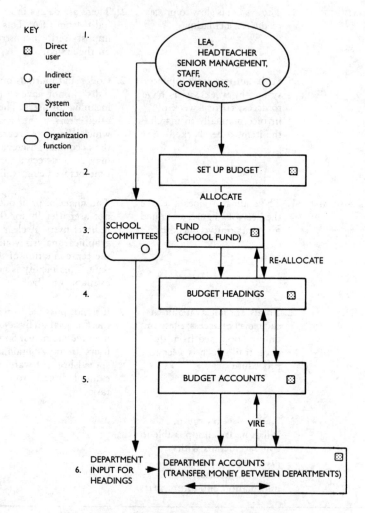

FIGURE 7.2   Task representation I – SET UP BUDGET. When money is vired, the
screen display shows the totals at each level change as the virement occurs. It is not
possible to see the previous amount allocated for comparison.

the alterations are made and provide a check on the changes as they are taking
place. This information may only be obtained at present by obtaining a print-out
at the end of the procedure.

Maintaining orders is a rigid system with the procedure to raise orders and
reconcile invoices following a set sequence of events. Errors and amendments
require the user to backtrack through the levels (Figures 7.3a and 7.3b). The direct
users have sole responsibility for this procedure. Reconciliation depends on the
links with the LEA. As there are often delays in receiving the 'tabs' information
and there are difficulties with matching this on the SIMS system, users generally
give this task least priority because of pressure of work. These delays mean that

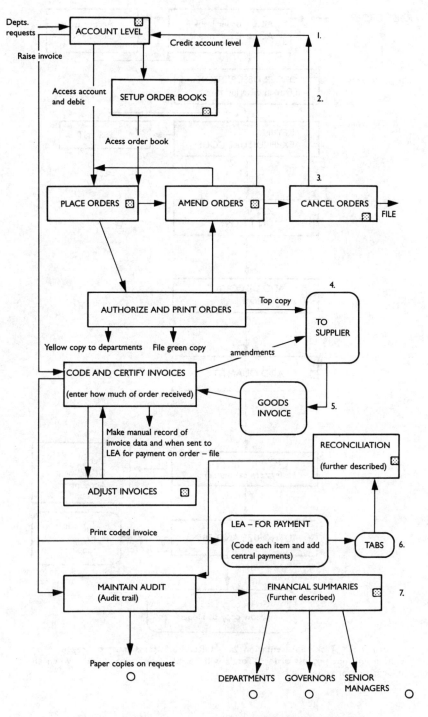

Depts. requests

Raise invoice

ACCOUNT LEVEL

Credit account level

1.

Access account and debit

SETUP ORDER BOOKS

2.

Acess order book

PLACE ORDERS

AMEND ORDERS

CANCEL ORDERS

3.

FILE

AUTHORIZE AND PRINT ORDERS

Top copy

4.

TO SUPPLIER

Yellow copy to departments   File green copy   amendments

CODE AND CERTIFY INVOICES

(enter how much of order received)

GOODS INVOICE

5.

Make manual record of invoice data and when sent to LEA for payment on order – file

RECONCILIATION

(further described)

ADJUST INVOICES

Print coded invoice

LEA – FOR PAYMENT

(Code each item and add central payments)

TABS

6.

MAINTAIN AUDIT
(Audit trail)

FINANCIAL SUMMARIES
(Further described)

7.

Paper copies on request
O

DEPARTMENTS   GOVERNORS   SENIOR MANAGERS

O   O   O

FIGURE 7.3A Task representation 2 – MAINTAINING ORDERS.

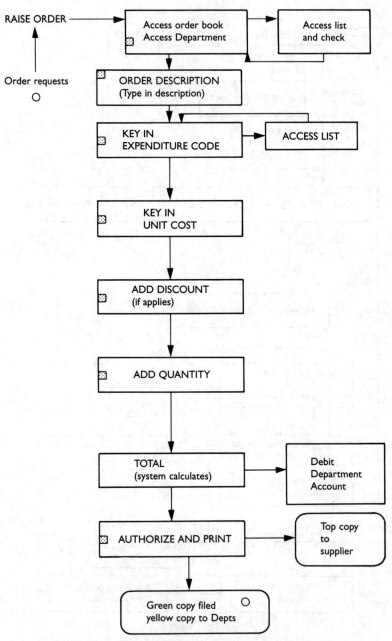

FIGURE 7.3B Task representation 2a – ORDERS.* Items must be keyed in or system will not process orders. Totals will be calculated automatically when all information provided.

the audit maintenance is inaccurate. The financial summaries from the system cannot provide a correct basis for management decisions by the indirect user group. The output is required by a range of indirect users but it is not in a user-friendly form and some modification is usually needed. This is an added task for the direct user. Our findings also revealed that most indirect users are unfamiliar with the format and language of the information.

DISCUSSION

This was a high-level task analysis that provided a broad overview of the system to support financial management and administration in LEA schools. The task analysis raised some important issues about the way the computerized system is being used to improve the efficiency in the operation of LMS. The sample size was small but the findings are supported by and extend the results of earlier work to evaluate computer systems in schools (Wild *et al.*, 1992).

The task analysis demonstrated that the computer system is at best being used as an electronic version of the manual paper system. It is not providing increased flexibility for informing management decisions. The users are not obtaining information fast enough from the LEA to make budget decisions and budget forecasts. The delay in making payments to suppliers due to the bureaucracy of the LEA is causing some suppliers to reject trade with schools. Computerized records are also causing some inaccurate school financial accounts and much information about the budget is out of date when received. Few schools are using the local cheque facility. A manual system has some flexibility, but SIMS is a rigidly created database that requires a set sequence of inputs to produce the required results. Keying errors, changes to input and delays in accounting cause serious problems in maintaining accurate, efficient records. The ability to vire between budget headings is the key to flexibility in resource management. An important issue is how this can be used and exploited effectively for short-, medium- and long-term planning objectives. The current system imposes some constraints on this requirement. A possible solution would be to introduce systems that offer budgetary planning over a longer time period, for example a three-year rolling system with past, present and future years held on the database (Barker, 1991).

The computer system has limitations and in many ways is causing more problems than the previous manual system. The lack of flexibility in the process of raising orders, checking orders, authorizing payment and reconciliation has magnified and made more complex relatively simple tasks. Management decisions cannot rely on information from the system due to an unacceptable time delay in receiving the information about the annual budget as well as the 'tabs' and reconciliation information. There are often errors and misunderstandings in finance from LEA records in the tabs due to the lack of narrative and coding in a different style to SIMS output. The outcome is that the information on the computer is not up to date to allow for an accurate current financial statement to be obtained. The situation will be alleviated to some extent when 'local cheque' facilities are used by schools, but for some schools this will not be plausible as they have so little real spending budget to manage. The role of the LEA as monitors and regulators of school expenditure should be revised to enable schools to have greater independence over their method of expenditure and accounting. The organization within the LEA Treasurer's Department is causing inefficiencies in school administration and decision-making. Some restructuring and reallocation of resources to improve the systems in schools may now be necessary (Levačić, 1992).

Direct users and indirect users are not getting adequate time to familiarize themselves with the full scope of the database. In particular, the potential to use the information to support management decisions and increase the efficiency of administration in the separate departments is not being fully realized. The information is being streamlined into rigid systems with access to only a few people. Enabling a greater number of people to become familiar with the power of computerized administration and its potential as a management support system is a desirable future direction. LMS must translate into desirable improvements for management of the schools [. . .] Many schools have undergone expensive training for a few operators, yet most schools would now benefit from wider training for more staff to gain knowledge about the new computer facilities. [. . .]

The environmental conditions of work are not satisfactory for half of the users interviewed. Users complained of dissatisfaction with their physical conditions of work and three-quarters complained of stress since the introduction of the computerized system. The LEAs and schools will have to pay serious attention to these unacceptable conditions. [. . .]

CONCLUSIONS

Some schools are not getting a fair deal in the allocation of IT systems. Progress with IT to support administration is based on school size. Large schools are coping better than small schools as they can afford to employ more staff with specialist IT and administration knowledge. Middle and small schools are most vulnerable and are not really able to make progress with managing their budgets, but are depending heavily on the LEA guidance. [. . .] Unless funding is made available to provide schools with the opportunity and potential to make an assessment of their long-term management, administrative and budgetary objectives the future progress to improve school management will continue to be muddled.

School administrators have seen the advantages of computerized records but are frustrated by the constraints of the current system. Forward planning requires flexible computer information modelling systems. Schools now need to have access to independent professional advice that will help them make their own assessment of requirements for financial management, administration and decision-making. A 'low-level' task analysis that assesses these needs would now be of benefit. With a clear understanding of their needs schools may obtain flexible computer systems that will support their short- and long-term objectives for whole-school planning.

SIMS has been implemented as a system that requires schools to communicate with the local authorities. Schools have received an equitable allocation of funding, training and support to initiate and develop IT administration systems for LMS. However, there are problems with the management of the computerized administration links with the LEA which are having consequences for schools to manage their administration efficiently. If schools decide in the future that the LEA does not support their needs and that mutual support between families of feeder schools will serve their needs better then funding to enable schools to assess their joint requirements will be needed. For example computerized systems that are compatible across the families of schools have obvious advantages in easing transfer of pupil records. The opportunity for schools to manage their own budgets but share some of the administrative costs may therefore be desirable. How such shared systems could be resourced, maintained and provide training and support, and yet be efficient and meet the user requirements is an important issue for the near future.

REFERENCES

Barker, S. (1991) *Bursarial administration modules*. Cirencester: Dolphin Computer Services Ltd.

Coopers and Lybrand Association Limited (1988) *Local management of schools: a report to the Department of Education and Science*. London: C. L.

Foundation for Information Technology in Local Government (FITLOG) (1988) *Report to the IT user requirements consortium for the LMS initiative*. FITLOG.

Gregory, R. (1979) *Personalised task representation*. AMTE (E) Report TM 79103. Copyright Controller. London: HMSO.

Harker, S. D. P. and Eason, K. D. (1979) *Open systems approach to task analysis*. HUSAT Report No 178b. Loughborough: University of Technology.

Levačić, R. (1992) Local management of schools: aims, scope and impact, *Educational Management and Administration*, Vol. 20, no. 1, pp. 16 –28.

LRM (1990) *Familiarisation for management training manual (SIMS)*. Dunstable: SIMS Ltd.

Mitchell, S. M. (1991) An evaluation of computerised administration in secondary school. MSc thesis, University of Technology, Loughborough.

The SIMS Approach (1991) *Information for local authorities*. Dunstable: SIMS Ltd.

Wild, P., Scivier, J. E. and Richardson, S. J. (1992) Evaluating information technology supported local management of schools: the user acceptability audit, *Educational Management and Administration*, Vol. 20, no. 1, pp. 41–8.

CHAPTER 8

The Resource Implications of Developing Flexible Learning

DAVID OWEN AND MAGGIE FARRAR

ABSTRACT

'Flexible learning' has been characterized as a general approach to education and training that encourages independent and responsible learners. The approach takes account of the differing needs and aptitudes of young people and focuses on developing a partnership between teachers and pupils. It was for these reasons that flexible learning commended itself to the staff at Haggerston School, reflecting the school's historical commitment to developing the learning opportunities for pupils of all abilities. Although the school has a clear philosophical sympathy with the approach, adopting flexible learning in a more structured way requires a commitment of resources. This chapter is an exploration of the resource implications of adopting flexible learning and attempts to cost its development at Haggerston School.

INTRODUCTION

As deputy headteacher at Haggerston School with responsibility for resources and curriculum development, the promotion of flexible learning comes within my brief. As a member of a senior management team (SMT) comprising headteacher, two other deputies and three senior teachers, I am expected to lead on matters concerning the curriculum and particularly to lead discussions on the resource implications of curriculum initiatives. I work closely with my senior teacher colleague, Maggie Farrar, who has responsibility for language and learning across the school as well as line-management responsibility for the special educational needs (SEN) and English as a second language (ESL) departments, the 'curriculum support' areas, in the school.

Haggerston School is a popular, fully subscribed, all-girls 11–16 comprehensive school with 900 pupils and a multicultural intake. The school has a teaching force of 54 full-time equivalents (ftes) and has in addition four staff who have been appointed under 'Section 11' contracts and are managed centrally by the borough.

The school is situated in the London Borough of Hackney which is considered to be 'among the most disadvantaged boroughs not only in London but in the country as a whole' (DES, 1990, p. 1). Hackney Borough Council assumed responsibility for education following the statutory demise of the Inner London Education Authority (ILEA) in April 1990.

Haggerston School is committed to the notion of 'curriculum-led' resourcing which has led to the linking of curriculum and resources within one senior manager's job. The steady development of curriculum provision in the school dates back to before we embraced the Hargreaves approach to curriculum planning. This approach stressed breadth, balance and coherence in the curriculum and commended a list of compulsory and optional areas to schools (Hargreaves, 1984).

These recommendations find significant echoes in the Dearing Report (1994) on the National Curriculum. Our historic commitment to curriculum development and a firm belief that to 'stream' or 'set' pupils is not in their best educational interests has led us to adopt flexible learning approaches to teaching and learning. As a school committed to mixed-ability teaching groups across the whole curriculum a continuous interest has been to make the curriculum accessible to all by ensuring that it is sufficiently differentiated.

Within the SMT we felt that the flexible learning approach articulated through the Technical and Vocational Education Initiative (TVEI) and its extension provided the most appropriate vehicle for continuing curriculum development. The key features of this approach are accessibility and differentiation within a mixed-ability environment. These support the school's professed aim to provide a variety of opportunities for pupils to achieve intellectually, personally, socially and creatively. The material published by The University of Sussex Institute for Continuing and Professional Education (Eraut *et al.*, undated) along with visits to a school adopting flexible learning, convinced us that our pupils would benefit greatly if staff used flexible learning approaches across the school.

However, we realized that funding the development of flexible learning across the whole curriculum was not possible under the school's current system for allocating resources to departments as separate units. Accessibility and differentiation, although widely acknowledged as every teacher's concern, were still largely addressed through the SEN and ESL staff. The SEN and ESL areas were not funded by formula, as were the other departments, but were given an allocation based on historical patterns and modified by supplications to the resources committee. It was also clear to us that the capitation allowance, however distributed to departments, would be insufficient to fund an initiative of such proportions. We would have to invite the governing body to examine the whole of the delegated budget and persuade them that money from the school's trading arm, the Haggerston School Trading Company, which was in the process of being set up, would need to be committed to the proposal.

The SMT, therefore, needed to address the following questions:

• How much would implementing the flexible learning initiative cost?
• From which sources would the costs be met?

- How could the method of allocating resources for curriculum support be modified in order to encourage the development of flexible learning across the *whole* school?

For flexible learning to have a major impact on the achievement of Haggerston's pupils, all of these questions would need to be answered.

UNDERSTANDING FLEXIBLE LEARNING

My senior teacher colleague and I visited a nearby school to see a flexible learning approach to the curriculum in action prior to raising it in discussion with the teaching staff. When the idea was first formally discussed at an internal meeting of the developing curriculum working group, teachers suggested that substantial pockets of flexible learning were already in existence in the school, for example the development of National Curriculum technology with its system of mentors. We felt that flexible learning would complement much of the school's current work and would attract funds through TVEI. We therefore set up a subgroup to explore understanding of the term across the school and to assess the place for such an approach in the school's future curriculum plans. No questions about the resource implications of implementing flexible learning were raised at this time and it was clear to us that flexible learning was seen as something that could be 'done' in some areas and not necessarily in others.

As the main 'change agent' in the curriculum area, it was my responsibility to provide colleagues with an awareness of the implications of such changes. I encouraged colleagues to find out about flexible learning and some reading material was distributed at the end of the meeting of the new subgroup. Staff accepted that flexible learning was not one technique to be applied by one teacher but was rather a general approach to the delivery of education and training . . . to promote independent and responsible learners by providing learning situations which are meaningful to learners and take into account their differing needs and abilities. The flexible learning framework we designed emphasizes a partnership between teachers and learners rather than focusing on the teacher and the subject. The approach stresses the acquisition of skills and knowledge through direct interaction with resources; the interaction between tutor and student as an extension of the learner/teacher partnership; and the role of the teacher as evaluator, enabler and monitor of learning experiences relevant to individual students' needs. The main thrust of flexible learning is to develop autonomous and responsible learners who are able to take responsibility for their own learning (Tomlinson and Kilner, undated). Several questions arose at the next meeting of the flexible learning subgroup:

1. How will greater access to computers and IT provision, critical to the development of flexible learning, be accomplished and how much will it cost?
2. How could the library, again important to flexible learning, be developed and how should the development be funded?

3. How will staff used to separately funded curriculum areas accommodate the idea of a shared curriculum and shared resourcing?
4. How could existing resources and spaces be better utilized?
5. What are the staff development implications of flexible learning?
6. What are the timetabling implications of flexible learning?

These questions indicated a growing awareness that a policy of flexible learning would have serious resource implications. The costs would have to be met from sources other than the existing capitation allowance for faculty spending.

PROMOTING FLEXIBLE LEARNING

The SMT asked the school's network manager to report on the current provision of IT across the school and make recommendations for updating this over the next five years. To take account of the school's move towards flexible learning, a ratio of one computer to seven pupils was set as the target, reflecting the advice of the Inner London Educational Computing Centre (ILECC). The network manager also stressed the need for staff access to hardware and a range of software. A detailed specification of the school's needs was drawn up by the network manager and tenders were invited from three computer suppliers. As the deputy head with line-management oversight of the network systems, I presented the plans to both the finance subcommittee and the governing body, having a professional computer consultant in attendance to elucidate as necessary.

The available literature suggested that the school library was of central importance in the development of flexible learning. It should be a resource centre with readily accessible reading and reference books and access to information through a CD-Rom. The area should be amenable to group work, individual research and whole-class work. We had concerns about the security of our library's existing stock. Loss of stock cost around £2,700 per annum, most of it due to an antiquated and inefficient system for retrieving overdue books and a poor level of security. To promote flexible learning we felt it would be necessary to improve the security of the library, to introduce at least one CD-Rom terminal and to make several network stations, linked to the central server, available for pupils' use. Since introducing a security system into the library, the losses have become negligible.

The media resources area would be at the hub of the flexible learning wheel and would need to be able to cope with the anticipated demands placed on it. The media resources officer (MRO) in consultation with the senior teacher, language and learning, was asked to produce a five-year development plan for the MRO area, taking into account the flexible learning policy. The projection appears in Table 8.1.

TABLE 8.1
Analysis of the five-year needs of the MRO area

	PRESENT	NEXT 3–5 YEARS	STRATEGIES	TARGET
Management support and policy	Media resources and library work to LEA guidelines. Is there a school policy on the use of the MRO?	Senior management support in the form of an agreed policy for media resources and the library to actively support flexible learning, library development plan now under way	Publicize resources area and library more effectively. INSET/induction for staff and pupils	Optimum use of media resources facilities and expertise in liaison with library to support flexible learning and whole curriculum
Staffing	Full-time MRO, full-time technician, part-time clerical support solely for curriculum work	Retain full-time MRO and technician; extend clerical support to full time for media resources and library with flexible learning in mind	Identify and utilize individual strengths within the resources area	Increased use of resource area facilities in support of flexible learning
Accommo-dation	1 media resources office, one print room with door connecting to MR room, door (seldom used) connecting to library	Allocation of more space. MR domain to take in library and learning support (SEN and ESL) spaces. Ideal solution: learning resources block or building	Joint report to SMT from library, MRO and learning support on use of space in support of curriculum; seek financial support from LEA, PTA, governors. Explore money-raising schemes	Functional learning resources suite with appropriate space allocation. More use of the area by staff and pupils
Information technology support	3 networked computers, 1 stand-alone in MRO area, no access in library, 1 networked station in learning support area	More networked stations for MRO, library and learning support. Flexible learning requires more access to utilization by pupils	Submit IT plan to SMT and network manager. INSET for staff on software available; identify and publicize software packages most appropriate to flexible learning	Maximum use of IT facilities to support learning process
Other audiovisual resources	1 TV and VCR between MRO, library and learning support; several audiocassette recorders in MRO area, 1 on loan to library. 2 carousel slide projectors in MRO area. No such in library or learning support areas	TVs and VCRs for library and learning support; audio players and slide projectors for library and learning support areas	All three learning support areas to submit joint bid to SMT via resources committee for extra AVA equipment to support development of flexible learning	A fully equipped learning resources suite to furnish the needs of the flexible learning initiative

We also agreed in the management team that the timetable should be used to encourage colleagues to explore flexible learning. In consultation with the heads of faculties and using a computer program we produced timetables for the next two years which emphasized the deployment of teaching teams and provided common non-contact time for colleagues to discuss teaching and learning strategies. We suggested to teachers that we had built into the timetables the possibilities for regrouping pupils to encourage both small-group and individual work very much in keeping with the current practice of the 'support departments'. Initially some teachers felt that if several classes from the same year group were timetabled together then sufficient resources may not be available. In practice, however, it has encouraged staff to discuss the optimum use of the available resources and to explore alternative teaching and learning strategies.

COSTING FLEXIBLE LEARNING

It may be that, like history, flexible learning is what happens whether recorded or not. Certainly the problems of disaggregation are real and the task of ascribing a cost to the implementation of the flexible learning, as with the introduction of the National Curriculum, is challenging. Nevertheless, we have made an effort to cost out implementation to date and have tried to estimate the order of expenditure that may be needed to ensure that the momentum for change is maintained. The costings, albeit tentative, have been calculated under several headings, courting the danger of counting some costs twice and perhaps missing those that may fall between two headings.

The 'shadow structure' at Haggerston School is the staffing plan to be implemented as existing postholders leave. It has been modified over the years by the head and the SMT in recognition of the changing demands made upon the school. The shadow structure recognizes, for instance, that there has been a change from a subject-based departmental system to one based on coalitions of previously autonomous subjects in clusters and then into faculties. This change was made in an attempt both to rationalize curriculum provision and to simplify the apportioning of resources in order to make the accountability lines clearer under local management of schools (LMS). The change has brought concomitant changes in the allowance structure (latterly the allocation of responsibility points) and an increase in the complexity of job descriptions to match. We have made changes in response to the National Curriculum and its assessment demands and changes in response to the Home Office review of the manner in which 'Section 11' funding has been applied as well as changes to reflect the expiry of the four-year transitional arrangements that accompanied the introduction of formula funding for schools under the LMS provisions of the Education Reform Act 1988.

Given this, we felt that structural changes to accommodate the introduction and implementation of flexible learning should be kept to a minimum. The move to flexible learning would have to be incremental. The only clearly visible structural changes already undertaken or envisaged in the school's development plan are outlined in Table 8.2.

TABLE 8.2
Staffing changes and costs

CHANGE	ESTIMATED COSTS OF FLEXIBLE LEARNING ASPECTS
Appointment of head of learning support/flexible learning manager[1]	£1,400 per annum
Establishment of flexible learning team[2]	£3,600 per annum
Staff development and INSET[3]	£6,000 first year only
Technician for MRO area	£1,800 per annum
Visits to flexible learning institutions	£360 first year only
Total costs	
For first year	£29,360
Recurring costs	£23,000

[1] The old incentive allowances have been used for ease of calculation. The shadow structure envisages three additional posts in a reconstituted support faculty where the head has responsibility for ESL, SEN and the development of flexible learning. Only the difference between a C and D allowance has been attributed to flexible learning here.
[2] The figure is calculated as the number of staff in the subgroup × the number of hours per year the group meets × the cost of a supply equivalent in £ per hour, excluding on-costs.
[3] Calculated on the basis that each member of staff would need a minimum of one (five-hour) day to become familiar with the philosophy and techniques of flexible learning.

The governors also approved expenditure of £25,000 per annum for five years, in the first instance on a leasing basis, to update and upgrade the school's network systems. The complete specification for this addresses the needs of the whole school. It is, however, possible to identify some elements of the IT plan which may not have been included without the commitment to develop flexible learning and to estimate the likely proportions of some integrated technical aspects of the system without which flexible learning would be unlikely to develop. These estimates appear in Table 8.3.

The installation of a security system and a CD-Rom in the library has already been mentioned but it is acknowledged in the SMT that further expenditure will be necessary in the library to make it more appropriate to the widespread use of flexible learning techniques, such as the provision of individual study bays, tape decks, videocassette recorders and laptop computers. Teaching areas across the school need carpeting and refurbishing to make existing equipment more accessible. A pilot study is under way in the mathematics faculty and the cost of creating an 'ideal' classroom is being worked out with the help of an outside consultant. When the costings become available, extrapolations for the refurbishment of the whole faculty will be made and a development plan submitted to the resources committee to assess the resource implications for the whole school.

TABLE 8.3
Information technology costs for flexible learning

ITEM	COST (£)
One CD-Rom server for the library including *Oxford English Dictionary*, the *Guardian* and *World Book Information Finder*	2,700
Software for pupil-centred curriculum use in history, english, maths and science	400
Software licences for 32 stations	3,500
Additional computer stations, cabling, software support and maintenance	10,000[1]
Total costs	
For first year	16,600
Subsequent years	10,000[2]

[1] Estimated on the basis that this figure represents the approximate difference between annual expenditure in previous years and that committed by the governors to promote flexible learning.
[2] This is estimated at 40% of the budgetary commitment to IT development agreed by the governing body through the leasing agreement of £25,000 per annum.

It has become clear to the SMT that all the additional resource needs of flexible learning cannot be met from the capitation allowance allocated to faculty heads despite the provision of an additional curriculum development fund. The governors' premises subgroup is currently drawing up plans to refurbish the school on a rolling programme and the needs of flexible learning will be advanced by the senior teacher who supports the headteacher in advising the governors on this group. Governors can only allocate the money at their disposal and it has long been felt at Haggerston that we would need more money than was likely to come from the public purse. To this end we have, in consultation with a solicitor, set up two registered companies – the Haggerston School Trust and the Haggerston School Trading Company. This enables us to generate additional income through the trading company and to covenant it to the school trust. The company directors include members of the SMT as well as governors and income generated is committed to furthering the interests of the pupils at the school. We have run two national conferences at Haggerston aimed at raising achievement in the inner city. The BP Oil Company donated £2,000 to the first conference on the understanding that we would use the money generated for the immediate benefit of the pupils. We chose to earmark the money for the flexible learning initiative and it was used in partial payment for the security system in the library.

To encourage staff to take an active interest in the initiative we felt it would be helpful to explore the use of the funding formula, used to allocate capitation allowances to faculties, to promote flexible learning. Although the amounts of money involved are relatively small, we felt that this move would alert middle-management colleagues to the initiative in a way in which no memos could.

RESOURCE ALLOCATION

Following the Education Reform Act 1988 and the move towards local management, schools have become attuned to 'the familiar themes in the Government's rhetoric and policy towards the public sector – efficiency, effectiveness, responsiveness and accountability' (Levačić, 1989). Effectiveness has been defines as 'the process of ensuring the organisational goals are pursued' and efficiency as 'the process of ensuring that operations are carried out at least cost [making] no assumptions about the value of the operations' (Fidler and Bowles, 1989).

Schools have been attempting to allocate resources efficiently long before the legislative imperatives of the 1988 Act. Marsh (1982) analysed the distribution of capitation allowances in a Devon school and devised a method of allocation that was claimed to represent the cost of conducting the subject in the school. By using a formula, Marsh claimed that the allocations were 'purely objective and indisputable once the curricular organisation [had] been established for a particular year'. However, even administrative procedures that rely on complex formulae are neutral neither in their impact nor, indeed, in their formulation: objectivity in the realms of administration is a myth (Forster, 1986).

Davies and Ellison (1987) examined the problems of resource allocation across a range of secondary schools in Cheshire in 1984/85 and concluded that a combination of both quantitative and qualitative methods in allocating resources appeared to be the most promising approach. With the now widespread use of computer-aided administration (CAA) packages in schools it is arguably even more important for school managers to be aware of the various approaches to resource allocation and their limitations so that what goes on 'behind the screens' is managed in accordance with the school's aims. The emphasis that currently obtains, and finds strong echoes in the Ofsted documentation, is on a rational approach to resource allocation. Although a formula may be applied with disinterest it would be difficult to sustain the belief that it was formulated without at least inadvertent reference to the political pressures that invariably exist within any institution.

It has been suggested (Boulton, 1986; Simkins and Lancaster, 1987) that resource allocation models should attempt to recognize the 'political' dimensions that exist in organizations and this is particularly so within organizations like schools which are staffed predominantly by professionals (Noble and Pym, 1989). This may lead to a proportion of the available resources being allocated by formula and the remainder via the submission of bids. The possibility that resources may then be allocated in proportion to the supplicants' bidding skills or political acumen rather than the perceived needs of the overall curriculum provision cannot be ignored.

As the deputy with responsibility for resources and in particular for preparing for LMS, I kept my SMT colleagues and the members of the school's resources committee informed of legislative changes and national attitudes to those changes.

Under the ILEA the school had been responsible for controlling a proportion of its expenditure under the authority's Alternative Use of Resources (AUR) scheme since 1973. To this extent the school was not unused to making decisions about resources. A finance committee existed to this end and developed into the more general resources committee (finance). Membership of this committee was not well defined, teachers coming along to meetings when matters of particular interest appeared on the agenda. 'Members' were assumed to represent their curriculum areas and were expected to 'fight their corner'; decisions were made by a show of hands. The head, although retaining the right of veto, was cast in the role of trying to ensure that a favourable consensus emerged from these meetings. A new headteacher was appointed in April 1992. As the school approached LMS, with the first delegated budget due in April 1992, the constitution of the resources committee and its method of operation were refined. The committee now formally mirrored the curriculum structures in the school with heads of departments forming the bulk of the membership.

The method of allocating resources was examined and the formula used to allocate funds to departments was subjected to close critical scrutiny.

THE FUNDING FORMULA

Historically, the global sum of money earmarked as 'capitation' was split on a roughly 70 per cent / 30 per cent basis with the larger portion for 'departmental' spending and the smaller portion for 'whole school'. The 30 per cent fund was used for supporting non-statemented special educational needs, for English as a second language, the media resources office and the school library among other things. The 70 per cent was distributed according to an 'agreed formula'. The formula contained a factor, T, that recognized classroom contacts by calculating the number of pupil-periods per week that a department taught. A second multiplying factor, the A factor, was fixed by the resources committee to reflect the need for consumable materials that a department was deemed to have. Thus science, for example, was assigned an A factor of 2.5 and history an A factor of 1.0. The origins of the values of the A factors were rather obscure but, in parallel with the early efforts at devising LMS formulae, the A factors could be (and were) calculated at this time to reflect the existing 'historical' allocations. The A factors were calculated (rather than assigned as happened in later years) to allow the allocations to replicate the proportions of the previous academic year. Multiplying the A factor by the T factor gave the departmental allocation.

Although concerns about the A factors and the large impact that small changes in their value had on the amount of money received by each department were felt, they were not seriously addressed up until 1989, perhaps because the calculations needed to illustrate the changes had to be made up to this time on an electronic calculator. The effort needed to compute the changes was presumably deemed to cost more than the perceived potential benefits of the exercise. The scene altered when the endeavour was computerized using a spreadsheet. It was then possible in meetings of the resources committee to explore on a computer screen the implications of any changes in the A factors or the impact of a reduction, say, in the number of pupils opting to pursue a particular subject or the overall impact of a change in the proportion of the capitation allowance allocated to departments.

The immediate consequence of this touch-of-a-button information was that attention was now focused on whether or not the formula was 'fair' and, latterly, whether it addressed the priorities identified in the school development plan. Members of the committee were invited to suggest other models for allocating resources. The committee suggested that the role played by the A factors might be examined and that the possibility of retaining a proportion of the 70 per cent departmental allocation for developing cross-curricular initiatives and supporting curriculum innovations (in advance of the National Curriculum) be considered. A figure of 5 per cent was suggested initially. The general feeling at this stage was that whatever model was used there would be 'winners' and 'losers' but that to rely on the 5 per cent held back to correct the anomalies or to furnish curriculum innovations was not a viable solution. This conclusion reinforced the management team's view that the whole school budget would need to be revisited in order to find extra funds.

CONCLUSIONS

As a management team we have become aware that our efforts to raise the awareness of middle-management colleagues to the idea of flexible learning, clearly need redoubling. Discussion about resourcing the curriculum still centres largely on departments/faculties and the role of the A factor in distributing resources, although money is now held separately for curriculum development and enhancement and was earmarked for wider curriculum support. A flexible learning development plan, within the overall framework of the school development plan, to be financed from the curriculum development fund, is now in place. It was suggested at this point that the need to develop flexible learning could be met by introducing an additional multiplying factor, F say, into the distribution formula. Faculties that demonstrated an awareness and a commitment to the initiative would attract an F factor rating greater than 1. Faculties that showed no inclination would be penalized either by being given an F factor less than 1 or, by default, by having a smaller proportion of the available money whilst retaining the original F factor value of 1. We felt, however, that if we did this we might convey the impression that flexible learning could be adequately financed from within existing faculty resources which is clearly not the case.

The school development plan currently envisages a time when a learning support faculty will exist within the newly constituted faculty structure that the school has embraced. The 'shadow structure' shows a head of learning support faculty on a D incentive allowance (4 responsibility points) with a job description that includes responsibility for the library, the media resources office and the development of flexible learning. With the SMT's growing awareness of the extent of both the curricular and resource implications of flexible learning it may be that the responsibility for its development will rest with a deputy headteacher, as it does now, for some years to come.

POSTSCRIPT

The work is jointly that of both authors, David Owen and Maggie Farrar. Thanks are due to Pat Collarbone, the headteacher at Haggerston School, who has enabled much of the work to proceed, and also to the SMT at Haggerston School: Sue Warrington, Pat Healey, Tony Purell and Edna Cullen.

REFERENCES

Boulton, A. R. (1986) A Developed Formula for the Distribution of Capitation Allowances, *Educational Management and Administration*, Vol. 14, no. 1, pp 31–8.

Davies B. and Ellison L. (1987) *School Organisation*, Vol. 7.

Eraut, M. *et al.* (Undated) *Flexible learning in schools.* A handbook from the research project 'The Effective Management of Flexible Learning in Schools,' University of Sussex.

Fidler, B. and Bowles, G. (Eds) (1989) *Effective local management of schools.* Harlow: Longman.

Forster, W. (1986) *Paradigms and promises – new approaches to educational administration.* New York: Prometheus.

Hargreaves, D. H. (1984) *Improving secondary schools.* London: ILEA.

Levačić, R. (1989) Rules and Formulae for Allocating and Spending Delegated Budgets, *Educational Management and Administration*, Vol. 17, no. 2, pp. 79–90.

Marsh, D. (1982) *Educational Administration and Management*, Vol. 10, no. 3.

Mathews, P. (1993) Cheques and Balances, on *Managing Schools Today*, Vol. 3, no. 3, pp. 42–3.

National Commission on Education (1994) *Learning to succeed: a radical look at education today and a strategy for the future.* London: Paul Hamlyn Foundation.

Noble, T. and Pym, B. (1989) Collegial authority and the receding locus of power, in T. Bush (Ed.) *Managing education: theory and practice.* Milton Keynes: Open University Press.

Ofsted (1992) *Framework for the inspection of schools.* London: HMSO.

Schools Curriculum and Assessment Authority (1994), *The National Curriculum and its Assessment*, London: SCAA.

Simkins, T. and Lancaster, D. (1987) Budgeting and Resource Allocation in Educational Institutions. Sheffield Papers in Educational Management.

Tomlinson, P. and Kilner, S. (Undated) *The flexible approach to learning – A guide.* London: Employment Department.

CHAPTER 9

Achievement-Based Resourcing

JENNY SHACKLETON, WITH RHIANNON EVANS
AND MAUREEN HANLEY

ABSTRACT

The case study charts the progress of a project to secure the upward convergence
of resources with student achievement. It indicates the perceived deficiencies of a
college which has been both under-resourced and underdeveloped, and emphasizes the need for higher-order thinking and expertise in both financial and
educational management than is generally available within individual colleges,
or the education sector more widely. The steps taken to make progress within the
organization and to have impact upon the college's operating environment are
charted in two ways: by describing the college-wide measures taken initially; and
then by reviewing the progress of the project which drove the college forward at
all levels. On the basis of practical experience of a form of achievement-based
resourcing, the case study then raises a number of implementation issues, and
emphasizes the critical importance of information technology for both cost-
effective learning and efficient management. It concludes by noting the need
for appropriate definitions of productivity in the context of student learning and
achievement.

INTRODUCTION

In 1987 I joined Wirral Metropolitan College, a very large and diverse further
education (FE) college in Merseyside, as its principal. It was immediately apparent
that the college was impoverished in a number of respects including support staff,
student services, equipment and environment, and suitable provision. Simultaneously the college was routinely returning some 3 per cent of its available annual
expenditure to the local education authority (LEA), foregoing over £1 million per
annum of additional available funding. At the same time, it had a reputation for
being over-resourced. As a very large college with 30,000-plus students and 1,500
staff, its size, diversity, inexpert and nervous management, together with the active
and largely undeserved hostility of the LEA, had prevented the development of a

resource capability sufficient to fulfil either the college's role and responsibilities or the LEA's educational policies. The development of the college since that time has in essence been an exercise in the upward convergence of resources with student achievement. The exercise has gone through several stages since 1987, and is in effect unending.

There were urgent reasons for reforms within resource management and more generally. These ranged from an inability to serve student and client needs adequately, to an increasing vulnerability for the college as a viable educational institution. The causes of these problems were deep and pervasive, and their removal was to require high-quality and long-term thinking.

The direct barriers to effective resource management included poor information within both the college and the LEA; changeable procedures within the LEA; internal secrecy regarding allocations combined with a lack of feedback to spending areas; and an adherence to historical roll-forward budgeting and gradualism in all things. These problems had produced their own secondary and widespread effects such as hostility towards external funding organizations; a fretful concern about new educational needs which just would not go away; a belief that women and junior staff were out of place and out of their depth in discussions about money; and a fearful and untrusting ambience.

It is perfectly possible within the FE sector for a manager to be contributing to these deficiencies whilst being regarded as a very sound resource manager. Most FE resource managers, including myself, have learnt to handle resources and budgets through direct experience much of which may be of the learn-or-die variety. My direct experience has come from working across FE and as an LEA officer, and has embraced both public and private resources. Often, and rewardingly, as one's understanding of an area grows, so does respect for certain of the players and for their vision and leadership. Disappointingly this has simply not happened for me with resource management in FE, where higher-order thinking and expertise, and the creativity essential to future development, have been depressingly scarce, whatever the arena. I have therefore always needed to step outside FE to higher education, other nations and other sectors to find the necessary ideas, techniques, support and stimuli to make progress in this area.

Further education managers often suffer from a type of 'operational syndrome', an inherent tendency to revert to operational matters irrespective of the requirements. This preoccupation with functional management is apparent across their range of responsibilities, but is reinforced in the area of resource management by a very proper concern to work within given parameters and not take risks. The financial context has largely been set by LEAs, and under their regimes many college managers have frequently been unable to distinguish between proper regulations and constraints, and arbitrary ones. Even where those managers have been able to make these distinctions they may have been very wise in not challenging the arbitrary ones and thus invoking hostility and penalties.

Therefore, I would argue that as a result of our history and current circumstances FE managers are significantly under-prepared conceptually, under-skilled and under-powered when it comes to making the most of the new opportunities and constraints which have accompanied the incorporation of FE colleges. Whilst this issue can be addressed in several ways, the insights I hope to convey by this investigation are:

- the need to redirect the focus of resource management by senior college personnel;
- the need to develop connections between resources and educational purposes and quality at the points at which those purposes and that quality reside;
- the need to design and apply new and appropriate safeguards for a college managing its resources in new ways;
- the need to learn from the resource management practices of other sectors and nations;
- that our most talented and creative people must be encouraged to take an interest in resource management in education, in order to move the sector forward.

LITERATURE

The knowledge and material brought to the college (henceforth called Wirral Met for brevity) in 1987 included the publications of the Staff College and Further Education Unit, both on resource management and the management of change. However, to build up our understanding and expertise in order to, in effect, transform the college, we found that it was essential to go beyond any of the material designed for the education sector.

We therefore took three steps. Firstly, we went to the publications written for industry and business, including the articles of the Strategic Planning Society. Secondly, we took ourselves outside the UK to the USA both physically and metaphorically by seeking out American and international texts. We were concerned with assessing the quality of educational provision by referring to the value-added dimension which is measured from entry to exit. Thirdly, we made contact with policy research organizations in the UK such as the various institutes of education. Within all of this we were seeking:

- a new educational ideal which might stimulate and sustain Wirral Met's efforts;
- fresh ways of thinking so as to counteract inappropriate and rigid thought and behaviour;
- examples of strategic management and strategic organizations.

Examples of strategies for implementing change at Wirral Met include the introduction of:

- a flatter hierarchy and devolved management;
- a strong middle-management tier with a corporate training plan;

- a college services faculty to act as the strategic arm of the college and thus facilitate the implementation of change;
- a research and development section to pilot, evaluate and embed potential initiatives;
- explicit strategic management techniques across the board with clear loci of accountability;
- the identification of high-level skills required by the senior management, and the distinguishing characteristics of superior performers.

PREPARING THE GROUND

Wirral Met had long been hindered by a lack of clarity and agreement regarding its role and purpose, and this was exacerbated by conflicts and confusions of values. The process of forming a mission statement was therefore an extended one, requiring a new respect for knowledge and thought. However, the core of the mission was evident from the outset and was ultimately stated as in Figure 9.1.

PERSONAL ACHIEVEMENT

(1) Personal achievement is every individual's right, and the college should organize itself behind the right.

(2) The establishment of personal achievement is a powerful aid to learning and motivation; it should be seen primarily in these terms, within a framework of standards.

(3) The physical, mental and psychological involvement of learners with their own development and achievement, and that of their peers, should be adopted as an organizing principle for the college.

(4) Personal achievement should constitute the core mission of the college. To encourage the college to be self-critical about its ability and preparedness to support personal growth, positive appraisal measures should be introduced and developed for learning, teaching and learner support.

FIGURE 9.1 **Mission statement.**

Of equal importance to the elevation of individual achievement was the acceptance of a collective responsibility to organize the college around achievement. Resource management was regarded as integral and crucial to that organizational shift. The college's critical success factors, which derived from an environmental scan and evolved with the mission, illustrate some aspects of the new approach to resourcing introduced at this stage (see Figure 9.2).

CRITICAL SUCCESS FACTORS

Capability and culture
Develop a federal organization
Create a computer-integrated organization
Ensure flexible working practices in exchange for adequate reward
Achieve equality of entitlement and esteem for staff
Foster innovative strategies

Quality services
Diversify client services
Become a leader in client care
Optimize technology for learning
Identify and sustain leading-edge products and services
Minimize college-induced problems for clients

Funding and resources
Minimize costs relative to service given
Optimize short-term returns
Optimize a system of funding through clients

Relationships and systems
Manage volatile situations
Think globally; act locally
Become a nerve centre for learning networks and systems
Encourage ideas which impact statistically
Help build the new local/national/regional infrastructure and superstructure

FIGURE 9.2 Critical success factors.

From the mission and critical success factors strategic plans over five, three and one year were formulated. Over time these have become ever tighter in their objectives, targeting and deadlines, to the point where regular and open feedback sessions have the effect of ensuring that action occurs and is reported and reflected on. To maintain the overall forward momentum and handle the large-scale decisions for achievement-based resourcing, four themes were adopted as driving forces:

1. student and client services;
2. the college and broader environment;
3. curriculum provision;
4. processes and systems.

The task of global resource management was to facilitate and enable the forward momentum through these themes. To ensure that appropriate decisions were taken and funded a programme of research and development, which itself needed to be resourced, was also necessary.

It can be seen from the above that Wirral Met chose to get moving by instituting a classic strategic management approach. This started with the establishment of mission, critical success factors, goals and themes. It then extrapolated these into objectives, tasks, resource implications, targets and outcomes. Whilst in the early years of its introduction there was a need to supervise the associated managerial processes, in time it was possible to give substantial autonomy over the choice of process, and to manage largely through the consideration of outcomes.

The college's critical success factors included the need to secure rapid results as well as long-term goals. A new approach generally requires a kick-start, and each of the four themes mentioned above was able to be analysed in terms of the time needed to realize it; its budgetary implications; and its impact upon the college's objectives. Figure 9.3 illustrates the way in which student services were defined in 1988. Though not entirely fulfilling their potential yet, all the services noted there are now in place.

Most of these services developed to support students from entry through to exit and can constitute an ideal starting point for achievement-led resourcing since their resource needs can be met in small allocations during the period when there is little support for radical approaches to resource management. Student services are also important for two additional reasons. Firstly, they represent a dramatic shift in thinking towards student-centredness. Secondly, they must be designed, introduced and enhanced before one attempts to remove the course as the organizational plank of a college.

Although student services are not entirely dependent upon accommodation changes, the latter must be addressed from the outset in order to sustain the momentum of change and respond to changes in student behaviour. The planning and design of suites of student services accommodation and resource-based learning areas requires time, as does the acquisition of sufficient resources to make the changes. Unlike student services, for which one can take resourcing opportunities as they arise within an overall assessment of costs, accommodation changes are more momentous and cyclical. So as not to lose opportunities for a year at a time one must always make physical adaptations both to match other developments undertaken to that date, and also to anticipate the need for change during the subsequent 12 months. Given the dynamic nature of achievement-based resourcing, any other approach means that accommodation changes lag ever further behind the other developments.

In the case of Wirral Met, applications for financial support from potential sponsors, and low-cost outline plans for alterations began to be made as soon as we had a notion of our requirements. This would lead to the exercise of considerable ingenuity at later stages; however, it was only in this way that we achieved the required concurrence of activity and pace of change.

Marketing	Open days; workshops; seminars; conferences; taster courses; prospectus; admission; corporate clients/individuals; visits/ conventions; referrals; systematic word of mouth; student network; learning pass computer network.
Enquiry	Commissionaire; receptionist; electronic noticeboard; student database; enquiries logged; student admissions officer; databases of units and qualifications available; other agencies; print-out of enquirers.
Planning and choosing	Assessment centre; personal profile; diagnostic individual assessment; financial advice; prior learning assessment; expert systems; preferred learning styles assessment; prospectus; mode of attendance; action plans; careers guidance; interviews.
Enrolment	Information to students; financial aid; fees; student handbook; follow-up early leavers analysis; records of achievement; flexible enrolment system; computer-based enrolment.
Orientation and induction	Short courses; student union; open learning packages; time management; study skills; learning to learn; building student involvement; access to units for learning and/or assessment.
Assessment support	Initial assessment; formative assessment; summative assessment; personal statements; personal development; assessment on demand; NCVQ database; learning framework database.
Learning support	Learning contract; study centre; learning centre; personal tutor system; core; formative assessment; learning framework; open/distance learning; computer network; volunteer peer tutoring; study circles; writing centres; transfer.
Personal support	Careers advice; personal counselling; childcare facilities; health centres; adult network; women's centres; personal tutor; advocacy.
Work-based learning	Work placements; simulated work experience; assessment; training trainers; training assessors; training supervisors; training managers.
Accreditation	Summative assessment; portfolios; records of achievement; prior learning accreditations; NROVA; certification; credit transcript; credit transfer.
Evaluation	Student feedback; input into college review; outcomes, exam results, destinations; exit and transfer programme.

FIGURE 9.3   Services to support learners at Wirral Metropolitan College.

CHANGE THROUGH RESEARCH AND DEVELOPMENT

Early implementation of the above changes involved challenges particularly for our administrative staff who were then unprepared and unaccustomed to such proactivity. However, the redesign of provision and the evolution of systems were initially subjected to a detailed research programme funded both internally and externally. A research programme which we entitled 'Learning Gain and Achievement-Based Resourcing' set out to solve the following two problems: to find means of enhancing learning and capturing achievement in such a way as to stimulate motivation, opportunity and capability; and to ensure that resources actively supported this process at all levels. The linking of the two problems was intentional, but still needs frequent explanation. The rationale for making the link was that until we could prove an active relationship between learning and achievement and resources, we were in no position either to argue for additional resources, or to ensure the cost-effective use of what we had.

Thus from 1989, Wirral Met has been piloting an achievement-based approach to resourcing with a representative range of provision across the college. The initial work was part of a project funded by the Department of Employment but subsequent work has mainly been funded internally.

Traditionally, the basis for resourcing has been the course, using inputs rather than outcomes as the important factors. The movement towards an achievement-led organization requires that resources should relate more directly to achievement. This involves the support of learning (rather than teaching) and the facilitation of outcomes rather than volume of attendance. It is therefore learners and their achievements that are being resourced. This rationale is entirely compatible with the model of recurrent funding currently being implemented by the Further Education Funding Council (FEFC) within colleges throughout England.

The investigation of the links between resourcing and achievement has rested on two assumptions. The assumptions are:

- That a system based on resourcing the learner is likely to be more efficient, that is, to produce more learning for the same level of resources or the same level of learning with fewer resources. The logic is that if students have an informed choice of approaches to study they will tend to choose those where they do best. Resourcing the learner is also likely to be more efficient if personal starting points are defined and not assumed.
- That a movement from resourcing the course to resourcing the learner is accompanied by a change in the mix of resources applied – which means in the current circumstances a relative decline in the proportion of teaching staff and an increase in the proportion of both materials and support staff.

Resourcing the learner entails the introduction of more precise definitions of achievement, as well as student support services which provide advice and guidance for progression through the curriculum. The first is now available at Wirral Met in the form of the learning framework, which is the college's credit accumulation and transfer system. It is a system for harmonizing the FE curriculum through outcomes and credit value, and it provides a method for recording the gains that students make from their learning. It is therefore a system for accrediting the full range of gains made by the learner as well as a system for credit accumulation and transfer within the organization. The framework allows for the estimation of credit value based on notional/average learning time. Notional learning time consists of three components: direct teaching time, supported self-directed study time and private study time. It is assumed that teaching time will not normally exceed two-thirds of the notional learning time. The concept of notional learning time is derived from the specific learning outcomes – knowledge, skills, understanding, capability, experience – that are associated with each particular unit/programme and it provides a useful basis for developing future resourcing structures for the organization.

Sophisticated support and guidance for the learner is an essential element of this approach, and the college now has a further rationale for its new services as a consequence. There is a centralized advisory service to provide information and advice. Development centres provide facilities for initial assessment, action planning and accreditation of prior learning/achievement. Careers advice and guidance are available throughout programmes of study and facilities are available to review and record achievement both during and at the end of programmes. The increased emphasis on advice and guidance is also crucial in ensuring a quality service for learners as well as a more efficient and effective service, and is recognized within FEFC's new national funding methodology through the award of resource units for the entry phase of programmes.

A further essential feature of an achievement-based approach to college management is an individual student-tracking system which has the potential of linking with the centralized management information system. It is difficult to decide the optimum level at which information should be aggregated into the central management information system, and in many instances decisions will depend on the size of the organization. In a college such as Wirral Met, the new FEFC requirements for tariffs will produce in excess of a million records, and it is likely that this information will need to be produced at intermediate level prior to being aggregated into the central system. A critical feature of any tracking system is that it provides the opportunity for college managers to have up-to-date, accurate information on individual learner achievements so that they can respond immediately to the changing needs of the student population.

Resourcing the learner also necessitates alternative strategies for allocating and managing resources at a section level. Curriculum managers now identify different categories of resources which are required to deliver target credits, and would commonly use some version of the resource grid illustrated in Figure 9.4.

Programme leaders now identify the target credits based on individualized initial assessment and action plans for a group of learners, and subsequently identify the resources which are necessary to deliver these credits. The college

Section_____ Programme_____							
Units	Target credits	Resources			Achieved credits	Modifications to resource allocations
		Teach	Resource based	Admin	Materials		

FIGURE 9.4 Resource grid.

operates a limited devolved budget system which is at the middle-management level. Section heads manage cost centres and have responsibility for deploying part-time teachers and supplies and services. A section head might, for example, decide to release a member of staff from teaching responsibilities to prepare open learning materials to support future delivery. In calculating the resources necessary to deliver programmes section heads do not take into account the cost of particular lecturers. Central resources which are potentially accessed by all programmes are top sliced from the overall college budget. At the end of a learning period, which is defined by the programme, comparisons can be made with actual credits achieved by the learners, and the necessary modifications to the resource allocation will be made. It may be, for example, that learners would benefit from additional time in a workshop, and consequently resources can be vired from the classroom to the workshop. The achievement-based resourcing approach requires that resource management is devolved to the level of the manager most closely responsible for the delivery of the programme, and it is important that central finance systems can support this responsibility. This parallels the proposals for managing the information services within the college. This alternative approach to resource management has clear implications for quality assurance systems, and it challenges many of the traditional quality indicators of an organization.

In parallel with the above developments, programme leaders have been considering whether programme delivery methods are the most appropriate and efficient for their particular discipline as well as for the typical learners who access these programmes. One of the best examples of increased effectiveness and efficiency within the college is in the hairdressing section. The advent of National Vocational Qualifications (NVQs) in hairdressing meant that the section had to review the way it was managed internally. NVQs are not time based. As such, staff had to devise a method which would cope with roll-on/roll-off enrolment and promote flexible delivery, as many students achieved units at different rates. The section adopted a case-loading approach with some tutors taking overall responsibility for the target setting and progress review. Resource-based learning was introduced and some tutors would be simultaneously supervising smaller groups of students who were studying towards different units. The end result was that students were achieving units continuously – no student was being held back or made to repeat work they had already covered while other students caught up. Staff resources were also used more efficiently.

The increased demand for, and introduction of, resource-based learning has implications for the traditional measures of staff activity. It will no longer be appropriate to identify tutor activity by the number of students and class contact hours. A more appropriate indicator will be the number of credits which a tutor is responsible for delivering/facilitating. If, however, new performance indicators are to be implemented successfully then external accreditation will become a necessary control. Indeed, the new funding mechanism currently being implemented by the Further Education Funding Council (1993) will necessitate this development anyway.

THE BROADER COLLEGE ENVIRONMENT

After two years of project activity the college was able to derive some firm guidelines for resourcing which would then underpin the subsequent work. These were as follows.

1. It appeared practicable to describe and relate the achievements of students in different study areas following different learning patterns through the development of a concept of credit or credit hour.
2. The same notion of credit hour could be used to help define the commitment of a lecturer when changes in learning style made class contact increasingly difficulty to recognize.
3. The substitution of a case load for a timetable facilitated the introduction of more flexible learning arrangements.
4. Conventional calculations of case loads for open learning work appeared to rule out increases in the efficiency with which teaching staff could be deployed and thereby the availability of additional resources for other forms of support.
5. A 'resourcing grid' could be used to illustrate the nature and extent of the trade-offs which could and should be generated as patterns of learning shifted. Such a grid could lead to a formula which might be used to avoid the constraints of being tied to a particular balance of learning resources. The sort of formula which might conceivably be devised would permit elements of resources to be vired freely from one category to another without constraints.
6. The adoption of a credit or credit hour could substitute for the full-time equivalent student as a measure for external agencies, to the mutual benefit of them and the college.

The full implementation of credit accumulation within Wirral Met is now bringing together all aspects of management behind a number of major questions. For example,

1. In a system of achievement-based resourcing, is it possible or necessary to classify a unit in terms of study mode? May not the significance of mode of study for resourcing lie at the (important) margins whereby students acquire additional credits at virtually no ongoing cost to the college? For instance, students using a computerized biology package, 'Bodyworks', will also be learning basic computer skills and may be eligible for additional credits in this area.
2. How can cost-effectiveness be promoted by enabling and encouraging course teams to be flexible in shifting resources between staff and material resources?
3. Assuming that clients will act in their best interests, what type of fee structure will (help to) facilitate achievement and provide incentives to learn?
4. Given the mass of feedback available once credits are in place, how is this to be handled internally and externally?

From the outset it was clear that the college's greatest managerial difficulty was a lack of adequate information. This was despite a relatively sophisticated administrative information system. The college, therefore,

- imported a critique of the then arrangements and approaches from surveys of the applications of new technology in UK manufacturing, and analyses of the uses of information technology in American community colleges;
- developed a rationale for computer integration as the basis of organizational integration;
- in keeping with the aims of student leadership gave as much freedom and resource as possible to a wholly fresh team of learning technologists.

This approach came from what we knew about making change happen. We acknowledged that unless students at an early stage were introduced to a pattern of learning upon which we could later graft the collection of student information, then we would never be able to collect the data which are essential to a credit-based approach. Thus a series of facilities and devices were introduced directly to students; these included the phased provision of a highly sophisticated 800-place (and growing) computer network, together with learning passes and learner organizers, free trials, learner season tickets, family passes and so on. These have all had their desired effect in terms of student demand, discernment, and also step-increases in personal achievement. 'Two for one' is now a realistic qualification offer made to the student without loss of quality. And whereas with predominantly course organization there are additional resource requirements for each extra handful of students, that need not be so with achievement-based resourcing.

CONCLUSION AND RECOMMENDATIONS

Resource management is underdeveloped in FE. To a considerable extent this was inevitable since the management of colleges by LEAs largely removed opportunities for active and reflective approaches at either college or LEA levels.

Further education is now subject to a dynamic funding regime which means considerable exposure for colleges. Those that have managed roll-forward budgets with little reflection will struggle with inappropriate definitions of efficiency and debilitating attempts at cost-cutting. In our case, paradigms and parameters were decisively changed. This investigation has been about one attempt to do this early enough to have some choices in the matter.

We have addressed the development of resource management in Wirral Met from the perspective of those accountable as senior managers for bringing about those developments. As the involved managers our emphasis has been on the practical measures required to introduce, sustain and evaluate wholesale change. The most striking difference between the approach taken to change since 1987 has been the emphasis now put on management as the practical application of intelligence, information and mission or values. In that respect the organization regards itself as action research led and uses project management techniques as a matter of course.

REFERENCE

Further Education Funding Council (1993) Circular 93/32. London: FEFC.

PART THREE

Managing People

CHAPTER 10

The Selection of Academic Staff

KEITH NORRIS

ABSTRACT

This paper presents the findings of a research project to develop an integrated system of staff selection that is fair to all candidates, reduces the risk of discrimination and results in identifying the most suitable candidate. The results of an observational study of the selection process used in relation to eight academic posts involving twenty-nine interviews in a large mixed-economy college are presented. Candidate perceptions were obtained by conducting a postal questionnaire and semi-structured telephone interviews. The findings of the study are analysed and evaluated against a model developed from the results of a review of previous research. Recommendations are made with respect to each of the five phases identified as being critical in establishing a fair and valid selection process.

INTRODUCTION

Recent changes in the college environment and the balance of managerial responsibilities have highlighted the importance of staff recruitment and selection. The changing nature of further and higher education has resulted in increased pressure for colleges to become more enterprising and flexible in response to clients' needs. In spite of significant developments in teaching and learning strategies education remains very labour intensive with over 75 per cent of the total budget spent on staff wages and salaries. Innovation and the quality of provision are therefore dependent on the actions and behaviour of staff.

The granting of corporate status on 1 April 1993 resulted in colleges becoming the legal employer with total responsibility for the selection, employment and management of staff. As well as having to comply with employment and equal opportunities legislation colleges need to ensure that their selection process results in the appointment of staff capable of responding to the challenges and opportunities presented by the increasing rate of change and competition.

The purpose of this study was to develop an integrated system of staff selection that is valid, fair to all candidates and minimizes the risk of unintentional discrimination. In order to achieve this three fundamental objectives were established:

1. to develop a model of a fair and valid staff selection process by conducting a thorough review of previous research;
2. to establish current practice used in the selection of academic staff in a large college of further and higher education;
3. to evaluate current practice against the model and formulate recommendations.

RESEARCH METHODOLOGY

A review of previous research was carried out to establish a theoretical base and conceptual framework for the case study. In order to provide a context to more recent developments it was considered necessary to revisit previous reviewed research and identify significant trends. A detailed search of literature published after 1980 was conducted using both computerized and traditional techniques. The computerized literature search was, however, less succesful than had been anticipated due to the difficulty in identifying key words that were sufficiently discriminating whilst not excluding relevant articles.

Although care was taken to determine the relevance of articles, the number and range of published studies necessitated making judgements as to whether to include individual papers based on abstracts presented in the various indexes. Whilst this inevitably led to some degree of bias it is not thought to have had a significant impact on the results of the review. Published works not based on research projects were avoided.

The identification of current practice was achieved by conducting a study of the selection process used in relation to eight academic posts involving 29 interviews. The posts were spread relatively evenly across the three faculties and involved appointments in creatived studies, business and management and technology. In each case my role was made explicit to all staff and candidates involved. I achieved this by including a statement on all letters inviting shortlisted candidates to attend for interview, and reinforced it by explaining the nature and aims of the study to all the candidates at the start of the process. Candidates were also reassured that any information obtained would be treated in the strictest confidence and that I would not play any part in the selection process. A number of the candidates indicated that they thought that the study was very worth while and that they were pleased to participate. None of the candidates objected to being observed.

The main element of the fieldwork was concerned with studying a large number of variables and the interaction of groups of people. In referring to this type of study Krausz and Miller (1974) indicate that observational design is more appropriate than questionnaires and structured interviews. The dangers of relying on structured interviews are also illustrated by the findings of Latham and Saari (1984, p. 573) who on investigating the untypical results following the introduction of structured interviews found that what they were told was happening did not reflect reality, leading them to conclude that 'the researcher should be present when the data are being collected. What one believes is taking place and what is actually taking place may not be highly correlated'. It was decided therefore that I should personally observe all the key elements in the selection process from the point where the initial shortlisting procedure is carried out by the head of school and the head of faculty to the final offer of employment.

As an existing head of faculty I would usually be responsible for the initial shortlisting of candidates and would also serve as a member of the interview panels for all posts within the faculty of technology. This was advantageous whilst at the same time presenting a number of problems. I was therefore already familiar with the overall process and had been directly involved in almost one-third of the appointments made over the previous three years. I found it relatively easy to predict the stages involved and to plan the observations accordingly. There was also a high probability of my being accepted by the other members of staff involved in the process. However, it could be argued that due to my personal involvement, it was inevitable that I had developed preconceived ideas which could bias the results. Although data collection, analysis and interpretation are not and cannot be value free (Watts and Ebbutt, 1987) acknowledgement of the problem, together with a conscious attempt to be as objective as possible, was deliberately sought to minimize its impact.

In considering the role of participant observer, Walker (1985) indicates that the approach adopted can vary along a continuum from complete participation through participation-as-observer and observer-as-participant to complete observer. Cohen and Manion (1980) make a similar distinction in referring to participant observation and non-participant observation. My experience of the process indicated that it was not possible to adopt the role of 'complete participation' and at the same time record the interaction and involvement of the candidates and other members of the interview panel. Furthermore, I considered it important to obtain the confidence of candidates which I thought would only be possible if they could be assured that I had no role in the selection process. I decided, then, to observe all the stages of the process but not to be actively involved at any point.

Previous research also identified the lack of studies that included candidate feedback (Arvey and Campion, 1982; Banfield and Fearn, 1984). I felt that it was important to acknowledge that selection processes involve candidates assessing whether the college meets their needs as well as the college judging the suitability of candidates for the post on offer. Two types of information were identified in this respect: firstly, to ascertain the effectiveness of the process in enabling candidates to judge whether the post satisfied their needs; and secondly, to give candidates the opportunity to express their views on the procedures adopted. I would not be available to talk to the candidates on the day of the interview, because I would be observing the process including the final decision-making phase. So I decided to use a questionnaire to obtain information from the candidates about the post and semi-structured telephone interviews to allow them to give their views on the procedures adopted. A 90 per cent response rate was achieved from the questionnaires and 95 per cent from the semi-structured telephone interviews.

A pilot questionnaire was designed based on the findings of my previous survey (Norris, 1984). In considering the size and scope of the pilot it was necessary to bear in mind several factors. Ideally the questionnaire should be tested with a representative group of respondents. In this case, it could be argued that the questionnaire should be piloted with all candidates who had just been through a selection process at the college. However, it was not possible to contact the unsuccessful candidates. The strategy adopted was to identify all members of the faculty academic staff who had been appointed during the previous six months. It was assumed that their experience of being interviewed would be recent enough for them to remember the process, they were easily accessible and the pilot could be completed in a short time. Although the pilot sample would not be truly representative, I believed that it would still fulfil its purpose of checking the rigour of the questionnaire. Nine members of staff were identified as being eligible: eight main-grade lecturers and one principal lecturer. Six were male and three female.

Due to the importance of the formal interview I considered it necessary to develop a system for classifying the type and balance of questions asked of each candidate. My review of previous research identified two major projects that had attempted to do this (Janz, 1982; Wright *et al.*, 1989). The findings of these studies were used to develop five categories of questions (see Table 10.1).

TABLE 10.1
The five categories of question

CATEGORY	DESCRIPTION
Credentials	Factual qualitative details about the candidate
Description of experience	Non-evaluative description of past experiences
Self-perception	Self-assessment of strengths and weaknesses
Description of behaviour in situations	Detailed description of specific events in the candidate's past or response to job-related situations
Job knowledge	Knowledge required to do the job, e.g. technical knowledge

The number and type of questions asked of each candidate were recorded together with the length of the interview.

FINDINGS OF PREVIOUS RESEARCH

Interview and selection procedures have received much attention over the past 70 years. One of the first published research projects was reported by Scott in 1915 who found little relationship between the judgements of six personnel managers. Although this disappointing result became a recurrent theme a number of important findings were established by the end of the 1970s. Interview bias and the resultant discrimination were identified as the major factors responsible for low reliability and validity of selection interviews (Webster, 1964; Schmitt, 1976). More encouragingly, however, there was a high degree of consistency across a number of studies, indicating that well-structured interviews based on the requirements of the job and organized in a way to ensure equality across candidates were significantly more reliable than unstructured interviews (Wagner, 1949; Mayfield, 1964; Schwab and Henneman, 1969; Carlson *et al.*, 1970; Latham *et al.*, 1975) also found that training interviewers significantly reduced interviewer bias.

More recent studies have concentrated on identifying specific types of selection process that have a high degree of validity and reduce the risk of discrimination. Structured interviews have been found to produce particularly encouraging results: 'patterned behaviour' (Janz, 1982; Orpen, 1985) and 'situational interviews' (Latham *et al.*, 1980; Latham and Saari, 1984). Both are based on a job analysis to identify incidents and behaviours that are critical to the successful performance of the job. This can either be done by direct observation or by discussing the requirements of the post with experienced practitioners. The incidents regarded as being most critical are used to develop job-related questions. The questions can be worded in a way that requires candidates to explain their response to similar situations in their previous post or to indicate what action they would take in future job-specific situations. In both cases they should be asked to explain the reasons for their action and the actual or expected outcomes. Each candidate is asked the same set of questions and their responses scored on a predetermined scale. An overall rating can be obtained by applying weighting factors to each of the job dimensions.

The validity of structured interviews has been found to be significantly better than that achieved from unstructured interviews (Wiesner and Cranshaw, 1988; Wright *et al.*, 1989; Gaugler *et al.*, 1987).

A considerable amount of work has also been carried out to establish complementary procedures that are at least as valid as structured interviews. Most promising of these are work sample tests, biographical data and assessment centre techniques.

Work sample tests have been developed in an attempt to devise selection criteria that relate closely to the job in question. This usually involves the applicant performing a task or number of tasks which are either taken from or are designed to represent the range of work carried out by the postholder.

In reviewing over sixty studies Robertson and Kandola (1982) developed four categories of work sample tests:

1. Psychomotor: this category tests candidates' ability to perform physical operations including scientific experiments, practical workshop tasks and computer operations.
2. Simulated decision-making: tests where applicants have to take decisions similar to those required by the job. This can include in-tray exercises and case study material.
3. Job-related information: tests in this category examine applicants' knowledge of areas directly relevant to job performance. These types of tests can include presentations to groups of staff/students and the production of written reports.
4. Group discussions/decision-making: tests of this nature involve two or more people discussing a particular topic whilst their performance is evaluated. They are used widely for jobs where an individual's contribution within a group setting is an important determinant of job success.

The predictive value of **biographical data** has been recognized for a number of years (Asher, 1972; Reilly and Chao, 1982). The processes adopted in assessing and using biographical data are, however, extremely varied. The majority of employment selection processes require candidates to complete some type of application form most of which is concerned with the collection of basic biographical information. In its simplest form the information collected is used to assess the candidate's suitability for the post by comparing the applicant's details with the level of skills and experience thought to be necessary to perform the job successfully.

A more sophisticated approach involves developing a detailed biographical profile by analysing the characteristics of a large number of employees together with their respective performance ratings. Each biographical item is correlated with the criterion and the best predictors selected and weighted according to their importance. Specifically designed biographical questionnaires are used to obtain the required information and various statistical models used to establish an overall rating.

There has been a significant increase in the number of British companies using **assessment centres** for the purpose of staff selection (Robertson and Makin, 1986; Shackleton and Newell, 1991). The assessment centre method has been defined by Smith and Blackham (1988, p. 15) as 'involving a small group of candidates being assessed on the basis of their performance on a range of exercises by a number of trained assessors'.

An essential feature of assessment centres is the use of a range of tests and exercises designed to enable applicants to demonstrate whether they have the skills and abilities appropriate to the post in question. The battery of tests used frequently includes a number of questionnaires designed to establish candidates' personality profiles, job simulation exercises such as in-tray, group discussion and individual presentations, ability tests such as verbal and numerical reasoning and some form of structured interview. A typical assessment centre comprises 6 to 10 candidates and is conducted over a two-day period. A team of trained assessors is used to observe the various exercises and rate candidates accordingly. At the end of the assessment programme the assessors collectively consider the performance of each candidate and agree on an overall rating. This can either be in the form of a numerical scale, placing candidates into one of a number of predetermined bands, or simply deciding which candidate(s) to appoint.

Despite the apparently objective nature of assessment centres there is some evidence that the decision-making process can be subject to a range of biases. This is most frequently due to assessors attaching more importance to particular assessment procedures, highly visible exercises exerting an halo effect, and distortion caused by assessors discussing candidates prior to the final assessors' meeting (Smith and Blackham, 1988; Norris, 1991). It is also important to use trained assessors and standardized procedures to ensure that all candidates are assessed under the same conditions (Frank *et al.*, 1988).

Where assessment centres are used in the selection of academic staff great care should be taken to ensure that the tests are designed to reflect the nature of the post and the duties involved. Performing a practical laboratory demonstration, leading student discussion groups and the presentation of a mini lesson, are examples of tests that can be used to reflect future job performance accurately. The battery of results from a range of tests and interviews should be carefully considered by the selection panel during the decision-making phase.

MODEL OF A FAIR AND VALID SELECTION PROCESS

I have identified five key elements that are fundamental to a valid selection process.

- A systematic job analysis should be undertaken to identify key aspects of the job. This can be done either by direct observation to identify the skills and behaviour patterns that are critical to the successful performance of the job or by discussions with experienced practitioners and managers responsible for the job.
- Shortlisting of candidates should be based on a systematic comparison of the job requirements and an analysis of applicants' attributes.
- Interview questions should be based on the requirements of the job, be predetermined and asked consistently of all candidates. They should be presented in a way that requires candidates to explain how they have responded in the past or would respond in the future to specific work-based situations.
- Work sample tests and biographical data should be incorporated into the process to increase validity and reduce the risk of unintentional discrimination.
- The decision-making process should focus on stated candidate ratings.

A model of this process is shown in Figure 10.1.

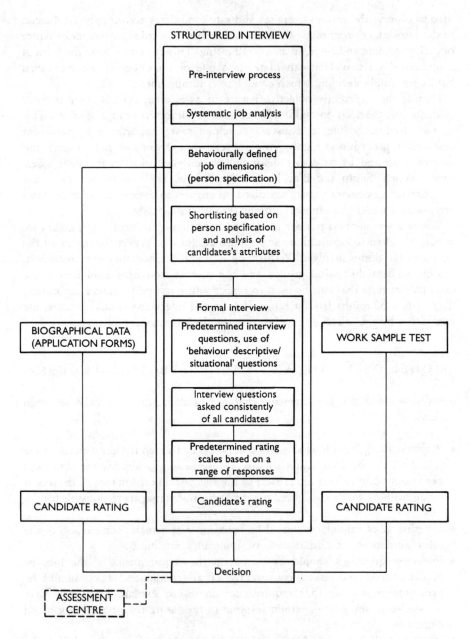

FIGURE 10.1   Model of a fair and valid selection process.

SURVEY RESULTS

Although I observed differences in methods used across the three faculties, the selection process for all the posts followed the same basic form. I identified five critical phases: job analysis and shortlisting, candidate briefing, pre-interview assessment, formal interview, and the decision-making process.

A job description containing details of the post, selection criteria and elements of a person specification was produced for each post. This, together with details of the school, faculty and college, was sent to applicants responding to the job advertisement. In the main the job descriptions were based on historical requirements and an 'informal' consideration of future requirements. A systematic evaluation of a lecturer's job was not undertaken either at institution or faculty level. Consequently the job descriptions varied in style and in the extent to which selection criteria were specified.

The results of my candidate survey indicated that overall the majority of interviewees were satisfied with the details they received. A significant number, however, stated that they had some difficulty in developing a clear understanding of the demands of the job and consequently in deciding whether it satisfied their needs. Inviting candidates to have informal discussions with the head of school prior to submitting an application proved particularly beneficial.

The recommended shortlist was produced by the head of faculty and the head of school for approval by the vice principal. Care was taken at both stages to ensure each candidate was considered on his or her merits. The lack of a standardized candidate analysis sheet, however, resulted in some discussions becoming unstructured with decisions based on an overall assessment of candidates rather than on a systematic analysis of attributes measured against pre-stated criteria.

In a number of cases the vagueness of the selection criteria, for example 'relevant qualifications', resulted in the quality of applicant determining the standard rather than the requirements of the post. In other cases the criteria effectively defined the minimum standard, for example 'management qualification at masters level'. In many respects it could be argued that comparative judgements are inevitable as the process is often concerned with selecting the 'best' candidates; specific selection criteria must, however, be defined in all cases.

Candidate briefing sessions were included in all the appointment processes. All the briefing sessions followed the same basic format in describing the nature and management of the college, the faculty and school structure and a detailed description of the post. They also included a tour of the college and school facilities varying in length from 30 minutes to an hour.

The vast majority of candidates indicated that they found the briefings extremely useful in assessing whether the post satisfied their needs. This stage of the process did, however, cause some problems on the two occasions where internal candidates were involved. The majority of the difficulties were due to the familiarity between the manager conducting the process and the internal candidate, resulting in differential behaviour and style of communication. In one instance the internal applicant was asked to show the other candidates around the practical facilities of the school. This resulted in two of the external candidates withdrawing before the formal interview. The problems encountered in the other process involving an internal candidate were not as blatant although on one occasion the internal candidate was asked to respond to a question raised by an external candidate. This in effect was an open acknowledgement by a member of the selection panel that the internal candidate had a superior understanding of the job requirements and presumably a better chance of being appointed. Feedback from the external candidates confirmed that both incidents reduced their confidence in the selection process. Although I believe there was no deliberate attempt to favour internal candidates, I think it is important to take great care not to give the wrong impression to the other candidates.

Pre-interview assessments were utilized in six of the eight appointment procedures. Four of the five techniques used – discussion groups, candidate assignments, oral presentations and scientific demonstrations – can be classified as work sample tests (Robertson and Kandola, 1982) with the fifth, a technical interview, being a variation on the formal interview. In all cases the candidates were advised of the requirements prior to attending for interview although in two instances this was not done very effectively. All the tests were well designed, had face validity in that it was apparent that the tasks reflected an important aspect of the job, and were carried out in a professional manner. Their effectiveness was, however, impaired by the lack of predetermined assessment criteria and standardized observation sheets. Consequently the quality of feedback presented to the selection panel varied considerably.

Over 80 per cent of candidates were in favour of using work sample tests and considered them to be very relevant to the demands of the post. However, I think candidates must be informed of the requirements of the tests prior to attending for interview.

The overall format of the **formal interviews** was consistent across all eight selection processes. The interview panel comprised the appropriate head of faculty and head of school, one member of academic staff from an area of the college not directly involved and the vice principal who chaired all the selection panels. A female member of staff was included on each of the interview panels.

Panel members were provided with copies of application forms for all the candidates and the job details prior to the interview. Analysis sheets of candidates' attributes taken from the application details were not provided. The area of questions to be asked by individual panel members and the order of questioning were agreed immediately prior to the interview. Each member of the panel was free to determine their own questions and to ask them in a form which they considered appropriate.

Each interview lasted an average of 25 minutes. I then classified the questions according to the five categories I had devised (Table 10.1). Almost half of the questions asked were 'self-perception' requiring candidates to assess their own strengths and weaknesses. A further 25 per cent were classified as 'descriptive of experience' requiring a non-evaluative description of their past experience and typically concerned with information contained on their application form. 'Description of behaviour in situations' questions accounted for only 14 per cent of the total questions asked.

For each post the areas of questioning were consistent but the balance and number of questions asked varied considerably from candidate to candidate. In one case the number of questions asked of candidates being interviewed for the same post ranged from 17 to 31. The balance between 'self-perception' questions and 'description of behaviour in situations' questions also varied considerably as did the wording and style of questions. In some cases panel members phrased questions more positively when addressing certain candidates. Full information about the number of candidates for each post, the average length of the interviews, and the balance of questions is presented in Table 10.2.

The **decision-making process** was conducted in two stages. Where the panel agreed unanimously that one or more of the candidates was unappointable or significantly weaker than the others, they were eliminated. Panel members then shared their views on the remaining candidates, taking each in turn. After all the candidates had been reviewed the chair summarized the views of the panel. Where a clear front runner emerged the chair confirmed with the panel that they wished the post to be offered to the particular candidate. Where this was not the case further discussions took place until a consensus decision was reached, usually by a process of elimination.

I noted that the decision was based almost exclusively on candidates' performance during the formal interview. Candidates' application forms and the job descriptions were very rarely referred to. Relatively little weight was given to the feedback from the pre-interview assessment.

CONCLUSION

The process observed was conducted within a well-defined framework and carried out very professionally by committed members of staff. Care was taken throughout the process to ensure that all the candidates were given serious consideration. The methods used within the framework, however, were not as fully developed as those represented in my model of a fair selection process. This is illustrated in Figure 10.2.

The job specification was not based on a clear job analysis. Although very thorough, the shortlisting procedure was largely based on an overall assessment of candidates rather than a systematic comparison of the job requirements and candidates' attributes. Interview questions were not predetermined, presented as situational questions or asked consistently of all candidates. The information used in the decision-making process was largely restricted to an assessment of candidates' performance during the formal interview with little weight given to the results of the work sample tests. Biographical data were only used during the shortlisting process. The lack of uniformity and the restricted range of information used in the final decision-making process significantly increase the risk of unintentional discrimination.

TABLE 10.2

Summary of question types asked across all candidates for each post

QUESTION TYPE	POST 1 (%)	POST 2 (%)	POST 3 (%)	POST 4 (%)	POST 5 (%)	POST 6 (%)	POST 7 (%)	POST 8 (%)	ALL POSTS (%)
Credentials Factual, qualitative details about the candidate	0	4	3	6	6	2.5	2	6	4
Description of Experience Non-evaluative, description of past experience	19	38	23	19	24.5	25	18	24	25
Self-perception Self-assessment of strengths, weaknesses, likes, dislikes and responses to hypothetical questions	51	41	26	12	33	40	44	47	41
Description of behaviour in situations Detailed description of specific events in the candidate's past or response to future situation	15	11	11	19	24.5	20	9	12	14
Job knowledge Knowledge required to do the job, e.g. technical knowledge	10	2	31	38	10	12.5	23	3	11
Others	5	4	6	6	2	0	5	9	5
Number of Candidates	6	4	2	1	2	3	3	6	27
Average number of questions	14	24	18	16	25	13	19	17	18
Average length of interview (mins) Excluding candidate questions	25	21	14	15	24	23	19	23	22
Including candidate questions	30	23	17	15	26	25	21	27	25

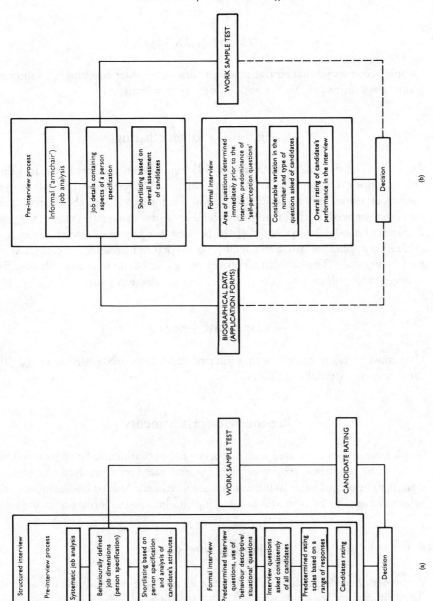

FIGURE 10.2 Comparison of the model of the selection process used at the college and that developed from the findings of previous research. (a) Model developed from the findings of previous research. (b) Model of the process currently used by the college.

RECOMMENDATIONS

I would recommend that educational institutions consider adopting the following proposals with respect to the appointment of academic staff.

Job analysis and shortlisting

An analysis of the role of academic staff be undertaken to identify the incidents and behaviours critical to successful performance. The results of the analysis to be used to establish behaviourally defined job dimensions. These should reflect the development needs of the institution as well as the immediate demands of the post. A standard candidate analysis sheet to be used in order to ensure consistency in evaluating applicants' attributes against the predetermined selection criteria at the shortlisting stage. The shortlisting process to be carried out by the appropriate line manager and at least one other member of the selection panel.

Candidate briefing

Care must be taken to ensure that internal candidates are treated in exactly the same way as external candidates.

Pre-interview assessments

Work sample tests to be used with respect to all appointments. The tests should be designed to reflect the nature of the post and the duties involved. Assessment criteria to be agreed prior to the test being undertaken. At least one member of the selection panel to be involved in assessing candidates' performance in the test.

Formal interview

A number of core questions to be formulated from the results of the job analysis. These questions to be presented as 'Description of behaviour in situations' questions, asked consistently of all candidates, and to account for at least half of the total questions asked.

Where possible panel members should agree a range of responses that constitute a good, satisfactory and poor response. Interview guides and standard recording sheets to be used.

Decision-making process

The decision to be based on a range of information including ratings from work sample tests and the analysis of candidates' biographical data. The results of the work sample tests to be in the form of comparative candidate ratings and presented immediately after the final candidate has been interviewed. This will facilitate panel members discussing the results together with the candidates' performance during the structured interview.

General

All staff involved in the process to be appropriately trained.

REFLECTIONS

I would recommend that a number of projects following the methodology adopted by this study are carried out in other educational institutions. This would increase the sample size and identify complementary and alternative practices. Observing the whole process proved extremely valuable in establishing the importance of each element and the interdependencies of the stages involved. A study of the systems used in the selection of support staff would provide valuable comparative data.

The use of questionnaires and telephone interviews was valuable in obtaining candidates' perceptions of the process, particularly with respect to those elements that cannot be observed. The study would, however, have benefited from a more systematic process of obtaining the views and perceptions of members of staff involved in the selection process, particularly with respect to their role in the decision-making process.

REFERENCES

Arvey, R. D. and Campion, J. E. (1982) The employment interview: a summary and review of recent research, *Personnel Psychology*, Vol. 35, pp. 281–322.

Asher, J. J. (1972) The biographical item: can it be improved? *Personnel Psychology*, Vol. 25, pp. 251–69.

Banfield, J. and Fearn, E. (1984) Selection for employment in the field of education: the experience of the interviewee, *Journal of Education Administration and History*, Vol. 16, no. 2, pp. 54–60.

Carlson, R. E., Schwab, D. P. and Henneman, H. G. (1970) Agreement among selection interview styles, *Journal of Applied Psychology*, Vol. 5, pp. 8–17.

Cohen, S. L. and Manion, L. (1980) *Research methods in education.* London: Croom Helm.

Frank, F. D., Braken, D. W. and Struth, M. R. (1988) Beyond assessment centres: variations on assessment centres cut costs while maintaining validity, *Training and Development Journal*, March, pp. 65–7.

Gaugler, B. B., Rosenthal, D. B., Thornton III, G. C. and Bentson, C. (1987) Meta-analysis of assessment center validity, *Journal of Applied Psychology*, Vol. 72, no. 3, pp. 493–511.

Janz, T. (1982) Initial comparisons of patterned behaviour description interviews versus unstructured interviews, *Journal of Applied Psychology*, Vol. 67, no. 5, pp. 577–80.

Krausz, E. and Miller, S. M. (1974) *Social research design*. London: Longman.

Latham, G. P. and Saari, L. M. (1984) Do people do what they say? Further studies on the situational interview, *Journal of Applied Psychology*, Vol. 69, no. 4, pp. 569–73.

Latham, G. P., Saari, L. M., Pursell, E. D. and Campion, M. A. (1980) The situational interview, *Journal of Applied Psychology*, Vol. 69, no. 4, pp. 422–7.

Latham, G. P., Wexley, K. N. and Pursell, E. D. (1975) Training managers to minimise rating errors in the observation of behaviour, *Journal of Applied Psychology*, Vol. 60, no. 5, pp. 550–5.

Mayfield, E. C. (1964) The selection interview: a re-evaluation of published research, *Personnel Psychology*, Vol. 17, pp. 239–60.

Norris, K. (1991) The recruitment and selection of academic staff. MSc dissertation, Anglia Polytechnic University, Chelmsford.

Orpen, C. (1985) Patterned behaviour description interviews versus unstructured interviews: a comparative validity study, *Journal of Applied Psychology*, Vol. 70, no. 4, pp. 774–6.

Reilly, R. R. and Chao, G. T. (1982) Validity and fairness of some alternative employee selection procedures, *Personnel Psychology*, Vol. 35, pp. 1–62.

Robertson, I. T. and Kandola, R. S. (1982) Work sample tests: validity, adverse impact and applicant reaction, *Journal of Occupational Psychology*, Vol. 55, pp. 171–83.

Robertson, I. T. and Makin, P. J. (1986) Management selection in Britain: a survey and a critique, *Journal of Occupational Psychology*, Vol. 59, no. 1, pp. 45–57.

Schmitt, N. (1976) Social and situational determinants of interview decisions: implications for the employment interview, *Personnel Psychology*, Vol. 29, pp. 79–101.

Schwab, D. P. and Henneman, H. G. (1969) Relationship between interview structure and interviewer reliability in an employment situation, *Journal of Applied Psychology*, Vol. 53, pp. 214–17.

Scott, W. D. (1915) Scientific selection of salesmen, *Advertising and Selling*, Vol. XXV, pp. 5–6, 94–6.

Shackleton, V. and Newell, S. (1991) Management selection: a comparative survey of methods used in top British and French companies, *Journal of Occupational Psychology*, Vol. 64, pp. 23–36.

Smith, D. and Blackham, B. (1988) The measurement of managerial abilities in an assessment centre, *Personnel Review*, Vol. 17, no. 4, pp. 15–21.

Wagner, R. (1949) The employment interview: a critical summary, *Personnel Psychology*, Vol. 2, pp. 17–46.

Walker, R. (1985) *Applied qualitative research*. London: Gower.

Watts, M. and Ebbutt, D. (1987) More than the sum of the parts: research methods in group interviewing, *British Educational Research Journal*, Vol. 13, no. 1, pp. 25–34.

Webster, E. C. (1964) *Decision making in the employment interview*. Montreal: Industrial Relations Centre, McGill University.

Wiesner, W. H. and Cranshaw, S. F. (1988) A meta-analysis investigation of the impact of interview format and degree of structure on the validity of the employment interview, *Journal of Occupational Psychology*, Vol. 61, pp. 275–90.

Wright, P. M., Lichtenfels, P. A. and Pursell, E. D. (1989) The structured interview: additional studies and a meta-analysis, *Journal of Occupational Psychology*, Vol. 62, pp. 191–9.

CHAPTER 11

Implementing Redundancy: Implications for Small School Management

LYNNE SLOCOMBE

It had been a difficult time at work, everyone distrusting each other. A time when you found out who your friends were. The worst thing was carrying on as if nothing was happening. Teachers were brilliant actors, they had to be.

(*excerpt from a short story written by a teacher about the redundancy process*)

ABSTRACT

This is a descriptive case study of the implementation of staff cuts in two small first schools. It is a multiple case study in that it looks at more than one instance of cuts and from several angles including that of myself as a participant-observer. It makes recommendations for human resource management practice.

INTRODUCTION

The purpose of the case study is to try to break down some of the mystique that surrounds the word *redundancy* in schools; to look, in particular, at how the model policy in one English county is implemented with particular regard to the reactions and feelings of those involved, and to provide information for those who may become involved in the future. Apart from acting as an awareness-raising vehicle, I hope the case study will highlight problem areas in the implementation of such staff cuts.

The context was changed from recording one particular redundancy study (the one in which I had been directly involved) to the involvement of a few schools, and also other personnel who had been involved, or were interested in, the redundancy policy implementation. The change of context was made for several reasons but mainly because I felt that there was (for understandable reasons) a reluctance to co-operate on the part of the teacher in the redundant post. I felt it was not ethically feasible for me to proceed without this compliance and, in addition, I did not feel that a single case could have been described without this. I decided that I could not give sufficient time to selecting and properly approaching another teacher who had similarly been in a redundant post.

I believed the alternative to be a multiple case study which would cover the main issues involved and would include views from many angles but with the exception of the key (redundant) teachers involved. Again, I was uncertain that this would be a successful formula but time constraints meant that I had to go ahead. The ethical dilemma seemed to resolve itself. Changing from the specific to the general was more acceptable to those involved and also, despite the small scale of the enquiry, there were many common aspects which emerged, including some recommended good practices.

The context of the resultant case study is, primarily, two schools in the county; I also talked to other members of the teaching profession who were, or could be, involved in a redundancy implementation. The views recorded include those of heads, teaching staff, governors, staff at the area education office, but not those teachers identified as being in redundant posts (further details on those contacted are given at the start of the Methodology section). The schools were first schools of mixed catchment areas, had non-teaching heads, and were experiencing falling rolls. One school had approximately 210 children on roll, the other approximately 135 on roll. At the time of the redundancy implementations (which both occurred in the same spring term), the county council had just circulated a draft 'Model Redundancy Policy for School Staff' and it is this policy which is referred to.

From the beginning I had promised to ensure anonymity for those involved in the implementations. As a result, in this case study the schools are not distinguishable from each other, and the views recorded are identified by 'role', for example parent-governor, head, chair of governors.

I was a parent-governor and a member of the redundancy subcommittee in one of the schools. Because I was conscious of having been so involved, I made some provision (noted in the Methodology section) to ensure that my study would be as objective as possible.

Despite searches through library sources, I did not find any appropriate literature readily available. I did look at books written on redundancy in commercial contexts but found nothing that I could relate to redundancy in education. In my analysis, I have noted particular aspects which make redundancy in education different.

METHODOLOGY

The instruments for the research were mainly semi-structured interviews with two heads, one deputy head, six teaching staff and two governors. I did not pursue interviewing those who had been identified as holders of redundant posts. I made a record of my personal experience and reflections and an analysis of policy documents. Other instruments were a short story written by a teacher, discussions at a seminar, and various phone calls. In the remainder of this section I look in detail at all these aspects.

Initially, I revised my existing knowledge of the redundancy policy, the matrix and the timetable of events (examples of the matrix and the timetable are discussed in the Analysis section), and made my own diary of the events in which I had been involved. I also revised my knowledge of the roles of those involved and then arranged interviews (allowing approximately three-quarters of an hour each).

At all appropriate opportunities I confirmed with those I was approaching for interview, my guarantee of anonymity for them. Because the subject of the study is redundancy, I was anxious that there should be willingness, on the part of those involved, to co-operate in the research – firstly, because I believed it was not acceptable to proceed without it, and, secondly, because the study would be incomplete without such co-operation.

At each interview I handed the interviewees a brief interview schedule which was in four sections: background and early warning; becoming involved; the process; afterwards. The questions were intended to help us to begin. I did not tape the interviews, but I did write up copious notes. I also left a copy (with a space after each question) and stamped addressed envelope in case interviewees wished to add any further comments and send them on to me afterwards. I emphasized that I wanted to hear anything they wished to tell me and would prefer to spend most time on what they felt was important.

I did not want those who knew me to feel pressurized to co-operate, so I tried to emphasize the voluntary nature of such co-operation and the confidentiality and anonymity. I also stated that in researching how the process was viewed by the parties involved, I was not providing an opportunity to put the record straight – it was not to be a continuation of the process but a reflection on it.

I opted to interview staff from the area education office first. From the first interview, with the assistant manager, I hoped to confirm my knowledge of facts, try to start to identify difficult areas, check information on budgets, identify unwritten practices, and see how she saw her role. I used a similar interview schedule, but this one also included aspects of the role of the adviser.

I then carried out the other interviews over a period of two weeks. They were conducted in an informal open way, and sometimes seemed to offer an opportunity for general reflection on the part of the interviewee. I tried not to lead but, as I had predicted, lack of time meant that I occasionally had to draw people back to what I *needed* to cover. I was, however, relieved that interviewees found it easy to talk about their experiences, and in a very dispassionate way despite the highly subjective focus of the study.

In the case of those interviewees known to me, there were moments when they would begin to say, 'you know yourself when that happens you . . . [feel/react in a certain way]'. At these times, I found it appropriate to 'lapse' into discussion – this, I believe, helped to prevent abruptly truncating a potentially sensitive flow – and I made it clear that we were talking 'off the record'. This is one tendency which emerged from interviewing as a participant-observer.

A few months after I had been involved in the redundancy process, I attended a seminar on redundancy run by the area education office on behalf of the county council. At this I learned more about what had happened in other schools. I also took note of the queries and expectations expressed by those attending the seminar (heads and governors) who had not, by that time, been through the experience. I used what I had gleaned at the seminar as part of my research: the questions and comments from others attending would partly identify those aspects which I should cover (these people were, in a sense, a typical sample of the 'audience' to whom any awareness raising of this case study should apply).

One of the teachers had written a short story soon after the redundancy process and she gave me a copy of this. The story relates the fictional experience of a teacher involved in a redundancy process and looks particularly at her thoughts immediately before she reads the letter which will tell her whether she is redundant or not.

I made various phone calls to check the accuracy of my account with those I had interviewed and to clarify points of fact with area education office staff.

ANALYSIS

The redundancy process is based on the draft policy prepared by the county council in negotiation with teachers' unions. It is very detailed and does give all information necessary to carry out the procedure correctly. The policy clearly identifies all steps to follow and no governors or heads expressed any complaint about its clarity. There is also extensive guidance, including a brief plan of the stages in the process (see Figure 11.1), offered by the area office before, during and after redundancy implementation. The policy quite clearly states that providing the 'procedures outlined in this Policy Document have been adequately followed . . . [and] . . . Governing Bodies act reasonably at all times in these matters' then the authority will meet costs of the redundancy. Where this does not happen costs could be recharged to the delegated budget.

Governors to whom I spoke on this were happy about the policy as a fair means of implementing redundancy. One interesting aspect, however, emerged from the views of one governor who was very familiar with redundancy procedures in the commercial world. He noted that, if one equates the governing body/local education authority (LEA) with top management, the governing body equates to the employer (with power to hire and fire) who, in this case, has played no part in the redundancy policy preparation, but yet implements it. All governors to whom I spoke were very much aware of the responsibilities of their actions, took them very seriously and agonized over many aspects of the procedure. Unfortunately, my collection of data did not include asking whether they would take on such a role again.

Key roles in the implementation of the redundancy procedure are those of the redundancy adviser from the area education office, in this case the assistant manager, and the head. These are the people who not only advise others on all aspects of procedure but also greatly influence the well-being and morale of the

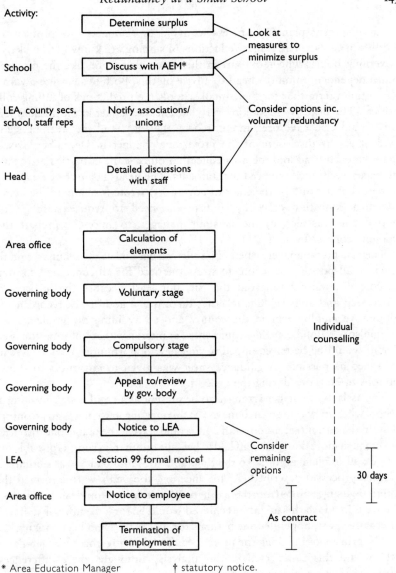

Activity:

School

LEA, county secs, school, staff reps

Head

Area office

Governing body

Governing body

Governing body

Governing body

LEA

Area office

Determine surplus

Discuss with AEM*

Look at measures to minimize surplus

Notify associations/ unions

Consider options inc. voluntary redundancy

Detailed discussions with staff

Calculation of elements

Voluntary stage

Individual counselling

Compulsory stage

Appeal to/review by gov. body

Notice to LEA

Section 99 formal notice†

Consider remaining options

30 days

Notice to employee

As contract

Termination of employment

* Area Education Manager   † statutory notice.

FIGURE 11.1 A summary of the redundancy procedure.

school staff and governors; their task is an extremely difficult one to carry out successfully.

The role of the chair and other members of the redundancy subcommittee is extremely important but they are not (nor could they be) people who influence the working of the school during the process. This becomes apparent when their roles are analysed later.

In the model policy, it is the governing body which is expected to 'seek as part of its development planning process to avoid or minimize any problem of staff surplus in cases where future reductions in staffing are known to be likely'. Both governing bodies who took part in this case study were, like the teachers, very much dependent upon the head to advise on this. Both heads were aware during the autumn term that for their small schools the predictions of falling rolls were critical. The heads were looking very hard at the budget in the autumn term and this would also have been monitored by the LEA, and the warning signs were evident at the disclosure of the provisional budget in December. Discussions between each head and the area education office staff, in particular the assistant manager, confirmed the need for staff cuts. The heads (as in the examples looked at here, but it could be the chair of governors) wrote formally to the manager of the area education office to confirm the need to reduce staffing. Informal notification was sent, by the assistant manager, to unions to prepare them for possible contact by staff.

The assistant manager, when I interviewed her and at the seminar, said that she tried on all possible occasions to stress the need for all concerned constantly to explore alternatives to avoid the cut, not least because the 'process can be harrowing and divisive'. She felt that there was a good track record for finding alternative employment in the county and so avoiding the implementation of compulsory redundancy. She commented at interview that 'information is control' – staff would be better equipped to find new opportunities if they were as fully informed as possible. A guidance sheet was given to governors to show other options to consider during the process.

The assistant manager arranged to be present at a regular staff meeting at each school when staff were given the news. At this meeting it was necessary to inform staff that, in the current situation, staff cuts would have to be made. She also needed to cover much more than this: staff had to become familiar, as soon as possible, with the process of implementation, so the timetable for redundancy was outlined and its various processes described. At the meeting, too, staff were informed that any alternative suggestions from them to avoid the situation would be considered; one of the ways in which this might be achieved would be for a member of staff to find an alternative post, hopefully one perhaps for which they had been looking.

The process of breaking the news to staff and to governors was similar at each school and this is reflected in the analysis, although where differences were observed they are clearly stated.

About the time of this first meeting, teachers in both schools were shown an alternative plan for their school, prepared by the head, which addressed the posts needed to run the school, but did not ascribe people to the posts. It could be described as a summary of the priorities extracted from the school's development plan. These rearrangements identify what minimum requirements are needed for the school to fulfil its legal obligations. Some teachers expressed the view that they would have liked to have been involved in compiling this. A letter was sent out from the staff of one of the schools to the area office manager deprecating the need for cuts which resulted in increased class sizes and the accommodation of rising fives in an already established first-year class.

All teachers to whom I spoke were extremely shocked to hear *confirmation* of the staff cuts, even those who had carefully interpreted budget trends in the previous year and who suspected what was to come. One head spoke of the 'shock and insecurity' the teachers expressed. Only one teacher mentioned that she had been on a training course in which redundancy had been included. None of the teachers had been involved in redundancy before. One teacher felt that the information had been 'presented correctly but unfeelingly', but there was general-ly a feeling that the matter was being handled capably and as sensitively as circumstances could allow, given the amount of information it was necessary for the teachers to be told. The assistant manager said that one of the very difficult parts of her role was 'ensuring that staff understand and are supported' and it is very much this part of her role that begins at the first staff meeting.

I also noted instances in the use of words such as 'suspicious', 'large amount of shortfall' and a concern that everything really had been done to avoid the redundancy. It is subjective analysis, but I suspect that these underlying worries were the expression of the teachers' internal panic and they were not issues which were followed up later. They do, however, show the depth of shock felt. The fact that the process prompted the writing of a short, sensitively written story is another indication of the depths of emotion aroused by the experience.

The assistant manager commented that teachers were currently probably experiencing a double culture-shock. Until very recently teaching had been regarded as a job for life. Before local management of schools (LMS) there had been no redundancy as such, only redeployment. So the teachers involved in redundancy in the current few years may be harder hit than in subsequent years. During the redundancy process, the assistant manager encouraged teachers to actively pursue other opportunities with her help. This help included counselling and advice, and approaching other schools to seek out existing or potential vacancies and asking for favourable consideration to be given to those from schools threatened with staff cuts. She hoped that this type of mobility would become a part of a teacher's outlook in future years and that minds would be more open, than perhaps they presently were, to new possibilities. The area education office planned to support such activity which they believed would be very much in the teachers' interests.

Governors' meetings were called in the spring term to appraise governors of the details of the situation. Governors were familiar with the budgets of the schools in which they were involved; however, the first experience of redundancy in one's own school seems to belie this. At the meeting at which I was present, governors were shocked, found it difficult to believe that there really was no alternative and we all tried to think of some other solution. One governor (working in industry), to whom I spoke at the time, felt that the redundancy was utterly regrettable when there was so little shortfall involved (in this case approximately £11,000): in his world of commercial work, the money would account for annual expenses for one individual on the staff. The response generally was the result of confronting how tight and inflexible the budget really was for small schools and very different from fields of work in which some of the governors were involved.

Governors in both schools immediately had to decide which method they would adopt to achieve the staff cuts: the model redundancy policy or last-in first-out (LIFO). Both governing bodies chose the redundancy policy procedure. LIFO seemed an unacceptable option at the time, although afterwards one teacher, and I agreed, said that in the school in which we were involved, LIFO may not have been such a fair option, but it would have avoided a great deal of stress for many and would have effected an identical outcome.

The redundancy policy meant that subcommittees had to be chosen: the redundancy subcommittee to select the redundant post and the appeals subcommittee to hear any potential appeal.

At both schools, the selection of members for each of the two types of subcommittee was done with regard to ensuring fair and mixed panels, for instance avoidance of governors with any ties towards particular members of staff, mix of men and women, people experienced in managerial and union work combined with those familiar with school/staff/parents. At one of the schools, the staff and the governors in question asked that those governors who helped regularly in school and were often working with, and so 'allied' to, a particular teacher, should not be members of the redundancy subcommittee. Here, the teachers asked for the deputy head to be a member of the panel as he was relatively new to the school and so could fairly and objectively represent them. The other members of this subcommittee were a welfare assistant, who was also the chair of the governing body, and a parent-governor. The subcommittee in which I was involved consisted of a governor with extensive experience and knowledge of union and council work and two parent-governors. One of the reasons why I was on the committee was that the other two were men and it was felt that there should be a woman to represent an all-female staff; also, as an active Friend of the school, I knew the school and staff well. The appeals subcommittees were chosen in a similar way. Once the subcommittees had been identified, governors involved in each type were instructed not to communicate in any way with each other on the matter. They also needed to remain relatively 'distant' from the staff.

In my interviews I was keen to find out from staff how they felt about non-professionals (in the teaching sense) selecting a post for redundancy, since I had had considerable reservations about this aspect. The teachers did not express any concern at all about this or about any of the panel members being unknown to the staff. The only reaction I gained on pressing this point was a possible influence of the head/assistant manager who would have been the 'heavies' compared to the 'lay' governors. One of the governors told me he 'would have preferred to have known staff but, as it was, it may have meant the decision was all the more objective'. Both redundancy subcommittees were joined at all meetings by the head and assistant manager and were advised on procedure at all stages; great effort was taken in and out of the meetings to ensure that the subcommittees understood all aspects of their task. At the meeting in which the decision was made all governors were clear on how to interpret the information – the matrices – they were given to consider.

The policy provides a 'base' matrix which can be adapted by schools to cater for their own operational needs. The major task of completing the matrices needed to be explained to all concerned. Both schools based theirs heavily on the recommended model and heads and staff consulted over just what areas for their school could be omitted and what added; any amendments could only be rows removed or added to the matrix.

One column was filled in by each member of staff individually and then in consultation with the head. Initially there was a tendency for teachers to undersell themselves. All staff said they were encouraged, by their head, to put more, and they then encouraged each other to do so. Much effort was involved by each teacher in completing these individual matrices: 'To prepare it seemed to be a review of your whole life, and it represented the whole of your teaching life.' This does seem incompatible with the outcome of the task – the simple columns in the final matrix. The example in Figure 11.2 shows the combination of the individual matrices and, while I am not able to state the post identified, this is a good example of the only document that each panel considered in making their decision.

The redundancy subcommittees were told to look at the operational needs of the school and heads/assistant manager stressed the need to consider the *weightings* of needs (for example, the extent of rising 5s education required) for the particular school. The policy has very specific guidelines about *nominating a post*. It is not a *teacher* who is identified as redundant. The subcommittees each decided by elimination: they considered their own development plan priorities, and by looking at the school's development plan would identify essential posts; less secure posts were then scrutinized. For our small schools this was done for the school as a whole; for bigger schools it would have to be done by, say, departments first. Neither subcommittee experienced any difference of opinion on the post finally identified, and members said they felt that, in that sense, the matrix worked in the way in which it was intended.

I asked in interviews with staff whether they believed that the matrix could disadvantage the younger teacher on the grounds that there would inevitably be less experience to note but no way of indicating potential. One young teacher felt this during the process and was reassured by the head that the decision would be made as objectively as possible. Unfortunately this led to an unintended feeling of security for the teacher as well as putting further pressure on the remaining teachers on that staff who misinterpreted the gesture and felt themselves more vulnerable because they had not received the same individual reassurance. It is difficult to see how this reaction could have been predicted, but it did show the sensitivity of the situation.

A second point with regard to the matrix and young teachers emerged. Where a young teacher is recruited and the staff already cover the core curriculum areas, the new teacher may, in the first instance, cover mainly non-curriculum areas (that is, not the core subjects) until perhaps there is a more major reorganization of subjects or the teacher becomes established anyway and changes will have occurred over the years. This was the case in one of the schools, where an experienced teacher felt that any selection of the post of the new teacher could be seen almost as a 'betrayal' since she had been relatively recently welcomed into the school.

SPECIFIC SKILLS AND EXPERIENCE

TEACHER NUMBER:	1		2		3		4		5		6		7		8	
MANAGING THE SCHOOL	a	b	a	b	a	b	a	b	a	b	a	b	a	b	a	b
INSET/Staff development		*[1]						*			✓					✓
Special needs			✓								✓					✓
Liaison: Middle school	✓							*	✓		✓		✓			
Preschool				✓		*		✓	*		✓					
Parents		✓		✓		*		✓	✓		✓			✓	✓	
Community involvement		✓[2]		✓		*[8]		*	✓		✓				✓	
Year group co-ordination		✓[3]		✓[4]		*	✓			*				✓[11]	✓	
Library		✓		*			✓	✓				✓		*		
Experience of Rising 5s				✓		*		✓		*		✓		✓[12]		
Experience of Key Stage 2	✓							✓		✓		✓	✓			✓
Experience of SATs		✓		*	✓		✓			✓		✓	✓		✓	
Management of SATs		✓				✓	✓			*		✓	✓		✓	
Management of Assessment				*[5]				*			✓				✓	

MANAGING AND DEVELOPING THE CURRICULUM

	a	b	a	b	a	b	a	b	a	b	a	b	a	b	a	b
English		✓		✓		*	✓			✓		✓		✓		*
Maths		✓				*				*	✓			*		
Science		*		*						*				*	✓	
Technology				✓[6]				✓						✓[13]	✓	
History	✓			✓		*		*		✓		✓		✓		
Geography	✓			*				*		✓				✓		✓
Art		✓		✓				*		*		✓				
PE/Dance/Drama		✓		*	✓			*				✓		*		
Music		*		✓				*	✓[10]			✓				
IT							✓								✓	
RE/Multicultural education		*		✓[7]		✓[9]		✓		✓		✓		*		*
PSHE		*		✓		✓		✓	✓		✓			✓		*

FIGURE 11.2   Reduction in teaching staff: criteria matrix
a = current including consideration of recent training; b = potential because of skills and experience;* = an interest.
1 = has led INSET for county; 2 = earlier expertise in adult education; 3 = development of team teaching; 4 = has taken on this role as additional responsibility; 5 = current course re-early years assessment; 6 = display expertise; 7 = equal opportunity – race and gender; 8 = course in residential social work (elderly, handicapped); 9 = equal opportunity – race; 10 = audiovisual aids; 11 = development of team teaching; 12 = ran a private nursery; 13 = display expertise.

The overall reaction to use of the matrix was favourable; governors and teachers I spoke to from both schools felt it was objective and no one was able to proffer a fairer system at the moment. The assistant manager stressed that the policy was a draft one, that it and the matrix system could be amended to incorporate improvements, and that the county welcomed improvements at any time from governors, staff or unions.

I asked teachers and heads how the school and staff kept going during the process. I was told that classroom work and work with the children went on as normal, that the teachers carried out their professional roles in this respect unaltered. In breaks and non-directed time, however, discussion very soon came round to the redundancy question. Much time in staff meetings was given over to such discussion and heads accepted this. One head said she spent an extraordinary amount of time discussing issues and explaining major and minor aspects of the process to staff but felt that this was the most supportive thing she could do. Both heads said that new initiatives, and chasing through any projects were shelved; the schools mainly ticked over on classwork. Short term, from what I was told, I found nothing to indicate that classwork or the children's education suffered in any way, although progression of any longer-term goals was delayed. Heads did not find that absence due to illness (stress) increased abnormally during the period.

Staff reaction was of a process going on somewhere away from them and some said a 'them and us' feeling evolved. There was no comment on any difficulty in relationship between staff and governors on the subcommittee who were known to staff. One parent-governor commented that the staff had some sympathy for her in having to do the job. The two parent-governors (I was one), who were members of the redundancy panels and whose children were still in the schools in question, were confident that their children's teaching would not be affected and this was confirmed in practice (that is, the children's attitudes towards school/teachers and their general disposition was unchanged).

The roles of the deputy heads were very different in the two schools. In the one school, the deputy head was not on the redundancy subcommittee, and so was not exempt from expressing any views, and yet was not in the running for being selected. The staff in this school did comment that she was in a 'difficult position'. The other deputy head was on the subcommittee at the request of the teachers so his position may have been a more comfortable one – he would have had immunity from commenting.

Every teacher felt vulnerable. I have already mentioned the effect of one head's misinterpreted discussion with one teacher. Another instance is where one experienced teacher thought, despite her experience, she could be chosen because she had become 'expensive'; her morale was further lowered by the thought that at her age she might be 'unemployable'. There was a feeling that a decision could be made from a financial point of view: that it would be better to retain a 'cheaper' teacher. This could not have been a way of deciding since the matrix takes no account of age or salary.

I asked teachers about whether they had responded to the encouragement to seek other posts or alternatives. For teachers in the county there was a very good early retirement package; other possibilities were secondments, job shares, permanent moves and promotions. Of the small number of teachers I was able to speak to, there were some who had been looking for a move anyway and they looked a little harder, but the teachers who did not want to move said they did not actively seek alternatives and just hoped they would be able to stay put.

The method for imparting the decision was to be decided by the teachers, and this prompted much heart-searching for both staffs. Teachers would be informed at the end of teaching on the day the governors would meet to make the decision; they would then be free to leave school straightaway. There was considerable deliberation before teachers decided on the method they felt best for them. The procedure for one school was for all staff to receive identical envelopes, all containing the same letter except for one which would have the letter confirming the post provisionally selected for redundancy. The other school opted for teachers to remain in their classrooms, and for the head to inform personally the teacher in the redundant post; at the same time the deputy head would inform the rest. There were differing needs within the two sets of teachers; some wanted to have the support of the others with all staying together, others needed to be alone. The head and assistant manager had checked previously on how all staff would spend the evening to ensure support would be on hand where needed. All teachers said it was the worst day of the whole process. Even those not chosen reported great distress – a probable release of the tension which had built up and concern for the one who was unlucky. The following day in school was also very difficult, some of the teachers said – predictably – it was easier to cope with classwork than to mingle in the staffroom: 'The [teacher] who had been made redundant was distraught, refusing to talk about it and avoiding her colleagues' (quote from teacher's story).

Governors were very concerned throughout the process and afterwards about the staff and morale in the school. After a very hectic period of subcommittee activity, I personally felt impotent, and I shared the feelings of the others in wanting to ensure that the teacher identified should not believe that she was in any way incapable. Our subcommittee asked for a comment to this effect to be included in the letter of redundancy. However, I believe our attempt to impart this message did fail. For us also, the possibility of appeal made it impossible to do anything, but at the preliminary meeting which took place regarding an appeal the subcommittee governors did express this view directly to the teacher, but again I suspect in vain at the time. In the event, the appeal option was not pursued.

I was told by teachers that some rifts which had formed among staff during the process remained afterwards. This form of aftermath was not addressed in any open 'debriefing' meetings of all staff. The lack of open discussion was 'as if it had never happened'. Some teachers recalled the great rush to help initially but once the process was over it seemed that the support had vanished. This was not the case in that area office and head's support continued to be offered, but presumably was now expected to be actively sought.

Despite the reiteration that it was the post made redundant not the person, one teacher remarked 'funny how it's always the person who feels redundant'. Both teachers who were in redundant posts, and given notice of redundancy, found alternative employment before the redundancy came into force, so they were not made redundant but resigned. As quoted from the seminar: 'Dismissal is only implemented if a redundancy situation still exists on the last day of service.'

Two more general aspects emerged in the reflections of those teachers who contributed to this case study. One teacher, who felt that the staff had not talked openly about the process afterwards, said talking about it all again probably helped in this respect – a form of catharsis. Another teacher, who was about to face the same process again, said it was useful to be reminded of what to expect; she did not anticipate finding it so traumatic the second time round.

CONCLUSION

I believe that some of the common aspects which emerged from my very limited research have provided indicators on where improvements in future implementations may lie. I have considered several of these in the Recommendations section which follows. However, there are two positive moves which are already taking place which make a fitting conclusion to this case study.

The first of these is a new practice which has begun at one of the schools. The school now operates a one day a week change of duties for all staff. The teachers all swop around responsibilities. This will enable them in future to offer a wider range of recent teaching experience.

Thinking in the area education office has also moved on. It is a form of redeployment revisited: schools and the LEA/employer engage in local redeployment with terms agreeable to schools, that is, the schools 'opt in' to this arrangement. It asks schools who have vacancies to try to accommodate those teachers who are identified in staff cuts in other schools.

RECOMMENDATIONS

1. Staff should be aware of details in the budget and, in particular, understand the connection between trends in numbers on role and budget share. Responsibility for communicating on this lies mainly with the head through staff meetings, although the chair and other members of the governing body should respond if their support is requested or deemed appropriate. The adviser from the area education office may also have a role in this (over and above advising the head in the normal way) if asked to become involved.
2. Early predictions, that is when the 'connection' becomes critical, as identified by the head and area education office, should be aired. This is not intended to be alarmist but if presented sensitively may prompt more urgent searching by those ready for a move, and so avoid the redundancy process having to be initiated. Again this task would most appropriately fall to the head.
3. Encouragement to teachers to look for new opportunities should be a continuous process, including ongoing career counselling/encouragement

which could be done mainly by the head, area education office and unions.

4. During any redundancy process, there may be a role for a 'neutral' governor, known to staff, to offer support: being available if staff want to talk things over (and this may also save a little of the head's time). It is important that those involved are encouraged to express their feelings and it may be that they would only be able to say certain things to a trusted neutral person. Governors should not assume that they can suddenly become confidants; ideally their duty is to have a reasonable understanding of the school and staff through regular contact – any out-of-character support would probably be met with suspicion, and would be better not offered at all.

5. Full staff discussions should be encouraged (see also (4) above), including debriefing sessions if these would seem to be helpful. A brief (not intimidating) redundancy package – a booklet for example – could be supplied by the area education office for the member of staff in the identified post.

6. Training and familiarity with redundancy implementation, including course/role play, should be available for staff.

7. A review of the policy made so that potential, in the case particularly of inexperienced teachers, can be included in the redundancy panel's considerations, either incorporated in the matrix or provided as additional information.

ACKNOWLEDGEMENT

I would like to thank all the teachers, governors, area education office staff and others who have helped me in the preparation of this case study.

CHAPTER 12

'The Photocopy Lady': The Role of the Reprographics Supervisor

TREVOR BURTON

ABSTRACT

This project analysed the job description and actual tasks carried out by a reprographics supervisor, a member of the non-teaching staff in an 11–18 college. The method was that of case study. The instruments chosen were: semi-structured interviews of the subject and her colleagues, a subject-completed task diary and examination of documentary evidence. The investigation confirms the great variety of the role of a member of the non-teaching staff found by earlier investigators and the major contribution that such staff make to the success of the institution. Very few training needs were identified (by the investigator or by the subject!), but a number of recommendations for the management team of the college pertaining to the subject and the work of her colleagues are made.

INTRODUCTION

The purpose of the study was to analyse the actual tasks performed by a member of the support staff of the college, in order to make recommendations for the future development and training of that person. During the study an additional purpose was added: to make recommendations to try to improve the contribution that the subject and other support staff could make to the college. The college concerned was Dixons Bradford City Technology College, an 11–18 inner-city school. The member of staff studied was Janet Knowles, whose job title was reprographics supervisor. She was the main reprographics technician and was also responsible for supervision of a full-time graphic designer and a part-time reprographics technician who also worked in the college office. Mrs Knowles had been a member of staff since the college opened in September 1990.

The two management issues involved in this study were staff development (in the context of non-teaching support staff) and efficient and effective deployment of human resources. In the context of the teaching staff, a study of this kind could be classified as appraisal. Indeed, many appraisal systems focus principally on the development of the individual. Since few training needs emerged from this study, I have used the data to suggest how the college can use Mrs Knowles' talents and, perhaps, the talents of other members of the support staff more fully.

LITERATURE REVIEW

The subject of non-teaching staff development has not provided an extensive body of research on which to draw. For example, Oldroyd (1991) in a handbook for staff development completely fails to mention non-teaching staff, as does Butler (1989) in an appraisal manual. Many sources refer specifically to 'teachers' and those that prefer the term 'staff', for example Lyons and Stenning (1986), rarely differentiate between teaching and non-teaching staff in any meaningful or useful way. However, there are some sources on which to draw to establish a context for this study. Riches (1981) has drawn attention to the wide variety of tasks undertaken by non-teaching staff, especially the school secretary, identifying 57 categories of tasks. This wide variety of tasks was confirmed by Park (1989). Riches (1981, p. 124) also pointed out how high are the pace and pressure of the job, quoting Lyons (1976):

> Few secretaries in industry would expect to undertake quite the range of activities considered 'normal' by a school secretary, and in addition, there is at least a notional responsibility for children, since, in a school, children are automatically placed in a position of dependence on adults.

Riches' last point applies equally well to all non-teaching staff. Her Majesty's Inspectors of Schools have published a review of non-teaching staff in schools (HMI, 1992). Several interesting points emerged: the already large variety of roles undertaken was becoming wider; non-teaching staff are rarely involved in appraisal; the quality and quantity of training varied widely across the country; the work of non-teaching staff was highly valued by teachers, *but* the effectiveness of non-teaching staff could be limited by low expectations or perceptions of their capabilities or potential. These last two contrasting judgements contradict Riches' (1988) suggestions that support staff are perceived by teachers and by themselves as having low status. HMI's recommendations were that there should be clear job descriptions for non-teaching staff; that the scope of their work should be widened; that they should be included in appraisal systems; and that suitable training should be provided for them. In an interesting case study that HMI reported on, centralization of non-teaching administrative staff led to improvements in the quality of reprographics equipment, more use of non-teaching staff in classrooms, the relief for the examinations officer from some clerical work and a recognition that the role of the school bursar is a senior management role, rather than a clerical one. If there is little training available and no career structure, as Riches (1988) points out, there may be a problem in motivating non-teaching staff – Riches' solution is to provide more frequent training; to vary the tasks undertaken and to increase the responsibilities offered: this agrees well with HMI's 1992 conclusions.

If the literature concerning the role of non-teaching staff in schools is slim, that concerning research into them is slimmer still. Riches suggests that since the setting is a social one, positivistic approaches should be discarded: his interests are in perceptions rather than quantifiable variables. Riches adopted the case study approach for his investigation. Nisbet and Watt (1984) suggest procedures for organizing a case study and outline the strengths and weaknesses of the method. They suggest that the case study is easily understood by a non-professional readership; that it can identify subtle and statistically insignificant influences; and that it is suited to use by an individual enquirer rather than a research team. The weaknesses of the method are that a study is not readily generalizable and that the selectivity of the enquirer is not subject to checks that can be applied statistically in large-scale surveys. Therefore, it is difficult for the reader, and the researcher, to disentangle the researcher's perceptions from any objective reality.

One suggestion that Nisbet and Watt make to overcome this subjectivity is that the researcher should *triangulate*, that is, information should be collected in a variety of contexts to allow checking in a way that is partly independent of the researcher. Park's study fulfilled the requirements of triangulation. She included three modes of inquiry: semi-structured interviews; a daily diary; and analysis of documents. She also interviewed several staff other than the subject of her investigation. Bassey (1984) recommends that there should be more emphasis by the research community on case studies, since these easily relate to practice and since the emphasis on generalizability is, in his opinion, misleading. However, Bassey's remarks are in the context of pedagogic research, rather than research into educational management. It is probable that in this different context, Bassey would maintain his stance even more fervently, given that management 'science' is far less developed even than educational psychology in practice.

METHODOLOGY

The method used was that of case study. I used the following research instruments for data collection: semi-structured interviews with the subject and other members of staff; informal task observation; and a diary completed by the subject.

Justification

Because the focus of this research is on the development of an individual, large-scale research methods are inappropriate as well as too costly. Since the setting is social, a more naturalistic method is required, in the ethnographic tradition. Also, since the individual's interests must come before those of the research, an experimental method has clear ethical problems. However, this would not necessarily rule out action research, if it were carried out with the consent of the subject. It is not a requirement that the study should be generalizable, though any observations that may relate to other staff should be set in context so that the degree to which they do (or do not) relate to others is clear. The case study method fulfils the requirements of naturalism, is ethical with respect to the subject's interests, and, it is hoped, will produce recommendations that can be related to the role of other non-teaching staff, even if those recommendations cannot be general recommendations.

The research instruments

In terms of research instruments, the more the merrier, for the purposes of triangulation. The limiting constraint I had was of time in which to carry out the fieldwork and to analyse the results. Initially, I began with an interview to try to determine whether Mrs Knowles' job matched her job description. I also sought to identify what training she had had, what she thought she currently needed and what she may need in the future. I also used this opportunity to discuss the task diary that I asked Mrs Knowles to keep. I chose a task diary to provide some objective measure spanning several days in the subject's work. While the diary seems an attractive method, it is full of pitfalls. Mrs Knowles was perfectly capable of completing the diary satisfactorily, but the pace of her job is very fast; some method of making the completion easy was needed. I constructed a pro forma for her (see Figure 12.1) which categorized the activities we had agreed made up her job, yet left some space for free comments to allow for unexpected categories (C, E and X) or for feelings about the tasks. I asked Mrs Knowles to complete the form on a half-hourly basis, and talked to her each day, as Park had suggested that support of this kind leads to better information collection. The period over which the diary was maintained was three days, chosen so that a single unrepresentative day would not unduly invalidate the analysis, but within the forbearance of the subject. During the diary period I also informally observed Mrs Knowles on task. After the diary period, I interviewed Mrs Knowles again, suspecting that she would have some insights into the usefulness of the method and its trustworthiness. In order to confirm Mrs Knowles' perceptions, I interviewed another member of the support staff, Mrs Richards. Mrs Richards worked for part of her time in the reprographics department under the supervision of Mrs Knowles. This interview was conducted using the same structure as for Mrs Knowles' interview.

Revisions to planned methodology

My original suggestions for the diary required completion every 15 minutes, which Mrs Knowles pointed out would be very difficult for her. She also

Date _____

From	To	Code			Comment
8.15	8.45				
8.45	9.15				
9.15	9.45				
9.45	10.15				
10.15	10.45				
10.45	11.15				
11.15	11.45				
11.45	12.15				
12.15	12.45				
12.45	01.15				
01.15	01.45				
01.45	02.15				
02.15	02.45				
02.45	03.15				
03.15	03.45				
03.45	04.15				
04.15	04.45				
04.45	05.15				

FIGURE 12.1 Task diary. R = reprographics work; SS = stationery supplies (internal); A = preparing artwork; W = word-processing; S = dealing with students; Q = dealing with staff enquiries; B = break (i.e. no work); M = technicians' meeting; T = teaching/assisting in the classroom; O = working in the general office; C = booking in jobs and sorting out the trays (admin.); E = answering telephone; X = setting up offset (maintenance). (The last three codes were added by Mrs Knowles.)

inspected the categories I had suggested, confirmed the appropriateness of most, discarded one and suggested some additional ones. The time I could allow for task observation was very limited and consisted of one half-hour and two shorter periods. Since I was being employed by the college it was not possible to devote any more time, and this casts doubt on the validity of observations made over such a short period.

Difficulties with the collection of data

The task diary, as expected, was more problematic than at first sight. The categories were originally meant to be able to provide a time analysis of the job, but Mrs Knowles made it clear that there were too many short minor interruptions in her working day for this to be valid. The categories were therefore entered into the diary according to the subject's perceptions. When Mrs Knowles was engaged on a long task of one or two hours' duration (for example, teaching[1] or reprographics work), the codes do reflect time spent. In most cases, they represent the subject's perceptions of the components of the job.

The interviews also proved demanding. Since I was conducting only two or at the most three interviews, piloting was going to be problematic. Informally, other teachers commented on my major questions, but no improvements were suggested. Carrying out the interviews was more of a challenge. I was very aware that both the subject and her colleague were, to differing extents, open to suggestions and leading questions. I found it difficult to draw a line between helpfully encouraging them to comment on the issues under discussion and leading them on to confirm my own part-formed hypotheses.

While I cannot claim to have avoided this pitfall, I was at least aware of it. I introduced each major topic and then tried to allow as much freedom as possible for the respondent to explore the issues. I also looked for confirmation by exemplification where I suggested an idea, so that the interviewee could produce some evidence to substantiate their agreement.

ANALYSIS

Interview with the subject

The interview with the subject took place according to the interview schedule shown in Figure 12.2. In general, Mrs Knowles felt that her job description as a reprographics supervisor was accurate. She said that she did all the tasks listed in the description, but that there were several minor tasks or roles that she carried out in addition to her job description (Figure 12.3). These additional tasks were contingent on her personal aptitudes and interests and provided some interesting facets to her work. The additional tasks identified included:

Q1.　Can we look at your job description and see how accurate you feel it is?

Q2.　Let's summarize the tasks you do that aren't in your job description.

Q3.　What training have you had so far since appointment? What training do you need now to help you cope with your job?

Q4.　There are bound to be several changes in the college which could affect your job. Can we make a list of them?

Q5.　What training could you get now to help you prepare for these changes?

Q6.　Can we look at this diary form to see if you will be able to use it?

FIGURE 12.2　Interview schedule.

- acting as a first-aider – this is mainly because her sister is the college nurse and because the reprographics department has a sink!
- mailing information to parents who do not live with the child;
- using a word-processor and database to produce mail-merged letters, e.g. cover sheets for annual reports personalized with the parents' and students' names;
- using desktop publishing packages to do simple artwork to supplement the work of the college graphic designer;
- correcting copy for staff using a word-processor;
- typing of minutes for the parents' association and doing the reprographics and correspondence for any event staged by them;
- typing, amending and printing of some standard letters for one of the year co-ordinators – this was a historical legacy of work that was begun when the

JOB DESCRIPTION

REPROGRAPHICS SUPERVISOR

To be responsible to the principal through the director of finance for:

- general supervision of the reprographics department and staff therein
- production of all internally reproduced materials
- general day-to-day maintenance of all reprographic equipment
- day-to-day liaison with relevant suppliers
- control and distribution of all stationery stock
- ordering and control of specific reprographic stock materials
- day-to-day administrative procedures to support the finance department
- support teaching of such lessons as might reasonably be required by the deputy principal (Curriculum)
- any other duties which the principal might reasonably request

FIGURE 12.3　Job description – reprographics supervisor.

college did not have a word-processor operator and which has continued;

- selling homework diaries, photocopying and stationery to student and staff (and therefore handling cash);
- advising senior managers about the purchase of any reprographics equipment: she would be very surprised if she were not consulted;
- acting as a quality controller for reproduced work (e.g. letters to parents) which leave college.

This last aspect of her work intrigued me. She is clearly exceeding her job description in a way which could have a great positive effect on the college's public relations. As Mrs Knowles put it: 'If it's not right, I won't let it go out.' She felt that this role was acknowledged and sanctioned by senior staff, who welcomed her questioning whether certain items should leave college. However, she has no formal role, and the formal quality control system that exists is paper based and handled by a member of the senior team before it reaches reprographics. Nevertheless, the system does let some errors through, and she sees it as her task to field these errors.

One aspect of her job description is 'the general supervision of the reprographics department and the staff therein'. The staff comprises a part-time reprographics technician who also works in the general office (Mrs Richards) and a full-time graphic designer. My informal observations of these staff indicated that the potential for awkwardness in personal relationships was present and that Mrs Knowles exercised considerable interpersonal skill in maintaining good working relationships. The previous job descriptions did not make clear the line of responsibility within the reprographics department, and she was pleased that this was rectified by the recent production of new job descriptions. When asked to sum up how she contributes to college, Mrs Knowles said, 'I'm support staff and I get a lot of job satisfaction out of that. The things I do directly affect what happens in classrooms. I'm always helping with school events too.'

Mrs Knowles has already had training provided. The college has always intended that non-teaching staff should have access to staff training and development. In fact, all staff are to be involved in appraisal as HMI has recommended, not just the teaching staff. Mrs Knowles' training has been focused on two areas: the first is the operation of the photocopying and offset equipment. This comprised a one-day course at the suppliers costing £45. The college has also paid £180 for her to enter for RSA word-processing Parts 1 and 2. This has been of great benefit as it has improved her knowledge of layout in written documents. The investment in purely monetary terms is modest, but Mrs Knowles did not feel that she was being treated ungenerously, simply that she had few training needs. The college is trying to develop its non-teaching staff and provide suitable training as the HMI Report (1992) recommends. She has also benefited from some less formal college-based information technology (IT) training, though this has been of most value at the extremely informal level of direct questioning of the graphic designer with whom she shares the reprographics room.

In terms of further training, Mrs Knowles could identify little that she needed.

Of course, the purchase of a full-colour printer (not an immediate prospect) would require training, but she felt that such a printer with the demands it would make on her time would reduce the support she could give to staff in her main role. This is clear evidence that she identifies strongly with the college and is committed to its success. She felt that her IT skills, although highly developed, could improve. She identified desktop publishing and use of a graphics package for doing simple signs: in this way, she could free the graphic designer to do more demanding work of an artistic nature. She felt perfectly competent to realize a simple design from a sketch submitted by a teacher. In terms of her financial role, she thought that no further training was needed, but that her system of stock control was unsatisfactory and advice on how she could improve it was needed.

Together, we identified four main changes that were likely to affect her job. These were:

- the use of School Information Management System (SIMS) to produce lists of students;
- the use of SIMS to produce reports;
- the part-time relocation of the graphic designer to give him a curriculum role;
- the expansion of the college as rolls rise.

Of these changes that were likely to affect Mrs Knowles, none had any training implications for her. The use of SIMS was, she felt, likely to affect the office staff, and any lists kept by Mrs Knowles would be small and independent of SIMS; therefore she would be unlikely to use it. Her work with the cover sheets of reports would in all likelihood be completely taken over by the SIMS system. The other issues did not have a training implication, though I found it fascinating that Mrs Knowles was identifying many other management issues as we discussed the changes.

Task diary

The categories used to analyse Mrs Knowles' job were as follows: reprographics work; stationery supplies; preparing artwork; word-processing; student enquiries; staff enquiries; administration for reprographics; answering the telephone; break; technicians' meeting; teaching or assisting in the classroom; working in the general office; and maintenance on the reprographics machine. When Mrs Knowles entered a code, my initial idea was to use that to represent a portion of time spent on a task. It soon became clear that this was unlikely to work well. Therefore the analysis cannot claim to be one of time spent on subtasks. Rather, the analysis shows significant components of Mrs Knowles' day-to-day job, as perceived by her. Figure 12.4 shows how prominent each category was over the three-day period of the task diary.

Clearly, Mrs Knowles' job incorporates much reprographics work. Basic reprographics and machine maintenance account for 34 recorded codes out of

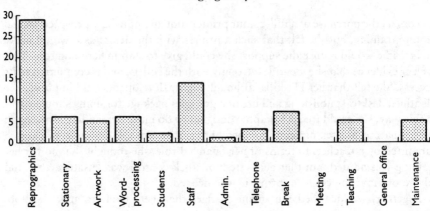

FIGURE 12.4 Analysis of codes in task diary showing how many times each code appeared.

83 that Mrs Knowles recorded over a three-day period. However, a substantial proportion of it is also taken up by a plethora of other tasks. Notable among these is the dealing with enquiries from staff, students and telephone callers which totalled some 19 codes. She is also asked to produce word-processed copy and some simple artwork designs in order to reproduce them (11 codes). The remaining codes are accounted for by reprographics administration (1 code), stationery supplies (6 codes), breaks (7 codes) and teaching (5 codes). Mrs Knowles' written comments in her task diary proved illuminating. The comments showed where she was exceeding her job description. For example, during the three-day period, she had to liaise with all teaching staff about the ordering of a lesson planner, redraft a letter to be sent out of college and discuss with the year co-ordinator of Year 7 what arrangements needed to be made for the incoming Year 7 students in August. (This last task fell to Mrs Knowles because of her involvement with the parents' association.) This clearly shows how she is using her many skills for the benefit of the college.

Interview with other staff

The other member of staff interviewed was Mrs Richards. She confirmed much of the interview with Mrs Knowles, giving me confidence that the methodology had allowed a valid investigation. Mrs Richards stated that Mrs Knowles' job description was accurate and also that she exceeded the description in several aspects of her work. Mrs Richards found it difficult to analyse Mrs Knowles' role and I found it difficult to extract information without planting suggestions. However, Mrs Richards was adamant about the quality control role played by Mrs Knowles and suggested that she contributed to this too. She particularly pointed out how keen Mrs Knowles was to ensure that letters to parents were perfect, giving an example: one letter was returned to a member of the senior team because it did not read well; the letter had to be withdrawn by asking the students who had already received it at registration to give it back in. This demonstrates that Mrs Knowles certainly has a quality control role which is acknowledged by the management of the college. Mrs Richards also confirmed the word-processing and artwork preparation which Mrs Knowles did in support of the reprographics department. Mrs Richards also said that she maintained a distribution list of families where the father and mother receive information separately because they live apart, and that Mrs Knowles had taken on responsibility for ensuring that these parents received the information. This confirmed what Mrs Knowles had said in her interview.

Mrs Richards is supervised by Mrs Knowles and I was interested to see what her perceptions of the Mrs Knowles' management role were. She indicated that there was a good atmosphere and that Mrs Knowles managed her well, giving directions that were clear and authoritative without being bossy. This tallies well with the previous interview with Mrs Knowles. She also said that Mrs Knowles prioritized the tasks well and that this was essential to the efficient management of what was occasionally an exceptionally busy part of the college. The first-aid role that Mrs Knowles plays was seen as a very minor part of her day-to-day work: 'Only what you would do as a mum.'

Mrs Richards generally confirmed Mrs Knowles' perceptions that she had few training needs and those she had were best met by informal on-the-job training. Mrs Richards suggested that it was often difficult for support staff to be able to analyse their own needs and to be aware of what training was available. She also confirmed that support staff felt they were considered equally when it came to allocation of funds for staff development. One point that came out of both interviews was that the support staff were very interested in the research being done and enjoyed taking part: if this is how they come to view appraisal there may be advantages for the college in terms of morale.

CONCLUSIONS

Mrs Knowles' job description describes her as a reprographics supervisor. This is substantially correct, for carrying out reprographics work and supervising others doing such work is a major part of her job. However, she also carries out many other tasks that go somewhat beyond the basic job description. Her role as a parents' association official provides an important, if perhaps unrepresentative, point of contact for school management which could prove very useful.

Mrs Knowles' training needs are currently few and probably best met by informal training by the graphic designer. She often works at a very demanding level and has been involved in teaching and been consulted by a year co-ordinator during the three days of her task diary. It is good that the college has not fallen into the trap of having low expectations of her. However, it is clear that she has unfulfilled potential.

Mrs Knowles is already taking on management responsibility and is successfully maintaining a good working atmosphere. It is possible that this management ability could be extended further, should there be a suitable opportunity within the college. Mrs Knowles' job description was important in that it gave her confidence to accept fully the management responsibility for the staff working in reprographics. It has clearly been a very positive move. Both members of the support staff I interviewed felt very committed to the college and were very well motivated. They felt part of the team of college staff. It seems clear to me that increasing the variety of tasks and level of responsibility has contributed to Mrs Knowles' job satisfaction.

RECOMMENDATIONS FOR THE FUTURE

1. Mrs Knowles' role in quality control should be strengthened by having it formally and publicly recognized. The existing paper-based system of quality control that requires the approval of a deputy principal has allowed some errors through. It would be worth evaluating whether using Mrs Knowles' talents differently may allow modification of system and improve quality control.
2. Mrs Knowles' role with the parents' association gives the college a valuable, immediate point of contact with a representative body of the parents. There may be other staff in college who can be a similar point of contact with other bodies and this should be explored.
3. Mrs Knowles has shown the ability to maintain a good working atmosphere by sensitive management of two staff. This should certainly be recognized and explored as an ability that could be of value to the college.
4. The college currently has achieved an ethos in which support staff feel committed to, and valued by, the college. This should be recognized and maintained as an important strength. The support staff need to continue to feel that, should any training need be identified, there will be funds available to meet it just as there would be for teaching staff.
5. Up-to-date job descriptions can help to ensure that potential management problems are avoided. The college should make sure that the job descriptions already in place are kept up to date and changed whenever there is a substantial change in responsibilities.
6. Help for support staff find it difficult to analyse their jobs and identify their training needs.

UPDATE

Mrs Knowles was interviewed briefly with the aim of establishing whether the conclusions of the investigation were still valid, if any of the recommendations had been acted upon, and how changes in the institution had affected her.

Since the investigation, Mrs Knowles' managerial responsibilities had changed. Both of the staff she managed had left the institution and had been replaced with others. She has begun to do more graphic design so that the new designer could be effectively inducted into his post. She has received informal graphics training from the new graphics designer and she has given on-the-job training to the new reprographics assistant. She commented on the recommendations made in the original report. These comments are arranged in the same order as the recommendations of the original.

1. She said that her role in quality control continued to be important, that more people were aware of it, but that it was not a formal role.
2. No other staff had been identified with outside contacts which could be of use to the college.
3. Mrs Knowles will receive some management training and have her management role increased as a result of appraisal.
4. The college has maintained and even strengthened the feeling that support staff have equal access to staff development. There have been specific steps taken to include support staff in college training days and to identify their training needs.
5. Her job description has been altered to include the first-aid responsibility which she was initially reluctant to have formally acknowledged. She has now been trained and is therefore more confident about it.
6. All support staff are being given specific assistance in defining their training needs through appraisal. The deputy principal responsible for staff development has also taken specific steps to include support staff in college training days and to identify their training needs. The support staff have also taken full part in the college's efforts to achieve the national 'Investors in People' award.
7. She still perceives stock control as a problem, and the situation has not improved since the original investigation. There is little consistency between academic departments in whether they order stationery from her or directly from suppliers. As a result, she finds it difficult to manage stock levels efficiently.

She confirmed that the conclusions of the original investigation were still substantially true.

ACKNOWLEDGEMENTS

I am grateful to the principal of Bradford City Technology College for permitting the study to take place, and to Janet Knowles for agreeing to be the subject of the study. I would also like to thank her colleague, Mrs Richards, who also took part.

NOTE

[1] Mrs Knowles was involved in the enrichment programme. This is a less formal part of the curriculum where students have free choice from academic or leisure-

based activities. Mrs Knowles offered the following: class of 18 mixed-sex students doing cross-stitch; making desserts with 12 students; and assisting an art teacher with textile work.

REFERENCES

Bassey, M. (1984) Pedagogic research: on the relative merits of search for generalisation and study of single events, in J. Bell, T. Bush, A. Fox, J. Goodey and S. Goulding (Eds) *Conducting small-scale investigations in educational management*. London: Paul Chapman.

Butler, G. (1989) *School appraisal in practice*. London: Longman.

HMI (Her Majesty's Inspectors of Schools) (1992) *Non-teaching staff in school – a review by HMI (Education Observed)*. London: HMSO.

Lyons, G. and Stenning, R. (1986) *Managing staff in schools – a handbook*. London: Hutchinson.

Nisbet, J. and Watt, J. (1984) Case study, in J. Bell, T. Bush, A. Fox, J. Goodey and S. Goulding (Eds) *Conducting small-scale investigations in educational management*. London: Paul Chapman.

Oldroyd, D. (1991) *Managing staff development – a handbook for secondary schools*. London: Paul Chapman.

Park, A. (1989) The school secretary's role and training needs, in M. Preedy (Ed.) *Teachers' case studies in educational management*. London: Paul Chapman.

Riches, C. (1981) *E323 Block 6: The management of staff (Part 5 Non-teaching staff in primary and secondary schools)*. Milton Keynes: Open University.

Riches, C. (1988) *E325 Block 4: Managing staff in schools (Part 2 Support staff)*. Milton Keynes: Open University.

CHAPTER 13

Introducing Appraisal

DEREK GLOVER

ABSTRACT

This case study traces the stages in the introduction of an appraisal scheme into Swan Mill, a large senior high school. Derek Glover explains the role of the consultant in the management of change with a school and supports his narrative with evidence from the participants. The process of change is related to the Fullan model of 'initiation, implementation and institutionalization', and conclusions are drawn from this which might inform the management of future change within the school.

INTRODUCTION

This work was undertaken whilst I was acting as a consultant to a number of schools within a rural local education authority (LEA) over a three-year period. In each academic year the senior management team of each school involved determined the topic for consultancy investigation. It had been agreed with the LEA that the consultant 'would hold a mirror to the school to provide help in enhancing whole school evaluation'. This case study charts developments in the third year of my involvement at Swan Mill School by which time I was seen to be a non-threatening critical friend. It follows investigations of the introduction of whole staff cross-curricular planning in the first year and the integration of individual, departmental and school needs in a professional development policy in the second year.

The aims were negotiated with the head and deputy heads following a meeting of the management consultative committee (MCC). This is a policy advisory body drawn from senior management, heads of department and year, and representatives of other staff. It was agreed that I would:

- monitor the progress of the introduction of appraisal;
- act as an independent witness of the perceptions of staff;
- prepare a brief report on the introduction of appraisal which might guide senior management in other change activities.

In addition, the report would form the basis of discussion at the management consultative committee and would be used to guide the professional development planning for the coming year.

It was agreed that the work would be spread across three terms with the field-work being undertaken on three days per term. The head was anxious to stress that 'it is the process by which ideas are challenged, problems resolved and policies developed which is more important than the final report'. He had also stressed throughout the period of consultancy association with the school that the researcher was an independent 'witness of our activities, without bias, and without any obligations to either the school or the LEA'. This did, however, mean that I had to reassure staff that I would not be acting as another arm of the senior management team. I was also aware that they needed to feel that objective judgements were being made and throughout the work in the school stress had been placed on the difference between intuitive and professional judgement (Hargreaves and Hopkins, 1991). All the staff involved knew that opinion without evidence could not be used, and would not be part of any discussions with the head or senior management team.

There were disadvantages in undertaking the role of critical friend. Several of the staff interviewed had been working with me over the previous two years. We enjoyed an easy relationship and the role slipped at times to being one of confidant. It was consequently necessary to recognize when discussion was not pertinent to the investigation but might be of great value to an interviewee who was ready to seize an opportunity for the discussion of frustrations. Selective amnesia was essential in all matters other than those under investigation. This problem might have been overcome if detachment had been preserved through the use of taped interviews, but on balance the honest opinion was of considerable importance, not only in ensuring the integrity of the report but also in being able to fulfil the role of holding a mirror to development for the senior staff.

LITERATURE REVIEW

Preparatory reading had been based on the professional development concerns investigated in the previous year. In particular, the view of the School Management Task Force (1990) is that professional development is more effective where it is school based, and an entitlement to support rather than an imposition from above. In attempting to achieve this the school had found difficulties with the reconciliation of individual and departmental or whole-school needs. They had followed the thinking detailed in the collection of papers by Bell and Day (1991) and sought to establish an annual audit of individual and group needs, to involve staff in the prioritization of the perceived needs, and to attempt to reconcile the needs of the individual and the school as a whole through integrated development planning. Swan Mill had undertaken a major review using the Guidelines for Review and Internal Development in Schools (GRIDS) technique (McMahon *et al.*, 1984) and had moved towards an increased collegiality in its planning processes. Professional development was felt to be owned by the staff and they were anxious to maintain that ownership of any developments.

This meant that, as consultant, I needed to be aware of contemporary thinking on the introduction of appraisal. There is a difference between the 'how to do it' approaches which outline processes as exemplified in Trethowan (1987) and Poster and Poster (1991), and the more philosophical views which attempt to place appraisal within the whole-school development process. Amongst these Mortimore and Mortimore (1991) highlight the problems and potential of appraisal in a brief article which comments on the national pilot schemes. Also, Fullan and Hargreaves (1991) set the parameters for worthwhile development by stressing that any scheme should be effective, efficient, and economic. They also warn against assessment procedures which may be too competence based and would thus undermine the professionalism of the members of staff. This issue is taken further by Whitty and Willmott (1992). These readings appear to point to the need for care in using appraisal as a means of staff control rather than of professional development – a worry which members of staff were to articulate later. These readings were important in assessing the philosophy and practice of staff development in a school which had tried to recognize individual staff needs.

The introduction of an appraisal system was also an example of the management of change within the school. The staff at Swan Hill were becoming adjusted to a major shift in policy-making as the head moved away from a bureaucratic approach to one where there was an expectation of a great deal of staff involvement. In the words of one of the heads of department, 'I suppose we could cope with any change of procedure or policy now that we have become aware that the head really did want us to change from the old ways of doing things – and actually meant that we were involved.' This attitudinal change had reflected the Lewin (1943) view of the unfreezing of the organization, and the staff were aware that there was an increased emphasis on the generation of change from themselves upwards.

This led to consideration of change models and some staff wanted to know more of change processes. Fullan (1992) based much of his analysis of change on a three-phase model of introduction, implementation and institutionalization and the staff of Swan Mill had been used to working in this way with most policy development beginning with a pilot scheme which then becomes refined and developed as policy. Whilst this is essentially descriptive, Fullan does discuss the enabling and inhibiting factors in change and the detail and practicality of this discussion was fundamental to the analytical work. The staff had been used to a pattern of change which had been imposed on a 'centre–periphery' (Schon, 1971) or 'research, development and diffusion' cascade model (Havelock, 1972) typical of training for GCSE and National Curriculum introduction. They felt unsure of an approach which appeared to fit the Havelock problem-solving model and yet were aware that they had used this in their previous work on cross-curricular curriculum development. The management of multiple initiatives within education was a great concern to all involved and the work of Wallace (1991) was fundamental in helping staff to recognize the need for a cyclic review of work under way. This was also important to the professional development co-ordinator for the school who sought throughout to reconcile competing demands on staff time and energy through the school development process.

METHODS

The investigation was an example of an observed development within the school – a case study in the management of change in staff development. It was not action research as I was not a participant in the process of change, except in so far as my involvement may have prompted reflection by the staff who were involved rather than their unthinking acceptance of changed procedures.

The aims required the maintenance of a diary of observation throughout the development period. To this end I attended Swan Mill on those occasions when there was to be consideration of appraisal within the formal staff meeting, and working group sessions. This provided the framework for analysis of events according to the development stages outlined in Fullan's three-stage model.

It was also essential to maintain a file of the documentary material used and developed during the process. This showed, for example, the parameters set by national and county guidelines, the degree of centralized decision-making despite the alleged collegiality of the planning process, and the language and style of communication between the initiators and the staff as a whole. Much of the material was used as the basis for later interviews with staff and provided a means of triangulation between the reality and rhetoric of intended and actual practice. All the individual and departmental responses to the annual professional development planning audit were also available. The extent to which stated development targets had been achieved was of importance in the initial appraisal interviews.

Throughout the period of development I interviewed the professional development co-ordinator as the scheme was proposed, agreed and implemented. A representative sample of staff was also interviewed including four appraisers who had themselves been appraised, four of the people they had appraised and four who had not been part of the first cohort of appraisal but who had perceptions of the process.

I discussed the possibility of using a questionnaire with all staff but the sensitivity of relationships in the appraisal process was such that the head and deputies felt that this might engender 'unproductive staff room discussion' and it was agreed instead that the interviews would be based on a structured format which dealt with the principles of appraisal, the introduction of the scheme, job description negotiation, classroom observation, interviews and target setting. In the event I gained more from the quality of discussion in interviews than would have been possible from a questionnaire – innuendo, body language, and facial expression provide prompts for further investigation which are not available in the detached completion of a questionnaire. Further, I was making a report at the end of the first year of the scheme when only half of the staff had been involved and quantitative evidence would have been of only limited value at that point.

ANALYSIS OF THE SCHEME

At the end of the work in Year 2, after investigation of professional development needs, I had concluded as follows.

> The system of professional development within the school is understood in terms of the annual audit, whole-school provision through teacher education days, and departmental provision through subject development either on teacher education days or through departmental meetings. There is some understanding of the ways in which the needs of individuals may be articulated and there is a readiness on the part of the senior staff to meet these needs within available resources. However, it seems that many of the staff feel that there is a need for a coherent system of professional development which reconciles individual and school needs. Appraisal was mentioned by several of the staff interviewed as a way forward and there appears to be a readiness to see such a system in action.

INTRODUCTION OF THE SCHEME

It was known that staff were willing to consider a change of system. The leadership of the school recognized that the change was to be introduced at a time when there was some national union resistance to an enforced change and so the initiation phase was regarded as being tactically and strategically important because failure at this stage might inhibit not only appraisal but future management initiatives. To this end the head and deputies spent several months considering alternative schemes of appraisal in the light of national and local authority requirements before establishing the principles which they considered to be fundamental to the system. In summary the head stated that appraisal was 'a developmental process with the individual member of staff at the heart of things as the driving force'. One head of department said 'The head went to great lengths to ensure that the system was appraisee led, building on the idea of the provision of a supportive focus for the individual but blending the needs of the individual and the school together.'

In an attempt to ensure that the staff did not feel excluded from the planning process, the head introduced the subject at an autumn staff meeting stressing that reaction from departmental meetings would be discussed by the management consultative committee before final details of the scheme were settled. He also recognized that there had been a county-wide agreement between the unions and the LEA on acceptable principles. He stressed that there was little value in discussion of legally agreed principles. However, the system had to be tailored to meet the needs of the individuals in the school. The principles of a top-down model based upon the known and supportive existing systems of line management, a maximum of four appraisals to be undertaken by any one member of staff, the allocation of time and resources for the process and the setting of the agenda by the appraisee were highlighted at this meeting and it was agreed that the proposals would form the basis of a training day in February.

At a later stage there was discussion between myself and the head on the professed collegiality of the approach which to three of those interviewed had been seen as 'being top down in a kindly way', 'imposed because a leopard cannot change its spots', and 'another example of collegiality in the things which don't matter and authoritarianism in the things that do!' The head maintained that collegiality was only possible 'if time is properly managed – we can't waste time on what we can't change'.

At the February meeting the head outlined the proposed scheme, modified in the light of individual and departmental comments invited earlier, thus emphasizing that there had been consultation. He then concentrated upon the practical aspects of the scheme – classroom observation, the appraisal interview and target setting. He attempted to reassure the staff that this was a means of reconciling school and professional development and would not be used for performance-related purposes. These issues were then dealt with in detail and with the use of video material and group discussions facilitated by a consultant from a college of higher education. This had the 'advantage that it showed us that a lot of other schools were already undergoing the process, and it enabled us to learn from other experiences' (teacher), but it 'shifted the attention from the school and the immediate environment to issues in general and somehow it met individual fears by vicarious experience' (head of department).

Concerns were, however, publicly aired and the strength of feeling about an imposed system, although courteously expressed, was something of a shock to the management team. They had proposed a tight scheme which they thought had considered all eventualities. It had, as its basis, a package of materials which outlined the timetable for the first appraisal, the recommended procedures, and copies of all job descriptions and proposed formative and summative documentation. 'It seemed as if it was all cut and dried but we know that it had been considered by MCC and the senior staff, and they always attempt to be as fair and staff centred as they can in these matters' (teacher).

Group and plenary sessions during the training day investigated issues arising from observation, interview procedures and target setting. The discussion showed concern at a new, and to some, intrusive, procedure, but staff were aware of the sincerity of emphasis on a non-threatening, faculty-based, consistent system backed by full guidance and documentation.

Staff raised the following concerns:

- the mechanism by which identified training needs would become part of the development plan;
- the ways in which the appraisee really had ownership;

- the way in which time could be made available without disruption to the teaching programme;
- the maintenance of sensitivity;
- relationship to the school's aims and objectives;
- the use of the appraisal documents in reference procedures.

All were answered in a firm manner suggesting that the head had considered the comments made to him in detail, had sought advice and settled policy with the deputies and governors, and ensured that there would be no wasted time in discussion of issues over which the school had no control.

Five of the eight interviewees commented that the staff did not own the scheme in the way in which it owned other issues such as curriculum development and cross-curricular implementation, but subsequent interviews suggest that there was appreciation for the way in which the scheme was introduced: 'as effectively as possible by people who knew what they were doing – it is the Swan Mill way' (teacher).

IMPLEMENTATION OF THE SCHEME

The scheme was scheduled to begin for the staff as a whole in the summer term but the head, deputies and some heads of faculty were scheduled both to be appraised and to start the appraisal of others in the final weeks of the spring term. This had the double advantage of building on the experience of senior management colleagues and developing a cascade model. This was dependent upon the senior staff maintaining a consistent approach and interview evidence suggests that this was achieved. Of the eight interviewees who had been appraised seven described the same process. Additional training was arranged at an MCC meeting to deal with the issues of classroom observation as this became a real concern for those with a full teaching programme, but 'we learned a great deal as we went along both from our own experience as appraisee and in discussion with the senior staff as the process went ahead' (head of faculty).

The full package of materials was distributed to staff individually by their appraiser at the time when arrangements were made for a pre-appraisal meeting. These materials had been developed by the various management groups over the past term – the Fullan requirements of involvement and time and resource allocations had been met by judicious use of staff training days and allocated time. Included within the package were sheets of information and help on the management of the appraisal process. These were of high quality 'to show the staff that we regard the process as being valued and worth investment' (deputy head). Five of the staff interviewed felt that this was not the most effective form of training, but the three others recognized that given the need for flexibility in the management of time, the professional approach which was being shown to appraisal, and the need for training to immediately precede involvement in a phased process, this was 'an efficient form of flexible learning' (head of faculty).

Self-appraisal was considered to be an important part of the process. The two-part form required details of post, qualifications, previous experience and professional development, and gave an opportunity for reflection on the job description, work satisfaction, work frustrations, the nature of senior staff support, outline targets and professional aspirations. Those who began the work at this stage 'had something of a sense of exposing private issues, a concern that I might be professionally vulnerable and a feeling that I had been there before in my regular self-assessment as part of the professional development review each year' (head of faculty).

However, the self-appraisal process has been welcomed as 'setting your own agenda and making sure that you are in control of what will happen' (teacher).

The pre-appraisal meeting, usually lasting about an hour, built on identified issues from the self-appraisal which was 'generally most frank and honest, with a tendency to under-rate' (head of dept) so that the two periods of classroom observation could be most helpful for the appraisee. Observation has varied greatly according to the relationships within departments, the personality of the staff involved, the age and ability of the groups being observed, and the pedagogic requirements of the subject. Comments included:

> I chose two of the most difficult groups on the basis that the appraiser might be able to give me some ideas on motivation and management.

> I wanted to share my thoughts about two groups either side of the ability divide – they posed some interesting questions for discussion.

> It was a matter of sharing the problems I had had with two groups in year 9 and it was really an extension of our departmental discussions for real.

> I used John, my appraiser, as a bridge in my work with the group – we have never had a fly-on-the-wall approach when we are looking at the way we do things.

Whilst the appraisees have been in control of the situation some appraisers have suggested observation where particular groups or approaches have been considered worth evaluation, but the 'right to reject my suggestions was clear from the start' (head of faculty as appraiser).

The observation lessons seem to have passed without comment by the students who are 'so used to sharing staff, having students in the room or simply moving from activity to activity that there was no sense in which I felt that they knew I was being assessed' (teacher).

There is evidence of a variety of approaches to observation based on the way in which the appraiser felt most relaxed. Staff report that some colleagues have observed without participation (fly-on-the-wall), others have been prepared to assist with part of the lesson (useful stooge), whilst others have been totally involved as co-teachers. Observers then complete a standard form recording objectives, activities, pupil motivation and learning, enjoyment, challenge and assessment.

The follow-up meetings have been much appreciated by all eight appraised staff. They appear to have taken up to three hours according to the subject and the nature of the lessons observed but 'it was worthwhile because we were able to discuss so many of the issues in class management which I hadn't thought about since leaving college' (teacher), and 'it extended so much of the strategic discussion which was needed if we were to manage the National Curriculum effectively' (head of faculty).

Practice has varied considerably between participants but there have usually been two further meetings, both of up to two hours' duration. One, for all participants, has been concerned with overall appraisal of responsibilities, performance, curriculum planning, classroom performance, outcomes, wider responsibilities, career, relationships and highlighted issues. Some participants have then moved directly to target setting as part of appraisal, others have had a period of time for reflection before doing so. However this has been managed there has been time for discussion, recording, reflection and agreement because 'having taken care over the classroom observation it would have been possible to have rushed the appraisal itself at the very time when colleagues need to express their views, build up their self-esteem, and develop a positive feel about the school and their future' (appraiser).

There appears to have been considerable care in target setting because

> it may be our only chance to make the points we need to make to secure the sort of support we need – it is one way of stressing our professional development priorities, and it will be our safeguard for the future when we might not be able to undertake what we really set out to do.
>
> *(teacher)*

The targets are initiative based requiring a statement of action by self, school and other agencies, strategies to achieve targets and the necessary liaison to secure these, support networks to be used, continuing professional development and a personal action plan.

> It is this which has the greatest impact because it is a challenge both to the individual and to the school. It actually gives the appraiser a continuing responsibility and it means that there is some come-back if the senior management haven't got the resources to allow the sort of training which is needed.
>
> *(head of department)*

The scheme has not been without its difficulties. Staff have attempted to put much of the process into out-of-school time so that they do not affect normal teaching programmes any more than is absolutely necessary. 'The end of term seems to have come upon us so quickly and if we are to keep to target the colleague to be appraised will have little choice of teaching groups to offer and this may not be fair' (head of department) reflects the logistical problem which occurs when colleagues have devolved responsibility for making their own arrangements.

Another issue which has to be resolved by each pair of participants is the timespan of the whole process. Where it has taken over six weeks, 'classroom observation and appraisal have become divorced and it is difficult to retain the enthusiasm I first felt', but where the process has taken a maximum of three weeks 'it has meant that feedback is real, that there is impetus to get the job done, and the observation is a lead in to appraisal' (head of department).

It will be a further year before all members of staff have been appraised once and before procedures are refined in the light of the first experience. However, interview evidence from the four preparing for appraisal suggests that the principles of ownership by the appraisee, involvement by the appraiser and continuing responsibility by both appraiser and senior management are embedded in the culture of the system at the school.

The senior staff have reassured staff in the cascade of appraisal both by carefully structuring the system so that nobody is responsible for more than four appraisals, and by stressing that ownership is with the appraisee. They have listened to the comments emerging as the process develops and recognize that the scheme must continue to be given a high priority as fundamental to staff development, and that there must be further training to meet the needs of staff in coping with the system. Comments included

> I know that I could have been more effective if I had better counselling skills – I listened but felt that I could have done so much more to help if I could have found the right words.
>
> (head of faculty)

> now that we are aware of the imperfections of our way of doing things I would like more training in the actual interview – judging just when to propose, how to bargain and with what, and making the best use of time.   (head of faculty)

Staff express the view that the scheme must also be seen to be the way in which professional development needs are articulated and prioritized 'because this is a two-way process and we believe that we are involved to improve our ability to improve the experience of the youngsters' (teacher).

The other concern is that the feedback mechanisms should allow the staff to influence policy because of the way in which policies within the school may help, or hinder, the work of the individual teacher. There is a belief that the appraisal documents, seen only by the head, could be a means of conveying personal and individual concerns in a more direct way: 'We can influence discussion through the normal pattern of meetings but in many ways appraisal gives us a direct line to the head. He has to respect our confidentiality but he needs to know what we feel – it is a useful way of keeping him in the picture' (teacher).

Above all, staff are seeking the support and resources to ensure that there is feedback from senior management through the line-managment system once targets have been agreed, and that there should be continuing support for the open discussion, the ownership of personal professional development, and awareness of the impact of whole-school policies which the scheme has engendered. The first school development plan prepared since appraisal has attempted to meet individual needs both from target setting and from the collected needs of the department but the professional development co-ordinator has priced this at some £23,000 in a year when, with the deliberate diversion of resources to support effective appraisal, only £9,000 is available.

CONCLUSIONS AND RECOMMENDATIONS

1. The process so far has been effectively managed and accords with the change processes outlined by Fullan (1991). Time and financial resources have been made available for the development of materials of high quality which have been used to achieve a consistent approach.

    It is suggested that those staff undertaking and awaiting appraisal should be given more training in the process – distance learning materials may be convenient but staff feel the need to discuss issues and to be reassured of their competence level.

2. Staff expectations of appraisal are high. There is a belief that the setting of targets implies an undertaking on behalf of the school and that the system will give them the professional development which the informal staff development interviews had been unable to meet.

    It is suggested that the context within which staff professional development is being managed should be explained again to staff and that appraisers should achieve a prioritization of targets so that these may be taken into account in the annual school development planning procedure.

3. The management consultative committee and the head and deputies have been praised by participants for the way in which the change was introduced in response to expressed staff needs and with a minimum of disruption to the teaching programme or to departmental developments.

    The greatest criticism has been of the way in which, although ownership was nominally with the staff, much of the documentation and procedure has a 'cut-and-dried' look. This might have been avoided if the documentation had been made available for comment by a wider group of staff than the management consultative committee in the preparation period.

4. There appears to be some need for more training in counselling skills which would be of benefit not only in appraisal but in many areas of staff development and in achieving greater effectiveness in relationships with students.

    In planning staff training days for the coming year some provision for this work would be beneficial to whole-school development and it is suggested that this be given priority, either through professional development funding, or through targeted work under the personal and social education training programme.

POSTSCRIPT

In the period since the completion of the consultancy all but seven of the staff have been through the appraisal process. The original documentation has been revised by a working party drawn from postholders and standard scale staff. Training days have been organized on the management of change and on 'learning to listen'.

REFERENCES

Bell, L. and Day, C. (1991) *Managing the professional development of teachers*. Milton Keynes: Open University Press.

Fullan, M. (1991) *The meaning of educational change*. London: Cassell.

Fullan, M. (1992) *The new meaning of educational change*. Toronto: Cassell.

Fullan, M. G. and Hargreaves, A. (1991) *Working together for your school*. Toronto: Ontario Teachers Federation.

Hargreaves, D. H. and Hopkins, D. (1991) *The empowered school*. London: Cassell.

Havelock, R. (1972) The utilisation of educational research and development, *British Journal of Educational Technology*, Vol. 2, no. 2.

Lewin, K. (1943) Action research and minority problems, *Journal of Social Issues*, Vol. 2, pp. 34–46.

McMahon, A., Bolam, R., Abbott, R. and Holly, P. (1984) *Guidelines for the review and internal development of schools*. York: Longman.

Mortimore, P. and Mortimore, J. (1991) Teacher appraisal; back to the future, *School Organisation*, Vol. 11, no. 2, pp. 125–43.

Poster, C. and Poster, D. (1991) *Teacher appraisal, a guide to training*. London: Routledge.

Schon, D. (1971) *Beyond the stable state*. London: Temple Smith.

School Management Task Force (1990) *Developing school management: the way forward*. London: HMSO.

Trethowan, D. (1987) *Appraisal and target setting: a handbook for teacher development*. London: Paul Chapman.

Wallace, M. (1991) Flexible planning: a key to the management of multiple innovations, *Educational Management and Administration*, Vol. 19, no. 3, pp. 180–92.

Whitty, G. and Willmott, E. (1992) Competence-based teacher education, *Cambridge Journal of Education*, Vol. 21, no. 3.

CHAPTER 14

The Role of the Assistant Headteacher

RUTH WARREN

ABSTRACT

This research investigates the role of an assistant headteacher (AHT) in Northside Academy. The investigation was conducted through the use of a diary and interviews, with analysis drawing on ambiguities of role described in the literature and on the AHT's job remit. The report concludes that the role is low profile and therefore often misunderstood, and recommends a reduction of the secretarial aspects of the work, an increase in the amount of contact with departments through the development of the faculty role, and the introduction of systematic training.

INTRODUCTION

Northside Academy, the school in which the research was carried out and where I was a subject principal teacher, is a large Scottish secondary school with over 1,400 pupils and around 100 teachers. There is a line-management structure with a rector, depute rector, and four assistant rectors.

These posts make up the senior management team (SMT). Each AHT is responsible for a number of subject departments of varying sizes, described as a faculty (see Figure 14.1).

The subject of my study, Mr Stewart, has responsibility for the curriculum and, along with the other AHTs, had just begun to work to a new remit (job description). Within the project there was, therefore, the opportunity to examine how clearly the new remit described the reality of his work.

My main reason for choosing to look at the role of the AHT in a secondary school was that many members of staff seemed willing to advance their opinions about this role. However, the statements made often conflicted with the remits of AHTs in the school. From these perceptions I hypothesized that there was ambiguity about the role of an AHT and that this was creating tensions.

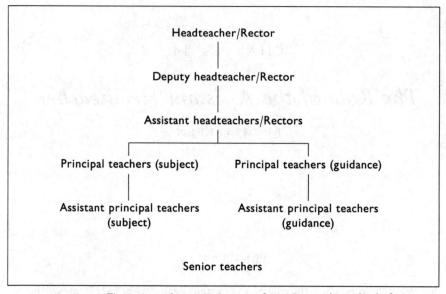

FIGURE 14.1 The pattern of promoted posts in Scottish secondary schools. Some education authorities use the term rector instead of headteacher. The number of promoted posts in a school is determined by the number of pupils. Headteachers/ rectors have discretion over the distribution of promoted posts within their schools. Senior teachers are given remits by the headteacher/rector. They generally have responsibility for an aspect of whole-school policy.

My research sets out to examine how far the ambiguities and tensions arise as a result of the perceptions of the role-holder and those with whom he works. It also examines how Mr Stewart resolves these ambiguities and conflicts, and goes on to consider further alternative strategies for the resolution of these within the role being studied, and in AHT roles in general.

REVIEW OF THE LITERATURE

In defining the role of any member of staff, a statement of expectations, in the form of a written remit, may or may not be available. In the school where my research took place, AHT remits existed despite the lack of any regional guidance on the role of AHTs. The use of written remits is cited as good practice by Her Majesty's Inspectorate (HMI) in its report *Effective secondary schools* (SED, 1988). Despite this clear approval of the formalization of roles, research has found that 'only 25 per cent of secondary headteachers were currently using job descriptions for deputes and AHTs' (Alexander *et al.*, 1992, p. 4). It is particularly relevant that Nias found that 'the evidence also suggests that clear statements of role expectations for oneself and others may increase trust in situations where ambiguity is fostering differences over fundamental aims, or obstructing the ethical conduct or means' (Nias, 1984, p. 119). This emphasizes the usefulness of written remits in practice, although the term 'clear statements' is more than a mere 'job description'. However, as Maw (1977) and Riches (1988) point out, exact role specification can be experienced by the role incumbent as constraint, and may reduce flexibility, or demotivate, so the need for clarity must be carefully balanced against this.

Much of the existing literature on roles stresses the importance of the 'role set' (those who interact with the role-holder). Different members of a role set have different levels of influence, depending on their personal and professional standing in relation to the role incumbent (Coulson, 1972; Bush, 1983; Maw, 1977; Riches, 1988; Walker, 1989). The influences of headteachers are considered to be the most important in the shaping of staff's role definitions. This is stated by Maw who says 'the head can be, and usually is, extremely powerful, because his expectations, whether formally laid down or not, affect the expectations that others are likely to have' (Maw, 1977, p. 95). Gross *et al.* (1966) point out the need to investigate not just the expectations of the role set, but also the relative importance that the role-holder attaches to them, in order to analyse the role rather than merely describing it.

Coulson goes on to make an important point, saying, 'the power and authority of role set members varies considerably, as does the extent to which they are able to observe how the role player actually performs his part' (Coulson, 1972). This latter point plays a part in understanding how perceptions affect role set members' views of the role examined. If a member of the role set does not often see or experience the work of the role-holder, they will find it hard to know what that person does, far less how well it is done. This is role ambiguity, which can be described as a lack of 'clear, consistent information regarding rights, duties and responsibilities of a person's occupation and how they can best be performed'. In addition, 'ambiguity may be in the mind of the role performer and/or the role set' (Kahn *et al.*, 1964). These writers suggest that the reduction of ambiguity requires that the role is made more familiar to the role set, and is another point in favour of a written remit. The importance of clarity of role to reduce ambiguity and tensions is stressed by Riches who says 'when a person's role is not clear, members of his/her role set may become insecure, lacking in confidence, irritated and even angry' (Riches, 1988, p. 77).

Much of the work of AHTs in Scottish schools is drudgery, and of a routine and mundane nature (Maw, 1977; SED, 1984, paragraph 5.3.3). The SED goes on to recommend the use of computer programs to reduce this, and later still goes on to say 'the main objective in the administrative areas of management should be to reduce the present emphasis on the many routine tasks that underpin the management of plant and provision in order that senior staff may give time and thought to the management of personnel' (SED, 1984, paragraph 6.3).

Lawley suggests that a way of minimizing routine work is to assess the administrative support required for the year and to have it available from clerical staff based close to the senior management (Lawley, 1988, p. 135). Riches, too, recommends spreading the workload and increasing efficiency by transferring routine administrative duties to secretarial staff. He goes further, saying that some activities, whilst laudable, might require a conscious decision not to carry them out because of lack of available time (Riches, 1988, p. 78). A problem with this is identified in the research reported in *Developing school managers, interchange no. 4* (Alexander *et al*., 1992) which found that teachers had difficulty in differentiating between management and administrative tasks, and also found that they tended to spend most time on routine administration. Obviously teachers would need to be clearer about which tasks were routine, and so could be delegated. The same report points out that the apparent lack of knowledge of management theory and practice amongst promoted staff makes them uncertain of their management roles. This points to ambiguity in the minds of the role incumbents, which fosters ambiguity in the minds of their role sets.

The research goes on to point out that some promoted staff have had formal management training, and that 'the extended promotion structure in secondary schools provides a form of management training on-the-job' (p. 5). They believed that the introduction of appraisal and school development plans would lead to the provision of detailed job descriptions and 'planned and targeted management training' (p. 8). Recommendations for change are clearly given: the need for clear time for management tasks, 'individualized job descriptions' coupled with 'target setting', and recognition of the importance of training to develop management skills development through school and authority policies and practices (p. 8).

The literature suggests that senior managers are generally expected to undertake too much in too little time (SED, 1984). Riches describes this as 'role overload' (Riches, 1988, p. 78), which he says happens all too frequently, where a person is given so many roles to fulfil that they are overburdened, and cannot necessarily cope with them all even by working extra time. If time and personnel are so short for the fulfilment of these roles then perhaps there is no place for retaining a teaching commitment, when such issues are examined in the cold light of day.

The specific aims of the project were:

- to identify and examine school and regional guidance on the AHT role;
- to record the actual work carried out during a week by one AHT;
- to find out how the role of AHT is perceived by the role-holder;
- to find out how the role of AHT is perceived by the role set;
- to identify the ambiguities and tensions experienced by an AHT;
- to examine how far these ambiguities and tensions arise from varied perceptions;
- to analyse how the AHT reconciles these ambiguities and tensions in the practical fulfilment of the role;
- to consider how the ambiguities and tensions identified might be further, or differently, reconciled through recommendations for change.

As the remits of AHTs are so varied, this research has been restricted to areas covered by the general and specific remits for the AHT who is the subject of this study (see Figure 14.2). Thus, certain areas, such as guidance, liaison with external agencies and leisure, which are included in the remits of some AHTs, are not considered in this particular study.

Mr Stewart's general duties

- Member of senior management team
- Member of principal teachers' forum
- Member of school development programme steering committee
- Assist with storm evacuation procedures and fire drills
- Promotion of good discipline and morale in the academy
- Communications with parents
- Interviews with parents
- Pupil discipline
- Dining-room supervision
- Corridor and stair supervision
- General movement of pupils in academy
- Attendance at parents' evenings
- Representing school on committees and at meetings
- Additional duties delegated by rector

Mr Stewart's specific duties

Mr Stewart will report to and will be directly responsible to the rector for the satisfactory administration and management of the following:

- The timetable
- Technical and Vocational Education Initiative (TVEI)/Further Education (FE)
- Scottish Examination Board (SEB) administration and management
- Health education courses S1–S6
- Education–industry links
- Arrangements for parents' evenings
- AHT Red House and Blue House – administration and discipline
- Faculty head (control of proper provision of courses, evaluation of course and resources, quality control of work and results, staff development needs)
- Corridor control and pupil movement including supervision at intervals and lunchtime

FIGURE 14.2   Mr Stewart's general and specific duties.

Similarly, certain interesting avenues, such as the influences of experience and training or comparing AHT roles in different schools, also had to be ignored, although these may offer scope for others looking for a different perspective from which to examine the role of the AHT.

RESEARCH METHODS

The two main research instruments were a diary kept by Mr Stewart and the use of interviews. The diary was selected as the most accurate method of gathering factual data on how the subject actually spends his time. The interview with Mr Stewart himself was a necessary follow-up to expand on his routine, both in terms of the individual week studied, and to put it into the context of the full year's work. Interviews with the role set were to gather their perceptions of Mr Stewart's role. Whilst questionnaires might have yielded some of this information, the interview technique allowed more open-ended responses, and probing where necessary. It is also the case that in the spring term, when the research took place, a great deal of paperwork is required, and it seemed more likely that oral answers would facilitate participation. Work shadowing would have been an alternative method to the diary, but was not a practical proposition if it was to be fully and effectively used. The issue was raised, but as no supply cover was available, work shadowing would have been limited to my non-contact periods. These six disjointed sessions over the week would have provided a much patchier picture of Mr Stewart's role than a complete diary of all work undertaken. Full-time work shadowing might have provided more detailed information *and* allowed the researcher to record it in an easily accessible manner.

Originally I had hoped to ask Mr Stewart to keep a diary (see Figure 14.3) for a fortnight, but time was a major constraint, and so a single week was the compromise. As he was attending an in-service course all day on the Wednesday of the week being studied we agreed to record the Monday of the following week instead. In order to facilitate the collection of data, and assist him in identifying planned and actual work, a simple diary sheet was devised on which he could record each day's events.

The published remit was broken down into a list of headings for interview questions and for the categorization of the activities undertaken by Mr Stewart during the week. His activities were tabulated and then recorded in the form of a pie chart to clarify the proportions of time which were actually spent on each activity.

The subject for interview were Mr Stewart, the other members of the SMT and four principal teachers from the faculty for which he was responsible. The interviews were carried out over a three-week period at times convenient to the interviewees. Most of them were conducted in a location that minimized disturbances. Recordings were made of the early interviews in case of the need to refer back, but copious notes were taken simultaneously, and it soon became clear that this was an unnecessary measure. The machine used for the recording was a personal dictating machine which was unobtrusive, and apparently uninhibiting, although the subjects recorded were close colleagues holding the same level of post as myself. The transcription of the tapes was never intended, as taping was a back-up process.

The interview schedule was used fairly rigidly to prevent the research from wandering too far from its original aims. Questions were devised using the aims to build up a series of items of relevance, and were open ended enough to allow subjects to express their opinions. The questions brought out answers in the fields in which the investigation was planned, but some of the 'why' questions caused confusion, whereas allowing freedom to answer the main question at length proved more fruitful. In the later stages of interviewing these 'why' parts were omitted.

Originally it had been intended that there would be a separate interview scheduled for Mr Stewart, but instead it seemed more relevant to use the same schedule with modifications to certain questions. This basically involved changing them from the third person to the second person, but some questions had to be

DATE:

	Planned	Actual
Before school		
Period 1		
Period 2		
Period 3		
Period 4		
Break		
Period 5		
Period 6		
Period 7		
Period 8		
After school		
At home		

FIGURE 14.3 Mr Stewart's diary.

omitted or required modification. This common interview schedule ensured the same ground was covered with all interviewees, and facilitated comparison for analysis of the date. The interviews took from 40 to 90 minutes and all except one were conducted in a single session.

The interviews generated an unexpectedly large amount of data which was tabulated under the various responses given. In the interests of meaningful analysis, it was necessary to ignore minority responses and so to concentrate on those put forward by several respondents.

RESULTS

These were grouped around the aims of the project.

The identification and examination of school and regional guidance on the AHT role

At the time my project was carried out, there were no regional guidelines for AHT posts. In Northside Academy, however, all the AHTs have written remits which have been circulated to departments.

To record the actual work carried out during a week by one AHT

Mr Stewart wrote his diary in terms of the time spent under each of the headings of his remit. In practice the TVEI element of the remit is just beginning, and so does not yet feature fully in his routine, so the time spent was 0 per cent for the week. Every other item appeared at some stage during the week. The SEB duties have been taken on by another member of staff, and supplanted by Scottish Vacational Education Council (SCOTVEC) duties. Some of those interviewed pointed this out, others were clearly unaware of this change, and some even confused the two bodies, assuming that SCOTVEC matters came under the heading of SEB duties. For this reason, SCOTVEC and SEB duties were paired when compiling the results. As the closely related house and faculty duties amounted to less than 1 per cent each, these, too, were combined. Minor duties such as preparation, taking classes for absent staff, form filling, arranging meetings and opening mail, do not appear in the remit, but are included in the results under the single heading of 'minor duties' to show how far clerical and other non-management duties impinge on the role-holder's time, totalling some 15 per cent of his working week.

The breakdown of the week into planned and actual work shows how far Mr Stewart has to be reactive, rather than proactive, as other set him unplanned tasks which require immediate action and the shelving of his own plans. These items were marked with an asterisk in the diary to identify them clearly. On all but one day there were two or more interruptions which had to be dealt with immediately, and led to other matters being moved to a later time in the day, or being omitted entirely. The total time which these matters occupied was over four and a quarter hours, representing almost 14 per cent of the entire working week.

To find out how the role is perceived by the role-holder

This information was gathered mainly through interview. Mr Stewart's perception of the time he should be spending on each of the items in his remit tied in almost exactly with the actual proportions recorded in his diary. The exceptions to this were the time spent in meetings, which was increased by the out-of-school meeting on the third day. The amount spent on timetabling was less than he projected, as the diary was recorded at a time when timetabling work was not at a peak. The amount of time spent on SEB/SCOTVEC work was also lower than the percentage he anticipated. Again this could be accounted for by the fact that it was not a busy period for such work. The skills oulined by Mr Stewart as necessary for his role included administrative skills such as organization of time, paperwork and workload through prioritization, and the ability to construct a timetable (which was specific to his remit) and to deal with paperwork associated with his role in co-ordinating SCOTVEC and SEB administration, which he said was greatest at the end of session. He also considered essential the ability to switch rapidly between tasks of differing natures, such as moving from the registration of pupil details for examinations to disciplining a pupil sent out of class. Amongst the managerial skills he identified were communicating well with others and making considered judgements on the evidence gathered through this communication. Other very general items such as 'making and implementing policy', which includes a whole plethora of information-gathering, management discussion, writing, consultation, monitoring and evaluation skills, were also identified. Some of the items were clearly personal rather than professional, for example 'being honest' and 'being able to take stick'. The overall impression I gained was that he did not appreciate or value the multitude of skills he was required to exhibit in the course of every working day.

The role he identified himself as fulfilling corresponded clearly to the paper remit. He mentioned 'being part of the SMT', 'faculty head', 'head of house duties' and 'heavy timetable and SEB loads in the summer'. He stressed that no items can be left out or considered a lower priority than others as they all have to be done. He said that the balance between them changes both seasonally, as in timetabling duties, and day to day, as in disciplinary and other immediate matters. He emphasized the fact that the role cannot be fulfilled in the contracted time and he identified tensions because of this.

Tension also occurred because of disciplinary conflicts between pupils and staff. When staff and/or pupils did not like decisions they vented their frustrations on him, causing stress. He found that the best way of coping was to go with the flow, as he felt little else could be done within a school. His personal priority was to do what was best for pupils first, and then what was best for staff, seeing his role as one of facilitator.

Interestingly, Mr Stewart did not consider his role ambiguous. He could see that others might think it was, because of their own expectations of an AHT. The small salary differential between AHTs and the middle-managers below them and the lack of clarity of the role meant that it was perceived as low-profile drudgery.

To find out how the role of AHT is perceived by the role set

This information was gathered entirely from interviews with Mr Stewart's main role set. Most mentioned the need for an AHT to communicate well and to be well organized. Duties specific to Mr Stewart which were emphasized included linking the SMT and departments through principal teachers, timetabling and disciplinary support. Views expressed mainly by senior management team members included having a whole-school view, being able to make considered judgements, and advising on the curriculum. Respondents were inclined to express these ideas in very general terms, and to highlight personal qualities, such as 'being highly principled', as well as professional qualities.

Other roles identified outside the remit for the AHT included attendance at pupils' social functions, linking the school with the local college, taking classes for absent colleagues and supporting and counselling colleagues.

Priorities were perceived very differently by most of the individuals interviewed. Most identified the timetable as a major priority, but after that other duties were each mentioned by only one or two individuals. The exception to this was that several respondents felt that discipline was low priority for Mr Stewart.

To identify the ambiguities and tensions experienced by an AHT

Mr Stewart's remit was not generally considered conflicting within itself, but some problems were identified – getting to classes, clashes between AHT and teacher roles, and the remit being too large. Most respondents felt that the role of the AHT was ambiguous, caused by others' expectations that he will work for them to solve their problems, and the fact that much of the role is hidden, so staff tend not to be sympathetic or to regard AHTs as fully a part of the senior management team.

There was strong consensus that the two obstacles most likely to be encountered by AHTs are lack of time and lack of flexibility on the part of other members of the SMT. Other factors mentioned by several respondents included not having all the information to make decisions, departments making increasing demands, and disturbances to planned work schedules. It was perceived these obstacles might cause problems including: seeming unsympathetic or unconcerned about departments; differences over timetabling leading to resistance to change so causing inflexibility; matters often being beyond the control of the AHT as he represents the rector and/or the SMT to departments; and lack of respect for senior management.

To examine how far these ambiguities and tensions arise from varied perceptions

The variety of responses was at times quite startling. In some areas there was clear division between the perceptions of members of the SMT and those of the principal teachers of departments.

For example, everyone interviewed considered communication between SMT and departments was essential but those on the receiving end considered the communication from Mr Stewart was lacking in both quality and quantity, and found the opportunities to discuss departmental or individual problems were very limited. He prioritized completing his administrative tasks rather than entering into complex interpersonal relationships. This was frequently interpreted by those seeking his help as unwillingness to become involved.

To analyse how the AHT reconciles these ambiguities and tensions in the practical fulfilment of his role

Most respondents felt that reconciling ambiguities and tensions was not always possible. At times, reconciliation was achieved by conceding to the power of the rector and depute to make decisions, or going with the general trend dictated by the majority of the SMT. Both of these allowed Mr Stewart to explain that decisions were not always ones with which he agreed, but that others, like himself, were bound by the final decisions made. At other times prioritization would determine his actions which he would justify in terms of having the whole picture which others might not have. This would not necessarily lessen the tension as others might still disagree with his decision. He felt that informing staff throughout the school about his actual role as AHT was the most effective way of dissolving tension. As I originally thought, there was widespread ignorance of the demands on him. Informing others helped to combat this.

To consider how the ambiguities and tensions identified might be further, or differently, reconciled through recommendations for change

Respondents' recommendations for resolving ambiguity and tension for AHTs included: being prepared to criticize others' ideas; raising awareness of the role of AHTs; enlisting the support of staff and the headteacher in allowing the AHT to carry out his remit; changing the contract or hours for AHTs; and developing a meaningful faculty role making training and role models available to AHTs.

DISCUSSION

In searching for a definition of the role of any member of staff, the tendency is to begin with the paper definition, the remit. The terms of the remit for this post are not necessarily explicit enough for all staff to understand. Certain aspects of the AHT remit might be clarified by including a degree of quantification in the job description – for example, the teaching quota and the input expected into disciplinary processes. During the interviews it became clear that certain aspects of the job description were being diffently interpreted by senior management and other members of staff.

Despite this, the relative amount of time respondents expected to be spent on the various areas of the remit shows a remarkable consensus of views, except in the area of discipline. The SMT considered that this was not a major area of responsibility for AHTs, but most of the heads of departments felt the AHT should be offering more support than they had experienced. This is clearly an ambiguous area, and the tightening up of definition of the role, as recommended in the literature, could help to reduce such misunderstandings. The caveat here is to ensure that in so doing the AHT does not become demotivated and prevented from developing his perception of his role. The fact that AHTs have a half-time teaching commitment was not familiar to the non-SMT members interviewed. This, and the sheer quantity of unplanned and minor duties, is the type of knowledge which might go a long way towards helping staff to empathize with AHTs.

The fact that Mr Stewart's perception so closely matched his diary record suggests that he is well aware of how he spends his time. That all aspects of the remit were covered during the five days shows the matters listed in the remit do, in this case, reflect what he does. As this is a relatively new remit, and he was well aware of my research at that time, it might well be claimed that he was unusually conscious of his role throughout that time. It would be interesting to cover similar ground again in a year or so, and perhaps to use a different technique at that time, such as work shadowing, to find how closely the work then reflects the remit.

The lack of time reared its head again and again. As time is so short, it was even suggested that an AHT could choose to use a remit as an excuse to be inefficient, as it could not possibly be fulfilled, so there was no obligation to complete any other than the most major tasks. There appears to be a lack of widespread under-standing of the time that an AHT already has committed before a week begins, with teaching, meetings and supervision duties accounting for well over half the AHT's week inclusive of time spent at home.

The major tension identified was being caught between the SMT and other staff, and some of the respondents who highlighted this pointed to the greater influence which the SMT is almost bound to have because of 'pecking order'. The literature goes further to say that the greatest influence is the headteacher, and this is clearly the case in any school, where the headteacher has the delegated authority to make the final decisions for the region. This being the case, the observation of respondents that Mr Stewart 'goes with the flow' is an astute recognition of the need for AHTs to allow everyday matters to flow, and to save their energies for major issues where contention is appropriate and constructive. Clearly an AHT who was in constant conflict with the interest of the SMT would suffer unthinkable stress and tension. There are, however, times when an AHT does have to question the ideas being discussed at SMT level, and to put opposing arguments to ensure that decisions which are taken have a sound factual basis, and therefore can be reported back to staff as the best available solutions.

Training was discussed by some respondents and is clearly an important issue in the literature. Similarly, the existence of good, well-trained role models will depend on the implementation of training strategies throughout education. In the region in which I did this study finance is available for those doing independent courses in management, such as those offered by The Open University.

CONCLUSIONS AND RECOMMENDATIONS

Mr Stewart's role was seen to be low profile, and consequently ambiguous in the eyes of many staff who prefer to project their own views of what should be done rather than to find out about the reality of his role.

It is clear that the major, and simplest, issue to address is that of awareness raising. Staff 'at the chalk face' have apparently little knowledge of the nature and functioning of management in Northside Academy. The major recommendation for addressing this is that this report be made available to staff. Another possibility is to encourage staff to work-shadow the AHTs, possibly during the times when pupils are on study leave and more non-contact time is available. This could include attending SMT meetings to experience management in action. Finally, the remits of AHTs need to be clarified to explain what the different tasks entail and how the work is distributed over the year, whilst ensuring that this does not overly restrict the role-holders.

The issue of communication was raised as a cause of ambiguity. One solution is the suggestion of the development of the faculty role into a more extensive and meaningful forum for the exchange of ideas in both directions. This would raise the profile of the AHTs who would chair these meetings, and would help to cement the concept of their managerial role in the minds of the staff in their faculties. It could also have the effect of widening discussion on policy and other matters, clarifying the reasoning behind decisions and thus lessening the tension for AHTs in disseminating and upholding SMT decisions.

The delegation of AHT functions to principal teachers, or below, could be problematic, in that overload is common throughout the profession, and the extra load needs to be spread differently, not just farther down. Consequently, the suggestion from the literature that routine tasks be mapped out and delegated to clerical staff, makes much more sense, and would free AHTs to develop the faculty role more fully.

The introduction of systematic training for AHTs is recommended in the literature, and some clearly hope this will become the norm as major national changes are implemented. Positive encouragement by regions and schools to participate in management training is essential if such necessary change is to take place on the scale required to train managers and provide future role models. In the meantime, Northside Academy could ensure that any information about management training is given suitable prominence, and that all staff are positively encouraged to apply.

POSTSCRIPT

My thanks for their assistance are due to all those who gave up their time and shared their views with me in order to help complete this research.

NOTE

The Scottish Education Department (SED) became the Scottish Office Education Department (SOED) in 1991.

REFERENCES

Alexander, E., Havard, J., Leishman, R. and Wight, J. (1992) *Developing school managers, Interchange no. 4.* Edinburgh: Scottish Council for Research in Education.

Bush, T. (1983) The role of vice-principal in further and higher education, *Journal of Further and Higher Education,* Vol. 7, no. 3, pp. 14–23.

Coulson, M. A. (1972) Role: a redundant concept in sociology? Some educational considerations, in J. A. Jackson (Ed.) *Role.* Cambridge University Press.

Gross, N., Mason, W. S. and McEachern, A. W. (1966) *Explorations in role analysis, studies of the school superintendency role.* New York: John Wiley.

Kahn, R. L., Wolfe, D., Snoek, R. and Rosenthal, J. (1964) *Organizational stress: studies in role conflict and role ambiguity.* New York: John Wiley.

Lawley, P. (1988) *Deputy headship.* Harlow: Longman.

Maw, J. (1977) Defining roles and senior and middle management in secondary schools, in A. Jennings, (Ed.) *Management and headship in the secondary school.* London: Ward Lock.

Nias, J. (1984) The negotiation of decision making roles in a new school, in S. Goulding, J. Bell, T. Bush, A. Fox and J. Goodey (Eds) *Case studies in educational management.* London: Harper & Row.

Riches, C. (1988) Management roles and responsibilities: the secondary school, in E325 *Managing schools. Block 2. Leadership and decision making in schools: roles and responsibilities.* Milton Keynes: Open University.

SED (Scottish Education Department) (1984) *Learning and teaching in Scottish secondary schools: school management.* Edinburgh: HMSO.

SED (Scottish Education Department) (1988) *Effective secondary schools.* Edinburgh: HMSO.

Walker, W. G. (1989) Leadership in an age of ambiguity and risk, *Journal of Educational Administration,* Vol. 27, no. 1, pp. 7–18.

PART FOUR

Managing External Relations

CHAPTER 15

Finding Out What Parents Think of Your School

PHILIP WOODS

ABSTRACT

The intention of this chapter is to stimulate interest in creating schools which are responsive to those who use (and work) in them. It offers ideas on working towards this aim which you may wish to consider in the context of your own school. The chapter draws extensively on the experience of a project which piloted in schools a process of 'school evaluation'. This evaluation process involved seeking parents' views of the school and taking action in light of those responses. Some of the practical ways in which pilot schools undertook this process are highlighted.

INTRODUCTION

Increasing attention has been paid over the last two decades or so to developing closer relationships between home and school. A wide range of initiatives and schemes have been instituted with the intention of bringing home and school closer together (Bastiani, 1993; Bastiani and Bailey, 1992), many of them grounded in a recognition that educational progress is more likely to take place where parents are involved in and supportive of their child's learning in school and at home. The emphasis in most such initiatives is on encouraging parents to be supportive and to become better informed, for example through visiting the school and being given better information. Indeed, in some instances education professionals have been criticized for adopting a so-called 'conversion' approach to parental involvement, seeking to change parents' attitudes and bring them round to the professionals' viewpoint (Merttens, 1993).

Less apparent have been initiatives which offer *parents* the chance to *influence* the nature of their children's educational experience and *schools* the opportunity to *respond* to parental views and wishes. A major project on home–school partnerships, supported amongst others by the National Association of Headteachers (NAHT), concluded that 'there is a need to work to establish a parental agenda [concerning education]. This would incorporate genuinely parental perspectives and concerns, rather than being merely a response to agendas set by politicians and the professional education service, as is currently the case' (Jones *et al.*, 1992, p. 74). Part of the reasoning behind the reforms since 1988 is that a more market-like environment, with greater stress on parental choice and competition between schools, will make schools more *responsive* to their 'consumers'. Successful producers, the argument goes, find out what their customers want and what they think of their product, and do their best to improve their product accordingly. These reforms have also given parent-governors an enhanced role on school governing bodies and thereby sought to increase 'consumer representation' in school decision-making. However, there is little evidence that these changes have brought about a significant increase in the influence of parental views and interests on schooling (Woods, 1993).

If parents are to be listened and responded to more effectively than they are at present, sustained and imaginative practical initiatives are needed which aim specifically to facilitate this. One such initiative involved a team of researchers, supported by Her Majesty's Inspectorate (HMI) and the Scottish Office Education Department (SOED), who set out to develop questionnaires for use with parents, pupils and teachers. The intention was to develop a set of instruments that could be used by schools for evaluating their own effectiveness *as perceived and experienced by these three groups*. This project (hereafter referred to as the 'school evaluation project') is about *seeking* and *utilizing for action* judgements on school life by those who are most closely concerned with schooling. It seeks to demonstrate how any school can:

● obtain the views and comments of parents, pupils and teachers;
● make use of those data to improve the school's policies and practices in response to these views and comments.

One of the things which is particularly good about this project is that it is grounded in consultations with those it set out to involve, and that the process of evaluation has been tested practically in schools. Initial drafts of the question-naires were discussed with parents, pupils and teachers. Refined versions of the questionnaires – and the whole process of school evaluation – were then piloted in 23 schools which represented different sectors of the education system (secondary, primary, special and nursery) and which differed by geographical location, size, denomination, and socio-economic area. This school evaluation project may thus be seen as a research and development programme consisting of multiple case studies.

On the basis of this practical testing in a variety of schools, detailed guides to school evaluation for use in schools have been published (SOED/HMI, 1992). They have been produced in two volumes, one aimed at primary and nursery schools, *Using ethos indicators in primary school evaluation*, and the other aimed at secondary schools, *Using ethos indicators in secondary school evaluation*. The guidance is extensive and detailed, much of it common to both volumes, and a great deal of use is made of practical examples of how pilot schools undertook school evaluation. The guides illustrate how practice may vary according to the differing nature and circumstances of schools and their communities. Any programme of listening and responding to parents, pupils and teachers needs to be designed in light of the characteristics and needs of the particular institution and parent body concerned.

In this chapter, aspects of the school evaluation project are highlighted and discussed, including some of the practices that pilot schools found useful. The primary focus here is on *parents* and how their views of the school their child is attending may be obtained – though, as has been noted above, the full school evaluation guides cover pupils and teachers too. You are encouraged to consult the full published guides for more detailed information on the school evaluation project.

OBTAINING PARENTS' VIEWS

If evaluation is to be genuinely that of the parents, the school needs to give them the opportunity to comment on those aspects of schooling of greatest interest to them (rather than what professionals think parents are concerned about). Hence in the pilot phase of the school evaluation project researchers discussed with parents what they would like to ask of the school, and what might be included in a self-completion questionnaire. The kinds of questions they were interested in were: Is my child

- enjoying school?
- happy?
- safe?
- successful?
- well behaved and learning good behaviour?
- able to get on with other pupils?
- being treated fairly by teachers?
- being given the fullest opportunities to learn?
- being helped to make the best choices?

(SOED/HMI, 1992, pp. 2/3,4)

The parent questionnaire which resulted from the pilot work is reproduced in Figure 15.1a–c. The questionnaire asks parents to give their views on a range of statements. In two sets ('communication and information' and 'parents and the school') they can indicate 'yes' or 'no'. In the remaining sets parents are able to choose from graded responses which allows a greater level of sophistication in the answers given and subsequent analysis.

The questionnaire reproduced is the version aimed at parents of secondary school children. Almost all the questions on the primary school version are the

1) What stage in the school is your child/are your children at? Please tick.

S1 ☐ S2 ☐ S3 ☐ S4 ☐ S5 ☐ S6 ☐

2) What languages do you speak at home apart from English?

....

Please indicate your view with a tick. For instance, if you think that your child always enjoys school put a tick in the 'always' column. If you have more than one child please choose one of them and answer all the questions in respect of that individual child.

MY CHILD	always	most of the time	some of the time	never
enjoys being at school				
finds school work interesting				
gets an appropriate amount of homework				
The school facilities and accommodation are adequate				
gets to talk to teachers about his/her homework				
is treated fairly by teachers				
respects his/her teachers				
is respected by his/her teachers				

Please indicate below whether or not you agree, or don't know, for each of the statements

COMMUNICATION AND INFORMATION	YES	NO	DON'T KNOW
School reports give me an accurate and helpful picture of my child's progress			
I get regular information about my child's progress			
Teachers are good at letting you know about your child's strengths and weaknesses			
I am happy about the kinds of things my child is learning			
I know that if my child is having difficulty he/she will be helped			
He/she is encouraged to work to the best of his/her ability			

FIGURE 15.1 Parents' questionnaire.

SECTION TWO

Please indicate below whether or not you agree, or don't know, for each of the statements

PARENTS AND THE SCHOOL	YES	NO	DON'T KNOW
Most parents show support for the school			
The school has explained its homework policy to me			
The school has explained to me what part I can play in my child's education			
Parents' evenings apart the only time I would have contact with teachers would be to sort out a problem			
I am confident that if I complain about something I will get a sympathetic hearing			
The School Board seems to be a useful thing for the school			
The PTA is good at keeping me in touch with school matters			
I think that parents should be involved in classroom activity			

SECTION THREE

This part is about meetings where parents visit the school, usually in the evening, to talk with individual teachers about their children's progress.

FORMAL PARENT-TEACHER MEETINGS	always	usually	sometimes	never
Meetings are arranged at a time which suits me				
The event is well structured and organised				
I get a chance to see the teachers I want to see				
I feel welcome and know where to go				
I am treated like a partner in my child's education				
I get a chance to speak honestly about what concerns me				
Teachers are frank with me				
I come away feeling I have learned something useful				

SECTION FOUR

The following are some statements made by parents in other schools. From your experience of your school, would you agree or disagree with them? For each statement say whether you strongly agree, agree, or disagree, or strongly disagree by putting a tick in one of the columns.

WHAT PARENTS SAY	strongly agree	agree	disagree	strongly disagree
"There is a good range of extra-curricular activities in the school"				
"School buildings are kept clean and in good order"				
"If parents complain teachers just close ranks on us"				
"I really feel they know my child as an individual"				
"Homework should be spread more evenly across the week"				
"Teachers are approachable and sympathetic"				
"There are some school rules which I don't agree with"				
"There shosuld be no uniform"				
"I don't know how I can help my child with his/her school work"				
"I would like to be more involved in important decisions about my child's future"				
"I wish someone had explained to me why they do a lot of the things they do in schools nowadays"				
"You are never made to feel as if you are wasting teachers' time when you visit the school"				
"Teachers are too tolerant of bad behaviour"				
"The head teacher is approachable and helpful"				
"Letters from the school could be improved"				
"The school has a good reputation in the comunity"				

same. The differences are that the primary questionnaire asks about the welcome parents get when they go to the school, whilst instead of this the secondary questionnaire asks about extracurricular activities, parental involvement in 'important decisions about my child's future', and whether parents get the chance to see the teachers they want to see. There is nothing sacrosanct about these differences, however. It could be considered, for example, a good thing to ask secondary school parents about their welcome to the school and primary school parents about extracurricular activities.

The final page of the questionnaire (not reproduced here) states that there may be a number of things about the school which the parents would like to mention but which have not been covered by the questions and invites them to write in the space provided. Providing this opportunity for unprompted comment is an essential and valuable part of the questionnaire.

Pilot schools used various tactics by which to involve parents in the evaluation exercise and encourage them to complete the questionnaire. Some decided to obtain a sample of parents, others went for a whole year group or all parents with children at the school. In one of the pilot secondary schools it was decided not to approach all parents but to 'choose a stratified sample of one in ten parents. The criteria used were geographical area, age of children and number of children in the family. Because of the relatively small number of parents, and the opportunity for follow-up letter and personal contact, it was easier to get a high return, close to 100 per cent' (SOED/HMI, 1992 (secondary), pp. 3/10).

Working out how best to approach parents can be a difficult and challenging task. It benefits from an understanding of the community of parents served by the school and where appropriate – as in the example below – consultations with parents themselves:

> [A pilot primary] school in an area of multiple deprivation had to address the specific problems of inadequate reading skills of many of the parents, coupled with a general lack of tradition of parents corresponding with the school. Many pupils did not read fluently: the written word is not a preferred means of communication in the district. The headteacher was very supportive of the whole idea of school self-evaluation, but was concerned about any exercise which might threaten the finely balanced relationship which was being established by a policy of non-demanding welcome for parents . . . . Parents of P1 children who visited the school regularly to meet the Home-Link teacher were consulted about questions which were seen as important about wording, and about how they felt other parents would react. They expressed interest in seeing the questionnaires and all asked to complete one to see what was involved. The Home-Link teacher was consulted. Possible alternative methods were suggested, including chatting to parents off the school premises, e.g. at local community classes. This was felt to be possibly a more effective way than expecting a high form return rate. It was agreed in the end to offer the questionnaire only to the parents of P7 pupils.
>
> (SOED/HMI, 1992 (primary), pp. 3/7, 8)

There are many different approaches to encouraging a good response rate. In one primary school, the class getting the best return was given a prize! The highest rate of return in a secondary school was 85 per cent, and in a primary school 100 per cent. A technique used in one school was to ask parents, if they did not want to complete a questionnaire, to indicate their wish by signing a statement and returning the uncompleted questionnaire; the secondary school doing this, which is situated in a very deprived area, obtained a 64 per cent return of completed questionnaires.

In another secondary school, a number of parents each had a patch within which they distributed school information to other parents. Questionnaires were distributed using this system which is already in place. In another school, parents were asked to bring completed questionnaires to parents' evenings, where extra copies were also available for them to complete on the night.

MAKING USE OF THE DATA

The purpose of collecting parents' views is twofold: firstly, to gain insight into how parents experience the school and what they see as its strengths and weaknesses; and, secondly, to utilize these findings to *improve* it wherever feasible.

Without seeking to do the second, there is little point in achieving the first. But gaining that insight is the initial stage following completion and collection of the parent questionnaires. In the school evaluation project both 'low-tech' (processing by hand) and 'high-tech' (computer processing) approaches were taken by schools (SOED/HMI, 1992, pp. 5/2–3). Experience suggested that with the former, 'To process one questionnaire by hand, once a familiarity and speed have been developed, takes about 90 seconds. One hundred questionnaires therefore takes one person about two and a half hours to process.' For the 'high-tech' approach packages for mainframe and microcomputers are becoming increasingly sophisticated and easier to use.

The school evaluation guides observe that it is also helpful if data are not analysed in piecemeal and fragmentary fashion, but are set within a framework or matrix. They outline a set of 12 headings and their respective indicators which can be used to structure responses to the questionnaires and analyse them under larger headings. The framework put forward is not intended to be definitive. Schools can modify this set, or develop another one, cross-referring – the guides suggest – to performance indicators outlined in *Using ethos indicators in primary school self-evaluation* (SOED/HMI, 1992). The 12 suggested headings are:

- pupil morale;
- teacher morale;
- teachers' job satisfaction;
- the physical environment;
- the learning environment;
- teacher–pupil relationships;
- discipline;

- equality and justice;
- extracurricular activities;
- school leadership;
- information to parents;
- parent–teacher consultation.

(SOED/HMI, 1992, pp. 6/2)

Each of these 12 indicators is defined in the guides and questions identified that are associated with them. Two examples are set out in the box below.

Examples of indicators and associated questions

<u>The learning environment</u>

Indicator:	the degree to which the classroom is seen as a stimulating working context and classroom learning is seen as satisfying and productive
Relevant questionnaire items from parents *include*:	*I am happy about the kinds of things my child is learning*
	I feel they really know my child as an individual

<u>Parent–teacher consultation</u>

Indicator:	the degree to which parents and teachers have opportunities to share their expertise and feel that it has been of benefit to pupils, parents and teachers
Relevant questionnaire items from parents *include*:	*I would like to be more involved in important decisions about my child's future*
	The headteacher is approachable and sympathetic
	Teachers are approachable and sympathetic

(SOED/HMI, 1992, Appendix 1)

Indicators like these may sound somewhat mechanical and to an extent contrived as attempts to encapsulate the complexities of school life. But it is clear from the discussion in the guides that these are suggested indicators and not intended as the 'last word'. They stimulate thinking about the challenging task of relating data (in the form of questionnaire items) to differing aspects of the school. Those wishing to conduct similar evaluation exercises need to consider carefully the structure of their analysis and how it might reveal areas for attention.

Examples of statistics that emerged from the pilot secondary schools, showing the range of parental responses to questions on involvement, are shown in the box below.

---

	agree/strongly agree
I wish someone had explained to me why they do a lot of things they do in school nowadays	55% to 79%
I would like to be more involved in decisions about my child's future	75% to 95%

Parents were generally extremely positive on the questions '*I feel I can go up to the school any time because I get such a nice welcome*', and on the question '*Teachers are approachable and sympathetic*', with typically around 70% in the 'agree/strongly agree' category.

(SOED/HMI, 1992 (secondary), pp. 7/13)

Findings such as these indicate issues on which significant numbers of parents are expressing some kind of negative view. Of course, the question of what constitutes a 'significant number' is one to which there is no objective answer. It need not mean a majority. As the guide observes, a school with 70 per cent agreement still might be concerned about the 30 per cent who disagree. Thus a school with such levels of agreement might wish to consider how it might make itself more welcoming and approachable to those parents who feel that it is not.

Although the focus here is on parents it is interesting to note, nevertheless, that often the differences between parents, pupils and teachers are particularly noteworthy and may prompt re-examination of certain policies and practices. For example, questions about information to parents highlighted wide discrepancies between parent and teacher evaluations: in one school fewer than half the parents agreed that 'The school has explained its policies on homework to me', whilst 9 out of 10 teachers considered that 'The school explains its homework policy to parents.' As the guides observe, 'a message sent is not necessarily equivalent to a message received, or understood' (SOED/HMI, 1992 (secondary) pp. 7/11). Other examples include differences of view between teachers and pupils on how fairly pupils are treated in school. Such discrepancies suggest areas for examination by the school. It may, for example, have been complacent about its policies and methods of communicating with the home and needs to explore with parents more effective processes. Or, on the question of fair treatment of pupils, a more searching review of discipline policy, involving both pupils and teachers, may illuminate concerns that would otherwise remain hidden.

The ways in which three pilot schools reacted to the data they had collected are outlined in the boxes on pp. 211, 212, 213, 214 and 215. The first of these, a nursery school, implemented a number of changes intended to improve communication and parental understanding of their part in their children's education. These changes cover three 'stages' in parents' and children's experience of the school. These are when they first start (entry); their time at the school; and the transition to primary school.

In a nursery school the staff decided that as a result of the evidence that many parents thought they would like to have more information about what was going on in the school, they should work on better communication with parents, and especially on better explanations on the parts parents can play in their children's education.

They were aware that they had to work with a wide range of levels of understanding among the parents and therefore planned to develop parallel forms of information giving.

On entry

When a child is offered a place, parents will in future receive:

- a visit from an existing member of staff or parent, to talk through hopes and fears, etc.;
- a picture book explaining life at nursery school, to be looked at with the child.

Then at the coffee morning for new parents a more detailed information sheet will be offered. This will include the sorts of things parents can do with their children to prepare them for nursery school and what to expect. The style of the meeting will be informal.

Throughout the session

Better communication about what goes on in nursery will continue with parents' evenings followed by daytime sessions. For example, after their discussion of the results of their survey, they ran a parents night at which the curriculum was discussed. Parents were given introductory talks in each main area by members of staff and were issued with worksheets to use in helping them observe what was going on in the nursery school. They were given the chance to walk round the school in pairs or in threes as they felt comfortable, with the task of noting down where each activity could occur. The staff were gratified to see pennies dropping as parents began to realize that skills like listening, questioning, discussion were part and parcel of every activity and not simply of any one area of the school's work.

'Now I see what you mean!'

After that parent's evening the headteacher received requests from a number of parents who had not been able to attend, to hold the same kind of workshop during the day. The school plans to do this in the coming session.

At transition to primary school

At the summer term parents' evening, at which transition to primary school was a focus, the staff decided to concentrate on reading, writing and maths, tying up what had been done at nursery school with what was expected at primary one. The staff planned to use the evening to broaden the parents' understanding of how each key skill could be related to everyday activities. There was discussion about how parents could follow up the activities at home. For example, when 'sorting' was discussed parents were invited to see the different sorting activities undertaken at school and then to offer suggestions about follow-up home activities, like sorting the dirty washing pile. They shared other skills like counting the cars going past the window. Parents were also shown the videos *Word Match* and *Shape Match*.

After this meeting particularly, parents reported that now they had got to know the nursery staff so well and could see the benefits of sharing information they would want to take this on to primary school.

(SOED/HMI, 1992 (primary), pp. 8/10–11)

In the next example from a primary school, the management team concluded that some of the responses were cause for concern. It decided that it had to respond to these by improving the school's methods of communicating with parents. Although there were indications that some parents wanted more extracurricular activities for children, the management team considered that such provision was inappropriate. It might be asked, however, whether the team should have taken more seriously this parental wish for extracurricular activities. For example, the school could have explored further with parents the kinds of extracurricular activities they were interested in. Perhaps parents and school might have been able to focus on, say, one activity which they all agreed was suitable for young children.

Primary one parents tended to think that more should be offered in the way of extracurricular activities for their children. The management team thought that by the end of a day at school, children are probably ready to go home and play or rest. Additionally they thought clubs tend to be for the purpose of developing specific skills, and infants are still at the stage of enhancing fundamental abilities. They thought, however, that parents could be reminded of the value to all children of some untimetabled time to reflect and please themselves.

These issues were thought by the management team to be largely a matter of explaining school policies. Some other aspects of the parents' responses were, however, more disturbing to them.

While nearly all parents (85%) said they were happy to approach school at any time because they got such a nice welcome, perceptions about the openness of the school varied between staff and parents. All the staff thought that the school had explained both its homework policy and the part that parents can play in the education of their children, but some parents disagreed; 61% of parents said that they would only contact the school in a crisis, whereas 79% of the staff felt that parents could visit freely. With one exception, staff felt that parents should be treated as partners, but 28% of parents thought that they were treated this way never or only sometimes, 39% of parents felt that they did not get regular information of progress, and 44% said that they would like more explanation of the things they do in schools nowadays.

The management team decided that these parental perceptions were a matter of some concern and spent a considerable amount of time considering strategies for more effective communication with parents. They came up with a number of possibilities:

- An afternoon a term might be fixed when parents could visit a particular class. The problem with that was that parents may feel constrained to come and there would be too large a number present to make the occasion useful. It was decided though that it should be discussed with staff.
- Older children might be asked to write down in their jotters three strengths and three weaknesses in their school work, with their teacher then adding her comment. The parents would then read this and comment as they wish. This would form a foundation for ongoing self-evaluation without being too time consuming.
- As part of the preparation for parent – teacher meetings, staff would be reminded of the value of a clear summarizing statement of the conversation, indicating to parents where the child's strengths are and what special focus is required for the coming term, as well as what areas still need to be worked on. This would help parents get a balanced picture of current progress and would help to prevent global generalizations.

The survey also revealed that parents and staff were agreed on the value of uniform: 66% of parents felt strongly that there should be a uniform and very few were against. Staff, with one exception, wanted uniform. Pupils' reactions were much more mixed with 28% thinking it should be worn always and 33% not wanting a uniform at all. The school now has a popular polo shirt, with a school sweatshirt, which is meeting with widespread approval from pupils as well as parents and staff.

(SOED/HMI, 1992 (primary), pp. 8/11–13)

Looking at the third example – a special school – it is interesting to note that the headteacher chose to deal with the findings in terms of numbers (rather than percentages) so that she would not fail to view them as representing real people: a reminder of the dangers of abstraction and of becoming mesmerized with figures to the detriment of the issues of everyday school life that lie behind them. It is also noteworthy with the special school that, owing to its particular circumstances, the headteacher decided to proceed with particular care since the problems highlighted were not capable of straightforward resolution.

At the special school one of the areas the headteacher decided to focus on was parents' experience and perceptions of the school. She started with totals in each column and identified those she thought were worth considering at greater length.

	Number of parents		
	Yes	No	Don't know
Most parents show support for the school	49	3	8
The school has explained its policies on homework to me	42	17	2
The school has explained to me what part I can play in my child's education	52	6	2
Parents' evenings apart, the only time I would contact teachers would be if there was a problem or a crisis	35	24	2
I am confident that if I complain about something I will get a sympathetic hearing	58	3	—
The school board seems to be a useful thing for the school	34	7	19
The PTA is good at keeping us in touch with school matters	53	3	5
I think that parents should be involved in classroom activity	21	27	12

One conclusion from the analysis was clear. It was important that all members of staff should be aware that a substantial minority of parents thought that homework policy had not been explained to them and methods had to be found to ensure that this number was reduced. The other areas of concern for the headteacher, that is contact with the school and involvement in classrooms, were much more problematic and therefore less amenable to straightforward statements of intentions.

In the special circumstances of the school the headteacher thought it important that she, and the other members of staff, should have some knowledge of the parents' perceptions of the everyday lives of their children, of their successes and achievements as well as their problems. The response of the majority of parents, however, confirmed her impression that they had a limited view of what would be helpful to teachers. The fact that the teachers (who had completed a similar questionnaire) tended to disagree with her compounded the difficulty of achieving any speedy resolution to the problem. She decided that, initially, she should highlight this response for discussion by the school board and by the teaching staff.

A significant minority of parents thought that parents should be involved in classroom activity, but half the teaching staff disagreed. The headteacher decided to approach the problem obliquely by asking the PTA to organize a meeting at which some of the staff could display some of their classroom materials and explain how they were used.

(SOED/HMI, 1992 (primary), pp. 7/9–10)

These cases illustrate the need to address carefully, imaginatively and with enthusiasm the question of how school policy and practice should be improved in light of what parents say about the school. It is apparent that the initiative for change as a consequence of school evaluation rests firmly with the school's headteacher and staff. This gives school personnel not only the chance to bring about improvements, but also the opportunity to ignore or explain away unpalatable criticism and to privilege the disadvantages for *them* of change over the disadvantages for *parents* of the status quo. Hence I draw attention, as an example, to the management team of the primary school (in the case above) which might be seen as too dismissive of parental interest in extracurricular activities for their children.

School personnel have to ask continually in the school evaluation exercise whether they are openly listening to what parents have to say and if they are prepared to do all that is genuinely feasible to make improvements. I would stress also that it is no good looking at school evaluation as a one-off exercise – 'Listening to parents . . .? We did that last year.' The implementation of change requires a preparedness to consult with parents and review the impact of planned improvements. Are the strategies decided upon by the school achieving what they were intended to? The responsive school must incorporate seeking, listening and responding to parental opinion into its natural management processes. A school evaluation exercise should not be an end in itself, but a beginning.

POSTSCRIPT

I am indebted to the work of HMI and the Scottish Office Education Department on which this chapter draws.

REFERENCES

Bastiani, J. (1993) Parents as partners: genuine progress or empty rhetoric, in P. Munn (Ed.) *Parents and schools: customers, managers or partners?* London: Routledge.

Bastiani, J. and Bailey, G. (1992) *Directory of home–school initiatives in the UK*. London: RSA.

Jones, G., Bastiani, J., Bell, G. and Chapman, C. (1992) *A willing partnership*. London: National Association of Head Teachers/Royal Society for the Encouragement of Arts, Manufacturers and Commerce.

Merttens, R. (1993) IMPACT: pride, prejudice and pedagogy: one director's personal story, in R. Merttens and J. Vass (Eds) *Partnerships in maths: parents and schools*. London: Falmer.

SOED/HMI (Scottish Office Education Department/Her Majesty's Inspector of Schools) (1992) *Using ethos indicators in primary school self-evaluation* and *Using ethos indicators in secondary school self-evaluation* (two volumes). Edinburgh: Scottish Office Education Department.

Woods, P. A. (1993) Responding to the consumer: parental choice and school effectiveness, *School Effectiveness and School Improvement*, Vol. 4, no. 3, pp. 205–29.

CHAPTER 16

School–Industry Liaison: Developing Local Links

LESLEY BROOMAN

ABSTRACT

This project investigates the management purposes in initiating links, the methods of forging links, and the nature of links established, between Rushton High School and Highcross Business Park. Analysis is based on interpreting the data collected in the light of the research methods used and previous studies of this area of school relations. The report makes recommendations as to how such a mutual partnership could be forged.

AIMS OF THE PROJECT

My project involved a review and evaluation of why, and how, Rushton High School was initiating links with the newly developed local business park. It was undertaken in response to the increasing importance in the school attached to developing school–industry links by staff at all levels in the management hierarchy; the need to enhance the student curriculum through school–industry links; concern about the direction of the initiative with Highcross Business Park; and concern about the nature of the influence of national education policy on the school's initiative.

The aims of the project can be summarized as follows:

- To outline the school's pre-existing links with employers.
- To assess the role of accountability factors in the school's motivations for developing links.
- To examine what strategies were used to initiate links with the employers and to evaluate the progress made.
- To identify whether the school's senior managers, staff and the local employers share the same perceptions and perspectives on the development of school – industry links.
- To recommend future action to strengthen and improve links.

BACKGROUND

The school

Rushton High School is an 11–16 co-educational comprehensive school on the edge of a large Midlands conurbation. It serves a community comprising a mixture of private and council housing, the latter in the form of large estates of small houses, maisonettes and high-rise flats mainly built to rehouse families from the inner city in the early 1970s. No large employers are established within the local community.

Rushton High's feeder schools show sharp differences in ethos which reflect the nature of the particular housing areas they serve. Rushton High School's intake has come increasingly from the primary schools serving council estates. Since 1989 the school has struggled to attract what had previously been a stable 150 first choices. Local parents, shown from research in feeder schools to be predominantly those of the academically more able students, are choosing schools outside the area. These parents quote concerns about Rushton High's examination outcomes, buildings and resources, the disproportionate number of male students (reflecting the presence of the 11–18 girls' school one mile distant), and the desire to move their children away from the social influences of the local community.

A new headteacher was appointed to Rushton High in April 1989 determined to address the community profile of the school, and thereby the issues of aiming to receive a comprehensive intake in terms of academic ability and socio-economic background, and the maintenance of the school roll at around 800 students. I was appointed to a deputy headship at the school in September 1989 with specific responsibility for 'curriculum in the community'.

The new headteacher completely reorganized the management structure of the school to support the implementation of the National Curriculum (NC). The structure is team based. Each curriculum team consists of one or more subject specialisms and is headed by a curriculum co-ordinator. Significantly for my project, the 'economic and industrial understanding' dimension of the NC was to be enacted across the curriculum through all subjects. The existing head of careers was retitled the co-ordinator for economic and industrial understanding, and the role was redefined to emphasize supportive work with all subject areas and the development of an 'industrialized curriculum'.

The business park

Until 1990 the school's local community was almost exclusively residential with no significant business/industry within a four-mile radius. For numerous social and economic reasons the community was targeted by the city council for regeneration and new development. As part of this programme, in 1990, with considerable financial support from the EU, the city's economic development department began the development of Highcross Business Park (HBP), about one mile distant from the school.

Enormous financial incentives were offered to British and foreign companies, many connected with the car industry, to move on to the Park into large, purpose-built premises and a complex of small units all within an expensively landscaped environment. In view of the residential nature of the area, only light and service industries were projected for the park. A new road was constructed to link HBP with a major trunk road and thereby the motorway network.

Five of the 16 companies already located on HBP are European, Japanese or Middle Eastern. The largest British company on site has relocated from the city centre. Half of the companies are small businesses offering specialist skills/products. The seven largest companies, in purpose-built premises, are developing manufacturing, distribution and administration on site. None are yet fully operational, but HBP is already becoming a significant local employer.

The recession has meant that a number of plots and small units on the park remain unoccupied. Two businesses have already closed down, but two are seeking to expand. There is some concern that heavier industry might be permitted to move on to the park if plots remain unoccupied, but, at present, the city's economic development department continues to promote HBP very actively, both in Britain and abroad.

LITERATURE

Much of the relevant literature for my project has its origins in the 'Great Debate' on education, generally acknowledged to have begun with James Callaghan's speech at Ruskin College in 1976. The 'Great Debate' was preoccupied with the issue of accountability, particularly the economic accountability of the education system. Concern focused on both the ideology and autonomy of educational professionals in deciding what was taught in schools, and how it was taught. This was within a climate of increasing acceptance for the view that the education system was failing to meet the economic needs of the country and not giving 'value for money'. The education professionals' apparent indifference to criticism, and resistance to being accountable, fuelled political and public dissatisfaction and the demand for change in education.

Since 1979 Conservative administrations, dominated by the ideology of the 'New Right', have put accountability at the top of the national education policy-making agenda. Accountability forms the core of the legislation of the 1980s, culminating in the Education Reform Act 1988 (ERA).

Kogan (in Glatter *et al.*, 1988, p. 139) suggested three normative models of accountability which are useful here to explain how the shift in the ideology dominating education policy-making produced a complete change in the ways schools were accountable. Kogan described his normative models in terms of accountability control, underlining how the dominant ideology defines account-ability. Kogan's first model is that of public, or state, control, 'bureaucratic accountability' (Glatter *et al.*, 1988, p. 141), which derives from contracts of employment and is carried through by a hierarchical management structure, both internal and external to the school, assessing competence in fulfilling contractual obligations. The second model of professional control has the teacher as an autonomous professional and the school as self-evaluating, entering into a dialogue with clients, and accounting, as relevant in the professionals' judgement, to different interested parties. In this model accountability is centred on the principles of practice rather than on its results. Within his third model of consumerist control, Kogan identifies two interrelated dimensions – partnership and market. In the partnership model, control is shared by providers (school) and clients (parents) in terms of responsibility based on a consensus of objectives and 'evaluative dialogue'. In the market model control is passed to consumers (parents), by encouraging schools to compete in providing better standards by removing their guarantee of 'trade' (Glatter *et al.*, 1988, p. 151), most notably via open enrolment. In having to compete in an open market to attract students, schools are encouraged into partnership with parents.

The 'responsively accountable school' (Elliott *et al.*, 1981, p. xiii) would have free and open communication with a range of interest groups about the aims and nature of education. The Cambridge Project was committed to the concept of such a 'neighbourhood school' having local accountability. Ebbutt saw it as a danger that it should be attempted 'to impose, unmodified, the *accounting* model of accountability from the tangible world of industry onto education' (Elliott *et al.*, 1981, p. 151). But this, I would suggest, was the outcome of the ERA.

It is interesting to note that in 1979 the East Sussex Accountability Project identified three facets to accountability: answerability, or moral accountability to clients, that is students and parents; responsive or professional accountability to self and colleagues; and accountability of a contractual nature to employers and politicians. By 1991, Broadfoot, addressing the same issue within terms of the forms of evaluative pressure on schools, identified four forms of accountability: professional – to colleagues; moral – to clients; bureaucratic – to authority structure; and market – to all stakeholders via performance indicators, as the basis of consumer choice (Moore and Broadfoot, 1991, p. 54).

In essence the legislation of the 1980s swept away the option for schools to exercise professional accountability through self-evaluation and responsiveness to clients, although professional accountability to colleagues remains. Accountability for the school is now imposed, direct and visible. The role of market accountability has become ever more significant through the performance indicators/consumer choice factors and delegated budgets to schools. Referring back to Kogan's three normative models of accountability, it can be argued that the professional model no longer pertains whilst the public and consumerist/market models dominate.

As Ball states, 'accountability is now firmly local. The onus is on individual schools' (Ball, 1990, p. 68), and as Kogan remarks, 'The head and staff will have their behaviour conditioned by the degree of success they can achieve in attracting pupils' (Glatter *et al.*, 1988, p. 152). Yet it may be anticipated that such 'conditioning' will be unequal within the school. Ball observes: 'The changed economic situation in which they now work has revealed the true antagonisms of management and labour in the school. These antagonisms have been obscured in the past by the powerful ideological effects of the concept of professionalism' (Ball, 1987, p. 135). As has been noted, professional accountability has been sidelined by public, consumerist/market domination and this could result in the 'conflict of loyalties' anticipated by Ball as the head and senior managers are preoccupied with satisfying demands imposed by governors, local education authorities (LEAs) and legislation, as opposed to the daily enactment of the curriculum that constitutes the focus of staff. Kogan records that no empirical studies have as yet assessed 'the effect on teachers' professionality by being part of a competitive scramble for students'. He goes on to note that although market accountability includes some aspects of professional control in the negotiative relations sought between professionals and clients, this would have a different power distribution and operate through different mechanisms (Glatter *et al.*, 1988, p. 152).

The notion of industry as an unsatisfied client of education was central to the 'Great Debate'. Literature from government sources, such as the Green Paper *Curriculum 11–16, better schools* (Taylor Report), laid the responsibility for the country's poor economic performance 'at the door' of the teaching profession through its preoccupation with liberal/progressive philosophy and failure to assume accountability for the 'production' of a workforce ready/willing/able to serve the economic needs of the country. Resultant social ills were thereby also attributed to educationalists. Certainly Jamieson and Lightfoot (1982) found that pupils identified sources other than school as having predominated in forming their attitudes to industry (E333 Module 3), but writers such as Weiner (1982) argued that the culture of British society at large is historically anti-industrial, schools merely being a microcosm of this.

Whether a social or solely educational factor in origin, Esland and Dale (1986, p. 7) cite the tension between the two goals of education – economic relevance and personal development – as being omnipresent, but do go on to state: 'As an educational innovation, the new vocationalism originated almost entirely outside the concerns and agendas of the education profession' (Esland and Dale, 1986, p. 9). From the late 1970s, national policy saw school–industry links as one of the few growth areas in education at a time of otherwise substantial cuts. The Technical and Vocational Education Initiative (TVEI) represented a break with the 'essentially incremental, apparently haphazard, pattern which had typified educational change' (Dale in Esland, 1990, p. 231).

The government, however, remained dissatisfied with progress. As a NC cross-curricular dimension, 'economic and industrial understanding' is now required to be enacted in schools, and links between schools and industry are clearly a vital component in this.

The literature relating to the nature of school–industry links themselves tends to focus heavily on the notion extant in the Great Debate, that of two distinct 'worlds'. Bridges (Elliott *et al.*, 1981, p. 125) identifies only one shared concern

between schools and employers, that of developing 'transitionary skills' to help
pupils move from one world to the other. Beyond this Bridges sees only
'differences of perspective', and does not consider that these 'gaps in attitudes
and values would in practice be narrowed by closer familiarity with each other's
world' (Elliott *et al.*, 1981, p. 141). Indeed, he believes that the gap would be
widened rather than closed.

Ebbutt on the same project team, however, adopted a more positive outlook,
seeing industrial experience for teachers and school experience for employers as
having the potential to 'refocus perceptions' (Elliott *et al.*, 1981, p. 148).

Both Bridges (Elliott *et al.*, 1981, p. 144) and Jamieson (Dale, 1985, p. 26) see the
focus and agenda of school–industry links changing with, as Jamieson terms it,
'the vicissitudes of the economy'. Reports on the education/industry compacts in
large cities would appear to reinforce this argument as the recession has seen
compact employers unable to honour the 'partnership contracts' guaranteeing
jobs with training.

Interestingly, but not surprisingly, more recent literature tends to be more
positive about the development of school–industry links. Marsden emphasizes
that for schools the needs and benefits of school–industry links are now clearly
demonstrable. He argues that this not only places the onus on the school to
develop the links, but also means that the school must have 'well-marshalled
arguments for why business should get involved, which can be "sold" to business'
(Warwick, 1989, p. 30). Here, far from the pre-ERA notions of business and
industry seeking influence and control over the school curriculum, we have the
picture of schools 'wooing' business and industry to enable them to fulfil statutory
requirements.

Bradshaw (Warwick, 1989, p. 65) argues for 'quality links' that establish
partnerships between schools and industry. Her 12-stage 'model for partnership' was developed from her work with four North Yorkshire schools (Figure
16.1). As an outcome of case study work, Bradshaw's model offers a valuable
means of comparison with, and evaluation of, the school–industry links at
Rushton High School.

The literature confirmed the focus of my project on links between a secondary
school and a business park as highly relevant within the current educational
climate. It highlighted the dominance of the national context in shaping and
directing the local. Both the accountability pressures and the need to develop
school–industry links are externally imposed and supported by legislation. My
aim was to address how far these factors account for Rushton High School's
initiative to develop links with Highcross Business Park (HBP), and to explore
whether the school's senior managers and staff and the employers share the same
perceptions and perspectives on these developments. Bradshaw's model for
'quality links' with industry offered a means of evaluating whether the Rushton
High School initiative reflects merely a senior management 'market' response, or
whether it represents planned policy to enact quality education through addressing not only the demands of public and consumerist/market accountability, but
also professional accountability via curriculum development and change.

Stage One: establishing the climate for change within the school;

Stage Two: exploring possibilities using a facilitator from the school and the industrial link agency;

Stage Three: generating ownership of school–industry links by getting one or more teachers involved;

Stage Four: providing a statement of intent for colleagues constituting a clear outline of what is going to be done;

Stage Five: searching for contacts with industry;

Stage Six: collaboration between education and industry representatives via a planning group utilizing a facilitator from a link agency if possible;

Stage Seven: undertaking a school–industry link activity;

Stage Eight: evaluating the activity ensuring that timescales and dates are set;

Stage Nine: reshaping the activity using the evaluation outcomes;

Stage Ten: engaging the support of management to sustain change;

Stage Eleven: publicizing progress and achievements to the whole school, parents, governors and the wider community – all stakeholders;

Stage Twelve: disengaging the school–industry links from the facilitator/link agency to be self-sustaining.

(Bradshaw in Warwick (Ed.) 1989, p. 65)

FIGURE 16.1 Bradshaw's 12-stage model for partnership.

METHODOLOGY

The research methods I used were:

- interviews with 12 staff of Rushton High School;
- interviews with representatives from 11 of the companies on Highcross Business Park;
- observation of the school's curriculum co-ordinators' meetings and staff meetings;
- review of school records of meetings, policy documents, schemes of work.

The choice of these methods was directly influenced by my position in the school as one of the three deputy headteachers. My role gave me an acute appreciation that the staff generally felt under extreme pressure, and paperwork represented one of the most despised demands on time. Most of the staff had been required to complete one or two questionnaires/audit sheets since January 1992. For this reason, and knowing that as a senior manager if I issued a questionnaire I would receive returns but possibly generate considerable ill-feeling, I rejected use of that research method.

A questionnaire had been very tempting as a quick and easy way to generate a great deal of data, but again, I felt my position in the school could result in some staff responding 'as expected' rather than honestly, and to have extended anonymity would not have allowed for analysis in relation to position in the management hierarchy, nor for interview selection.

I also rejected use of a questionnaire with the employers. I considered that the contact time required to put the questionnaire into context would be considerable, and far better spent as structured interview time. Moreover, as existing links are relatively new, I felt the personal contact of interview would obviate the possibly 'threatening' nature of a questionnaire, as well as contribute to enhancing working relationships.

My position in the school gave me enormous advantages in terms of access, both to staff and employers, since my responsibilities include contact with both groups at all levels. I also have the flexibility within my day to facilitate interviews to suit the interviewees' convenience, and to attend all meetings and receive documentation as a matter of course. The fact that my project arose directly from a current school issue meant that both staff and employers identified with its relevance.

Interviews

In selecting both staff and employer representatives for interview, I took into account the nature of my professional and personal relationship with individuals in terms of their preparedness to express honest opinions, given my assurance of confidentiality. I felt this was fully justified as it did result in individuals talking openly and frankly whilst no vital scope was lost to the project by not identifying specific individuals and their role responsibilities.

In the case of both groups, interviews lasted between 45 minutes and 1 hour and took a semi-structured form based on interview schedules consisting of open-ended questions to encourage the exposition of views. Figure 16.2 shows the interview schedule for staff as an example. Although the interview schedules were different for staff and employers to enable them to be relevant in language and emphasis to the respective groups, the questions ranged over the same issues.

The interviews represented a very large time investment. The length of interview time proved important to put individuals at their ease and to offset a 'getting-through-the-questions' atmosphere. In all but three interviews with employers, individuals appeared comfortable and eager to express their views.

The staff selected for interview included representation of all levels of school management, with the exception of senior management since their views are well known to me through our meetings and school policy decisions are outcomes of senior management working together as a team. In the case of three curriculum areas, I interviewed both the co-ordinator and junior members of the team to explore any differences in perception/perspective.

The 11 employer representatives selected for interview came from a range of companies, from those employing fewer than 20 staff to those with a workforce of hundreds. Five were from British companies, four European, one Middle Eastern and one Japanese. Such a range was selected to facilitate exploring any differences

(1) Were you aware of the existence of Highcross Business Park before the training day?

(2) Are you aware of school policy relating to school–industry links?

(3) Are you aware of any existing links between the school and business and industry?

(4) Does your curriculum area currently have any specific links with business and industry?

(5) What do you see as the main reasons for forging links with Highcross Business Park:
(a) for the school?
(b) for your curriculum area?

(6) What advantages would school–industry links have for employers on Highcross Business Park?

(7) What barriers to links do you perceive?

(8) What do you regard as:
(a) possible positive outcomes?
(b) possible negative outcomes?

(9) In what ways do you think links could be successfully developed?

(10) What are your personal views about links with business and industry?

FIGURE 16.2 Staff interview schedule.

in attitude and approach to school–industry links based on size and national origin, although no such differences were revealed. In all cases I went to the employer's premises to conduct the interviews.

Although initially I had some qualms about committing virtually all my research time to conducting interviews, these were dispelled by the outcomes. I certainly found that I gathered sufficient data for my project and I also gained enormously in terms of personal relationships, particularly with the employers. The data collected would also be of direct and immediate use to the school's curriculum development. The quality of data would have been improved if employers' perspectives on school–industry links had been probed more deeply, but I was unwilling to risk future relations when it was evident that all those interviewed were hesitant and unclear in many of their views. Possibly the greatest benefit of the interviews will be that they were thought provoking and will give rise to companies clarifying their aims and objectives.

Observation of meetings

Meetings proved an interesting although limited source of data. Two frank discussions revealing individuals' personal convictions, and group dynamics, particularly the ability of key individuals to affect the ambience of full staff meetings, were significant.

However, I found it difficult to remain in the role of observer. Although the role, and its reasons, were explained at the start of meetings, a number of staff were clearly uncomfortable with this, and since I would ordinarily have been an active participant in the meetings, the artificiality gave way to my involvement on more than one occasion. However, despite these lapses, having approached meetings with the intention of observation I was far more alert to procedures and outcomes in terms of who achieved them and how.

ANALYSIS

Pre-existing links

Data from staff interviews indicated an essentially 'go-it-alone' approach to school–industry links prior to the HBP initiative. Several curriculum co-ordinators and incentive allowance holders saw school–industry links as vital to delivery of their curriculum areas, particularly at Key Stage 4. However, in the absence of any formalized whole-school policy, they relied on being alerted to possible contacts by the co-ordinator for economic and industrial understanding and the deputy heads. Three curriculum areas had contacts, via individual staff, with employers for specific aspects of their programmes of study, some of whom they had used for a number of years. Links took the form of talks, demonstrations, set projects, competitions. All links were tightly focused and teacher led. Only one of the employers was from the local community. There had been no consideration of a team approach to school–industry links, or to broadening the existing employer input.

At a whole-school level, the co-ordinator for economic and industrial understanding referred to the increasing difficulties of securing work experience placements for all Year 10 students due to the recession and the number of employers tied to compact partnerships. (No compact opportunity currently exists for the school.) Work experience placements are renegotiated each year. Careers and recruitment talks are arranged annually for Year 11. The industrial co-ordinator reported monthly meetings with the link engineer who is making direct input in the technology area, and half-termly with the SCIP representative who has provided an economic and industrial understanding review schedule intended for use with all curriculum teams. Whilst the TVEI partnership group continues to meet each half-term, the industrial co-ordinator views it as 'dying on its feet' in the wake of financial delegation. Larger schools have secured individual sponsorship arrangements with major businesses which see a greater and better-focused return on investment in such arrangements rather than through the TVEI.

I knew from senior management team meetings that six staff have undertaken an industrial placement through the government's Understanding British Industry (UBI) initiative. Although individuals' placement reports have been available, there has been no co-ordinated utilization of experience and contacts gained at whole-school level.

The school's existing links are generally arrangements between individual staff and employers which address specific curriculum issues in specific areas. There would certainly appear to be pockets of quality, most notably in the technology area where a school–industry project is embedded into the curriculum and is subject to ongoing joint evaluation. However, existing school–industry links are not set within the framework of a whole school policy, nor perceived as having the potential for extension.

Accountability issues

The school development plan (SDP) identified promotion of the school as one of the two whole-school priorities. This was in direct response to the falling number of first-choice students taking up places at the school since 1989. Competition for students comes mainly from four much larger schools, two with sixth forms, one single sex. Two of the co-educational schools have established school–industry links with large national companies from which they have obtained very impressive resources and curriculum input.

Promotion of the school embraced a wide range of issues, but the senior team identified the development of school–industry links as a major new initiative in external relations. I was surprised to find that, with the exception of one standard scale teacher and one curriculum co-ordinator, staff considered the main reasons for forging links with Highcross Business Park (HBP), to be those centred on promoting the school to attract students; a higher profile in the community; and access to the media, resources and sponsorship. Even in relation to their own curriculum areas nine staff emphasized school–industry links' potential contribution to improved examination results and the school's standing in relation to other schools, that is market accountability factors, above actual student experience.

Staff are keen to protect their own school and livelihoods; professionalism might be said to have been overlaid with the necessary realism to run the school as a business, Ebbutt's 'accounting' fear seems to be evidenced as a reality (Elliott *et al.*, 1981, p. 151). Kogan's speculation about power distribution in external relations is also relevant. In relation to school–industry links, the school has the need, and therefore has to assume the initiative with employers. It could be said that the school is being 'responsively accountable', but its motivations are very different from those envisaged by the SSRC Cambridge Project team.

Strategies and progress with links

My role responsibility for 'curriculum in the community' meant that I had day-to-day management of the development targets relating to promotion of the school, including school–industry links. As premises were built and occupied on the business park, I sent student reporters to interview employers and then to distribute copies of the half-termly school newsletter.

When promotion was identified as a development priority, seeking to build links with the group of employers now 'on the school's doorstep', assumed a new importance and timescale. The management of the development was seen as crucial if links were to be effective. The strategies devised can be seen to have some parallels with Bradshaw's suggested model for 'quality links' referred to in Figure 16.1 (Warwick, 1989, p. 65).

Bradshaw's Stage One refers to establishing the climate for change. This had been achieved in the school through the commitment of the senior team, the involvement of staff and awareness raising of promotion and marketing. Two staff meetings contained heated exchanges about the 'morality' of marketing the school, but nearly one year later, two curriculum co-ordinators, among the most vehement opponents of promotion, said in interview that the climate created by financial delegation made marketing a necessity. The SDP promotion priority confirmed that change was being sought.

The exploration of possibilities at Stage Two using a facilitator, was carried out through discussion with the local community education development officer (CEDO). Although the CEDO had no existing knowledge or contacts with the HBP companies, she was highly skilled at forging initial links with organizations and recognized the potential benefits both to the school and to her wider community role. She agreed to help in any way that she could: this included some initial visits to companies with me, advice on the identified curriculum project and financial support.

The school now moved to Bradshaw's Stage Five of searching for contacts. This was because the strategy of face-to-face personal contact with each of the 16 companies on HBP was decided upon. The intention was to identify a contact in each company as a link without requesting anything but 'talk time' of the businesses. The approach was justified in that most companies expected to be asked for something. Once assured that the mission was not mercenary, all companies were extremely welcoming, especially considering that no prior appointments were made.

As the visits were made, so a project revealed itself through the difficulty in locating businesses and moving around the park – no site plan or directory was available. The production of one would be a valuable curriculum project for students, and would enable the school to give something to the businesses whilst working together co-operatively.

The school now addressed Bradshaw's Stages Three and Four – ownership and statement of intent. All staff were fully apprised of developments. Discussion at meetings indicated strong support, and the humanities, expressive arts and technology curriculum areas committed themselves to active support of the project involving students from Key Stages 3 and 4. As the profile of school–industry links was raised the industry co-ordinator presented a draft school policy statement for economic and industrial understanding. The statement set out the rationale for addressing economic and industrial understanding as a cross-curricular dimension, specified the school's aims and objectives and strategies for monitoring and evaluation, and listed broad guidelines and support for curriculum areas to develop their own targets and action plans.

Collaboration, as Bradshaw describes it in her Stage Six, did not occur, but further personal and telephone contact with employers drew very positive responses to co-operating with the directory project. The aim was to keep employers' time commitment limited and well focused through the use of carefully structured, desktop-published letters, pro forma and short 'tick box' questionnaires. As the students visited to collect data, many companies gave them works tours, literature and refreshments. 'Spin-offs' of this activity at Stage Seven were collaboration between the technology co-ordinator and one of the companies, representatives from other companies contributing to the school's 'Women's Day', and the pledge of work experience placements from nine companies. Student involvement proved invaluable. Two or three students were 'partnered' with each individual company. They were thoroughly briefed and their importance as first-contact students and ambassadors for the school underlined. Knowing individual students overcame many employers' initial anxieties about young people and fostered awareness of the educational benefit of the activity. Moreover, the knowledge gained by students gave me additional insight into individual companies and helped me to plan for interviews.

Stages Eight to Twelve of Bradshaw's model have yet to be addressed. It cannot be said that real change has occurred as there has been no genuine, structured collaborative work between the school and the group of employers. A number of companies made a point of expressing their pleasure in receiving students and facilitating the project, but whilst the school to date has gained a level of response from the employers, it has failed to gain any commitment to ongoing partnership.

PERCEPTIONS AND PERSPECTIVES

Staff

Of the 12 staff interviewed only two had been unaware of the existence of HBP before the training day. All members of staff perceived value in school–industry links, but position in the management hierarchy did affect how important such links were held to be. Neither of the standard-scale teachers interviewed could see any personal role for themselves. One incentive allowance holder is already involved in using business input in the classroom and regards it as a crucial motivating factor for students, as well as extending understanding in ways that the school alone could not do. This teacher has organized these school–industry links herself. Contrastingly, an incentive allowance holder in another curriculum area has no experience of school–industry links, and whilst aware of the curriculum need, cannot conceive of strategies to make them a viable proposition.

Within the same curriculum area, another incentive allowance holder has organized school–industry links on his own initiative following a UBI teacher placement, but has often found having business representatives in school for classroom input 'embarrassing'. This teacher feels a lack of support from the co-ordinator, and finds timetable constraints difficult to manage. Consequently, the contact has waned; the business concerned has not taken the initiative to continue contact.

The co-ordinator of this same curriculum area, in common with all the curriculum co-ordinators interviewed, identified school–industry links as vital to both the school and student experience, but constantly cited having 'no time' to develop such links. All curriculum co-ordinators foresaw enormous benefits from links with HBP in developing curricula which students would regard as more relevant, thus improving motivation and application to work, not least because they would have sight of expectations of them post-16 in terms of attitude, conduct, responsibilities, knowledge base and skills from adults other than teachers.

The constant reference to time restraint which staff perceived as the major obstacle to developing school–industry links highlighted the need for the school to prioritize formalizing whole-school policy development for all forms of links (not merely the HBP initiative).

The view was prevalent among staff interviewees (10 of 12) that school–industry links had currently no obvious benefits to offer HBP employers, other than some public relations gains in the wider community mentioned by four middle-managers. Staff were somewhat cynical of the school–industry movement as a whole, feeling that political and business commitment was tied heavily to the prevailing economic climate and not to the improvement of education. One curriculum co-ordinator commented that as an HBP employer she would see no realistic 'return on investment' through links with the school 'of whatever nature'. Such a view underlines those explored by Bridges (Elliott *et al.*, 1981, p. 144).

However, nine staff interviewed demonstrated the perspective that the nature and scope of employer contributions should be prescribed by the school staff. None of these nine staff wished to see any business initiative about curriculum input. Curriculum co-ordinators in particular did not consider that employers' perspectives could open up new horizons in the curriculum. The demands of programmes of study and the need 'to get through programmes and assessments in time' were cited by co-ordinators, along with the perception that they would be undermined by employers 'trying to tell us what to do' whilst not understanding that 'we don't have their sort of time and resources to work with'.

This clearly reflects Bridges' (Elliott *et al.*, 1981, p. 126) 'differences of perspective', and in no way opens the way for Bradshaw's 'quality links'. The whole notion of negotiation with employers was missing from the staff perspective.

Employers

Only one company contact interviewed had previously been aware of the existence of the school, and none of the companies has any form of policy or programme relating to educational links. Even a company which has relocated from the inner city, where it was involved in a compact partnership, has no formalized school–industry links policy. Although the company was clearly keen for links, it was also evident that it did not wish to commit to another formalized partnership.

None of the employers interviewed considered that educational links could be identified as a company priority. The main obstacles to this were the need to be fully established on site first; the recession hitting the car industry; and the small size of some companies. Eight of the 11 company contacts expressed awareness and interest in school–industry links focused on developing 'transitionary skills' in young people. These would enable them to know and understand the different expectations of work. Companies also 'had an eye' to recruitment possibilities. Careers talks, mock interviews, work experience placements were all volunteered with genuine enthusiasm. These reflect the areas in which employers feel competent and secure, and there was also the motivation of the personal pleasure and satisfaction to be gained from contact with young people, reflective of Marsden's argument (Warwick, 1989, p. 31). There was, however, the view that 'I wouldn't have your job for anything', and a clear reticence to be involved in anything outside the world of business and existing expertise.

Only one company had a view of the potential gains for the school beyond support in developing 'transitionary skills'. All companies demonstrated an expectation of the school dictating what was wanted, and of themselves as either agreeing or not as was appropriate. The progress to date of the directory project fully reflects this perspective in that all companies responded to the school's direct request to receive students and to provide specific data for the directory through a tightly controlled procedure. Extension to this has been dependent on the staffing and size of individual companies, the nature of their business and the quality of personal relationships between company contacts and students/staff.

Contacts from four of the companies expressed committed personal views to the notion of a limited partnership with the school, but felt their companies could not support such partnerships in the current economic climate. Such 'investment' was considered as too long term in respect of 'pay-off'.

Overall, the interview data highlighted that neither the school staff nor the employers were unwilling to co-operate. However, the development of school–industry links was severely hindered by the lack of understanding of aims and objectives, both within each others' areas of work, and of any potential partnership. The threat to 'professional autonomy' of industrialists seeking to dictate curriculum content was not substantiated by the employers who acknowledged the professional expertise of teachers. It is disappointing to note, however, that neither group envisaged joint negotiation, planning and evaluation. It is evident that time for face-to-face contact to forge the relationships and understanding upon which 'quality links' could be founded is the crucial, and very expensive, factor.

CONCLUSIONS

- My project shows that accountability factors, particularly consumerist/market accountability, as defined by Kogan, were the key motivators to the school initiating links with Highcross Business Park (HBP). Concern to attract students was paramount with curriculum development potential, secondary for staff at all levels of the management organization of the school.
- Before the school took the initiative to forge links with the companies on HBP, the school's links with employers had been largely *ad hoc* arrangements reliant on middle-managers assuming the initiative for individual curriculum areas. No whole-school policy statement and action plans had been developed or implemented.
- The school's strategies of initiating relations with HBP employers through: personal contact on employers' 'territory'; seeking to give something tangible to employers; student involvement; retaining the initiative; making minimal demands on employers' resources; have engaged the co-operation of all the employers with the directory project, and facilitated the establishment of a personal contact in each company.
- These strategies, however, have not 'sold' the notion of a mutually beneficial partnership at the level of Bradshaw's 'quality links', to either the school staff or the local employers.
- Both the school staff and employers identify the main barriers to links as time and the current economic climate. Neither group perceives employer involvement in curriculum development as a priority, or as desirable. From the perceptions and perspectives of their own 'worlds', both groups accept that the school should retain the initiative and responsibility for developing links.

RECOMMENDATIONS

The school's senior managers should give positive focus to the evident commitment of staff at all management levels to accountability factors by clarifying aims and objectives to facilitate achieving 'quality links' with HBP. Senior managers should clarify and support the role of the school–industry links facilitator.

A management lead could be given through the following:

- identifying economic and industrial understanding as a whole-school priority;
- committing to an INSET programme with the whole staff on the nature and potential of 'quality links' with employers in relation to curriculum development;
- giving active support to the co-ordinator for economic and industrial understanding for the formulation and implementation of a whole-school policy and curriculum area action plans for school–industry links;
- establishing, and being represented on, a task group consisting of volunteers

from each curriculum area with a clearly defined brief and timescales;

- ensuring ongoing communication of developments to all staff;
- monitoring staff commitments to support effective time resourcing and management;
- seeking the support of a facilitator from SCIP through the co-ordinator for economic and industrial understanding's existing contact;
- establishing contact with public relations personnel at the city's economic development department to explore the potential of links;
- keeping the governors fully informed of developments and fostering the recognition with them and HBP employers of the value of employer representation on the school's governing body.

The school should host a school/HBP employers' day on the completion of the HBP directory to:

- present companies with copies of the directory;
- enable displays by companies and by students centred on the work of the business park;
- create an informal, social atmosphere to facilitate contact between staff, students and employers;
- put out a 'tick box' questionnaire to employers to gain feedback on the directory project and an indication of their predisposition to ongoing school–industry links;
- invite all the school's business/industry contacts, officers of the LEA, and representatives from the whole range of community groups to raise employers' awareness of the potential networking through school-industry links.

This day could be quickly followed up with personal invitations to employer contacts to meet with staff to discuss perceptions and perspectives on school–industry links.

It is not practicable in terms of time to build and sustain 'quality links' with such diverse companies. Individual companies which demonstrate greater commitment to the nature of partnership sought could be targeted. This would increase the likelihood of successful outcomes, and thereby sustain commitment. Regular half-termly meetings could be held with individual companies.

The annual update of the directory and fieldwork on HBP should constitute a unit of work in Key Stage 3 (Year 9) Geography.

During the next two to five years the school could seek to agree formal partnership contracts with two employers on HBP.

ACKNOWLEDGEMENTS

I would like to thank the headteacher and staff of Rushton High School and the personal contacts I have at each of the companies on Highcross Business Park, for their kind help and co-operation with this project.

REFERENCES

Ball, S. J. (1987) *The micro-politics of the school – towards a theory of school organisation.* London: Routledge.

Ball, S. J. (1990) *Politics and policy-making in education – explorations in policy sociology.* London: Routledge.

Dale, R. (Ed.) (1985) *Education, training and employment – towards a new vocationalism?* Oxford: Pergamon.

Elliott, J., Bridges, D., Ebbutt, D., Gibson, R. and Nias, J. (1981) *School accountability – the SSRC Cambridge Accountability Project.* London: Grant McIntyre.

Esland, G. (Ed.) (1990) *Education, training and employment Volume 2: The educational response.* Wokingham: Addison-Wesley.

Esland, G. and Dale, R. (1986) *E333 Policy-making in education – Module 3. Industry, vocationalism and employer's needs.* Milton Keynes: Open University Press.

Glatter, R., Preedy, M., Riches, C. and Masterton, M. (Eds) (1988) *Understanding school management.* Milton Keynes: Open University Press.

Jamiesoan and Lightfoot (1982) in E333, Module 3 (1986). Milton Keynes: The Open University

Moore, R. and Broadfoot, P. (1991) *E333 Policy-making in education – Module 5. Curriculum and policy-making.* Milton Keynes: Open University Press.

Warwick, D. (Ed.) (1989) *Linking schools and industry.* Oxford: Blackwell.

Weiner, G. *et al.* (Eds) (1982) *Gender Under Scrutiny: new enquiries in education.* Milton Keynes: Open University Press.

CHAPTER 17

'Image Meets Reality': Marketing Courses for School-Leavers

JEANNE COBURN

ABSTRACT

This study looks at strategies used by an FE college to identify how it was perceived by school-leavers. The results of three small-scale projects are analysed, and suggestions made for future use of this information.

BACKGROUND INFORMATION

Charles Keene College mainly serves the city of Leicester although students come from the whole of Leicestershire. The mix of students and staff represents the cultural diversity of Leicester City. Slightly under 50 per cent of its full-time students are in the 16–19 age bracket. It has a history of working with all groups of the local community from employers to small community groups. The vocational spread is across engineering, business and management, science, humanities, the arts and sports and leisure studies. Particular strengths utilized by both the local community and local industry are engineering skills, English for speakers of other languages, equal opportunities, policy training and foreign languages. Programmes on offer range from basic education through to HND and degree-level (in association with De Montfort University) and are studied by a wide variety of modes. Following a reorganization in 1991 a new faculty (the faculty of enterprise, marketing and the community) was set up to develop and maintain proactive relationships with each market segment of the college's client base.

When I was appointed to the post of the head of the new faculty, one of my first tasks was to become acquainted with the college and its environment. In addition I had to support my division leaders, also newly appointed, in the development of their roles. These were distinctly different in nature but each with a common aim (that is community liaison leader, community education organizer, head of short courses, head of training, schools liaison officer and head of marketing services).

Each division took responsibility to reflect the college's image to their market segment and to ensure an adequate flow of information both to and from their clients. This ensures clients get information about the college quickly, regularly and effectively and that the college gets feedback efficiently from clients about the programme, quality of service image and publications to feed into our quality assurance system (see Table 17.1).

TABLE 17.1

Faculty of enterprise, marketing and the community: basic market segmentation

INDUSTRY AND COMMERCE	COMMUNITY	OVERSEAS MARKET	SCHOOLS
Employer	Recreation and leisure	EU	Pupils
Employees	Community groups	Eastern Europe	Parents
Chamber of Commerce/	Ethnic minorities	Far East	Teacher
Trade	Return to work,	Middle East	(inc. careers staff)
Business clubs	e.g. unemployed	Other	Career service
Community Business/	e.g. women		
Community Enterprise	Special needs including		
Youth business advice	people with disabilities		
	Adult training advisers		
	Training schemes [ET,		
	YT, EDEC, etc.]		
	Councillors		
	Local authority officers		
	Adult careers guidance		

It was recognized by the faculties staff and myself that the public image of the college as portrayed by the corporate literature was incompatible with the college ethos and image as perceived by staff and students. I felt it necessary to carry out a full-scale revision of the visual identity as part of an internal and external marketing drive, which would establish the faculty's place within the college, and the college within the community.

Standard texts on marketing and the newer texts on the marketing of education give useful background information on the approaches used in this case study and suggestions as how to build image and write publicity. However, every client group is different and the only way of determining their needs is to ask.

The developments outlined below have been part of the ongoing work of the faculty. The approach is always pragmatic, being a necessary balance of resources, both human and financial, theory, practice and politics, both internal and external. It should be remembered that whereas the tangible result of each stage has been a change in the way information about the college is presented to consumers, the intrinsic value has been in closer relationships with, and feedback from, the particular market segment addressed. A more detailed knowledge of what influences our clients choice can lead to improvements in our programme (new areas or new delivery modes) and better communication (particularly where evidence of misinformation is uncovered). It is also worth pointing out that this case study addresses the school-leaver market which is just one segment of the college's client group.

PROJECT ONE

Initially small groups of staff were asked to carry out a SWOT (strengths, weaknesses, opportunities and threats) analysis on the college (Table 17.2). Some were asked informally as part of discussions I had with other senior staff during my induction into the college. As part of the staff induction package given to all new staff a three-hour slot 'Marketing your Course' is given over to basic marketing training. At this I introduced the SWOT technique which, with teachers working individually, invariably produces more weaknesses and threats. By careful prompting and the pooling of ideas, enthusiasm is kindled and long lists of strengths and opportunities are produced. At the same time the first of a series of marketing audits on particular teaching divisions of the college was being carried out by the head of marketing services and a local education authority (LEA) officer. The information was pooled and the common threads summarized. As part of informal market research, members of the faculty are encouraged to discuss with students their perceptions of the college and their courses. (This is informal and completely unstructured; a separate formal course evaluation is carried out by course tutors.) The comments that came up repeatedly were the friendliness and approachability of staff, the professionalism of staff and the

TABLE 17.2
Examples of results of a SWOT analysis carried out in 1991

STRENGTHS	WEAKNESSES	OPPORTUNITIES	THREATS
Staff: friendly, welcoming professional	Work experience not universal	Incorporation Decline in birth-rate slowed	Competition from: Schools
Students: friendly, enthusiastic	Lack of detail on progression	Impartial advice *vis-à-vis* A-level or BTEC	Sixth-form college Adult education
Centre of excellence for certain provision	Difficulty in contacting school pupils	Training credits	Other FE colleges Private providers
Vocational	Traditional 36-week year (mainly)	Increasing political interest in 16-plus education	Internal competition of one course with another
Choice of work or HE as outcome	Difficulties over pastoral care for part-time students		
Adult environment			
Caring			
Multicultural			
Flexible attitude			
Accessibility of site			
Programmes for all attainment levels			
Physical environment and facilities			
Car park			

'something for everyone' welcoming atmosphere. Incidentally they make mention always of the 'hard work – but it's worth it!'

My deputy and I reviewed the sources and distilled them into key words that it was felt should be reflected in all our publicity. These were: professional; caring; approachable/accessible; multicultural; quality; forward-looking; flexible. All members of the faculty agreed that these not only reflected the college accurately but also were equally applicable to all market segments. They echoed the ethos the principal felt the college had developed. In view of the fact that the college is situated in inner-city Leicester, the multicultural slant was felt to be particularly important, and mirrored closely the ethos of the college.

Results

As a result of this preliminary work a design brief (see Table 17.3) was given to a number of design consultancies outlining the main constraints and asking for suggestions for implementation on a variety of items.

TABLE 17.3
Extract of design brief

To Incorporate	Wyvern logo, Charles Keene College, Address, Telephone nos, Fax nos, Leicester
Suggest	Implementation for range of stationery:
	Letterheads
	Compliment slips
	Business cards
	Memo pads, etc.
	Typestyle
	Paper
	Implementation for leaflet
	design (A4 sheet)
	Adverts
	Signage
	'T' shirts/sweats
	Carrier bags
	Balloons, etc.
	Files
	Later implementation for brochures, etc.
Image	Caring Approachable Professional } Quality Leicester(shire)'s College Forward-looking Flexible
Constraints	Low implementation cost. Must work in black and white for in-house production of much of the material.
Timescale	Full implementation two years Publicity within one year

During the months following the acceptance of one particular tender the new corporate stationery was introduced. The first large project was the design of a leaflet outlining full-time courses for school-leavers.

From experience we knew that this target market needs the information presented in a clear concise manner. Young people are put off by long passages of script and will not 'plough through' lots of information to find the details of the course they are interested in. Research into the decision-making process by school-leavers shows that the primary influencers of career and college choice are parents. Therefore any literature aimed at the school-leaver also has to be acceptable to parents.

It was therefore decided to produce a simple course guide containing course listings, progression routes, entry requirements and the name of the course tutor for further details. These would be aimed primarily at the 15-plus school-leavers but secondly at their parents and careers guidance staff. It was intended to use these widely at career conventions, career fairs and exhibitions; to place them at all information points, libraries and schools; and to mail them to individual enquirers with the appropriate back-up detailed course information sheets. Because of the large numbers needed, approximately 20,000 per year, a low unit cost was essential.

The design house was briefed as to our needs and that the college image and ethos was to be firmly positioned by this leaflet, the first of a range to be produced for each market segment. The leaflet was produced as a three-fold (six sides of A4 folded towards the middle) ending up as A4 size in one colour. The first cover was based on a set photograph of a group of smiling, young students showing the full cultural and gender mix of the college (see Figure 17.1).

The leaflet was very successful, being popular with staff, students and prospective students. Many people only loosely associated with the college commented positively. Over the next year it was updated and produced in a warm orange – felt by an informal poll to be a warmer and more welcoming colour. It also engendered a rash of improved leaflets from our rival colleges! To back up this factual information college newspapers were produced three times a year which contained lots of general information on a wide range of college activities and included students 'speaking' for themselves.

PROJECT TWO

There was a general concern that the college had only informally gathered views on the information we sent to schools and on the pupils' perceptions of college. As incorporation approached there was a noticeable increase in competition between colleges. I felt a more informed and formal approach was needed in order to understand the changing perceptions of potential students. The need of the local university for project-based work placements for its business studies students provided us with the ideal opportunity for the necessary research.

The advantages of using a university student for the research were many (other than the financial one for us and the offering of a live project for them). Firstly, a

FIGURE 17.1 Charles Keene brochure (before).

FIGURE 17.1 Charles Keene brochure (after).

student would be nearer in age to the school pupils and less likely to be seen as a figure of authority, therefore they would be more likely to get real answers to questions. Secondly, a university student would be more acceptable by school staff who often view further education as competition, but may view helping a student with a project as educationally valuable. The student was interviewed for the post (as is the accepted practice in order to mimic the 'real' world as closely as possible). She worked with us for just four weeks: in week one she briefed herself on the college and the project and planned visits to schools; in weeks two and three she visited four schools; in week four she wrote up the project. In addition she work-shadowed each member of the faculty for a day and helped out with the day-to-day business (mailshots, leaflet deliveries, telephone, fax, adverts, etc.). It would have been preferable to have done the planning prior to the placement but university examinations made this impossible.

Method

Research into attitudinal factors influencing choice can be carried out by a variety of methods. Quantitative methods need a well-designed questionnaire and a large sample size. Postal questionnaires get a relatively low response rate when sent to named respondents; sending a bundle to a school may well have given us no responses. Even if a large number were returned we had neither the time nor the software easily available in college to analyse the results with any degree of sophistication, neither did the student contracted to do the work.

The method chosen was to conduct small focus groups in schools from which students came to college. A range of schools were approached and four agreed to provide time to groups of 8 to 10 young people to discuss their perceptions of further education and the usefulness of the information the colleges supply. The four schools were in different areas of the city but represented the population of the city closely. They were asked to provide a typical ability, gender and ethnicity mix of 14/15-year-olds at the end of Year 10 (by this time Year 11 were on exam leave). Obviously the choice of young people had to be left to the school. It is interesting to note that, although the college offers a large link course programme, not one of the participating pupils had attended one and a disproportionate number had a stated intention of going on to A-levels.

In order to start discussion a range of prospectuses from further education colleges across Britain were handed out, followed by the course guide, newspaper and leaflet from Charles Keene College (the leaflet was brand new, in teen magazine format and in full colour produced to introduce GNVQ to school-leavers). A simple list of prompt questions was compiled, nine about the prospectuses and further education generally, six focusing on the Charles Keene literature (see Figure 17.2).

Each interview was tape recorded so that the researcher could concentrate on encouraging responses and contributions from each participant rather than on trying to note down essential points. Later, notes were made from each tape.

LITERATURE

(1) SEX: Male   Female

(2) ETHNICITY: White   Black   Other

(3) AGE: 14 years   15 years

(4) What do you feel about the print within the booklet?
Is there too much?
Is there too little?
Is it unattractive to look at?
Layout?

(5) In your opinion, does the booklet provide enough information about the college concerned; should, for example, you be interested in enrolling there?

(6) Did you find the booklet uninteresting to read/preferred to look at the illustrations instead?

PUBLICITY

(7) Did you find the illustrations unattractive/interesting to look at?

(8) What types of information and ideas would you put into a booklet if it were to be aimed at your particular age-group to make it more appealing? e.g. colour, young people, illustrations, print type

(9) Would you be interested in going to that particular college after reading the prospectus?
If yes/no Why?

CHARLES KEENE COLLEGE {underline}

(10) What interested you most about the prospectus/newspaper and GNVQ?

(11) What did you find the least interesting/most unappealing aspect about the prospectus/newspaper and GNVQ?

(12) From the three forms of advertising, which would you select as your most and least favourite?
Why?

(13) If you read a CKC prospectus/newspaper and GNVQ, would you be interested in joining a course there?
If yes/no Why?

(14) Does your opinion of the college affect the place at which you will choose to study?

(15) How many of you are considering going to sixth-form/further education establishment after completing school/college?
Number: Particular course:

FIGURE 17.2 School/college questionnaire.

Results

One of the most interesting results, although not documented, was that the university student, herself an ex-BTEC national student, did an excellent PR job informing the young people that there are other ways to higher education than the A-level route. The exercise also made another group of young people aware of the college prior to the usual careers round.

The initial analysis of the findings was carried out by the researcher and presented in a formal report. A great deal of information was recorded in the report, mostly confirming our expectations and experience as to what was preferred by young people in terms of information sources and some confirming our worst fears about the pupils' perception of further education.

> Equal opportunities – liked that/not too much information. Easily read and they liked the colours within the booklet.

> Liked the leaflet, the colours stand out – liked the pictures. It was found to be different as it tells you what is inside from the front like a magazine and attracts you.

It was at the end of the project that the real shortcomings of using an undergraduate researcher became apparent in that a detailed and succinct analysis was not presented; however, the report was detailed enough to compensate for that, although it was difficult to judge whether the weight of evidence was for or against on each point. The conclusions reached regarding college information were:

- The use of full colour and photographs was essential.
- Good, bold graphics and different typestyles were seen as positive.
- Young people should be featured, as they were not attracted by the idea of a mixed age group and would not associate with photographs of 'old' people.
- The entry requirements for courses should be made clear and they were unhappy about such statements as 'at the discretion of the tutor'.
- The right balance between too much and too little information needs to be struck.
- Student profiles and comments about the courses were appreciated.
- Clearly stated advice line numbers were appreciated.
- The clear multicultural emphasis was welcomed (by the majority).

The final general conclusion reached by the researcher was that the school pupils, all at the end of Year 10 and therefore before their in-depth careers programme, were misinformed about further education. Many of them had a negative attitude towards further education, stating that their teacher said it was not academically good, that it was a 'rubbish place to study' and that there was a 'bad atmosphere' amongst the students. However, all were impressed by the range and variety of courses.

As a result of this feedback the college redesigned the front cover of the course guide, in full colour and more in line with a 'teen' magazine. A 'mag paper' (cross between a magazine and newspaper) was planned to provide chatty magazine-style information aimed solely at the 15/16-plus market giving more information regarding choices between A-level/BTEC, school/FE and about student life and how much they enjoyed studying here. It was hoped that this would answer some of the information needs of the pupils before they made their choices and give a flavour of the bubbling enthusiasm with which current students describe the college.

PROJECT THREE

As our student researcher was finishing we were offered an opportunity to take part in an electronic focus group to assess the effectiveness of college publicity materials. The group was run by MASC, a joint venture of Maguire Associates and the Staff College. The electronic focus group (known more popularly as the 'people-meter') was first used for advertising and programme development for TV and more recently for political research. Maguire Associates have used it to provide immediate quantitative feedback on audience reactions to images messages such as those contained in prospectuses, videos and other educational marketing publications. Up to 100 members of the target audience can look at these types of material whilst each indicates their reaction by moving a dial which is wired to a computer. Their reaction may be calibrated and analysed according to any predetermined demographic variable. Responses are recorded on-line, allowing visual materials to be replayed with the graphical measurement of audience reaction overlaid on them, segmented by the chosen variable. Especially effective and ineffective images are instantly highlighted and strengths and weaknesses can be identified which are not apparent using more conventional methods.

Method

A group of approximately 50 end of Year 10 pupils from an inner-area Birmingham comprehensive school were used as the test audience. For our purposes the gender and ethnicity mix was ideal, very similar to our own immediate catchment area. The staff from the participating colleges also took part. The audience was segmented, electronically, into staff, student female, student male, student white, student of ethnic origin. The audience was then shown slides of a set of front covers, a view of the inside pages and samples of copy from each of a range of publicity. In addition three college videos were watched and audience reaction tested.

The audience was asked to move a hand-held dial between 0 and 9 for each slide and during the videos. After the slides had been shown an audience 'interview' was held with the dials being used as an agree–disagree meter. The whole proceedings were videotaped. After the pupils had left, the video was replayed with the responses overlaid on the visuals.

Results

Eleven separate items were tested, two of which were Charles Keene materials. Comments on the front pages reinforced our earlier findings that a combination of strong colour and photographs of young people enjoying themselves attracted young people. Not surprisingly female pupils reacted more strongly to photographs of young females than males but, unexpectedly, they also reacted positively to images of the building, unlike male pupils.

Again their comments on the inside pages reinforced our ideas that the informal layout was preferred (comments such as 'I like it 'cos it's not in boring straight lines'). When it came to copy, their preference was for text addressed to them ('when *you* are a student here *you* . . .'); short statements as bullet points making it easy to read; statements about success and how the college could help them with that success; information on social activities; and, again, they did not like the usual further education statement of something for everyone, they weren't very interested in crèches and studying with 'old' people (that is, over 20!).

SUMMARY

As previously stated, the approach used in these projects has been developmental; at each stage the information gained has produced a tangible improvement in our publicity material and informed our schools marketing team. Initially, the internal market (staff and existing students) was approached in a semi-structured way, the information gained being pooled to produce a design brief. It is important to note that design briefs contained details of the image to be promoted in addition to preferred layout, graphics, etc. This approach gave 'politically correct' publicity material that was very well received in college and by adults who were conversant with further education.

The second approach was to use focus groups of Year 10 pupils from representative schools, this project being run by a local university student on placement. The pupils gave their opinions frankly, no doubt encouraged by the nearness in age of the researcher. Useful information regarding publicity resulted in an increase in the use of colour (correspondingly more expensive) and graphics and informed our developing schools liaison policy.

The third approach was a new technological development of the second. Using electronic 'people-metres' the reactions of a large number of young people to publicity material can be monitored and analysed. Whilst this method proves a powerful and sophisticated tool, its widespread use would be uneconomic.

THE FUTURE

Utilizing all the information gathered will be a slow process. The more easily achieved target of rewriting the text of our leaflets is under way. The new course guide for school-leavers will contain slightly more information, have a less formal approach and will be in full colour. The college newspapers this year will be more closely targeted at different sections of our client base and will be used to reinforce a positive image of further education in general and Charles Keene College in particular.

In line with our strategic plan our schools liaison policy is being reviewed currently, both in the light of the feedback provided above and current changes in the 14–16 curriculum. We will be introducing more taster days for Year 10 and information targeted specifically at them rather than Year 11. The college staff have a tendency to distance themselves from schools, possibly from a mistaken fear of competition or just mutual suspicion. This will have to change but it will be a slow process, working individually with different schools and members of staff. The Dearing Report (1993) may well act as the catalyst for this change. We need to take as much care over the 16-plus transfer as secondary schools do over the 11-plus transfer; the college curriculum being seen as a progression from the school curriculum. At the same time, the essentially adult approach and atmosphere of an FE college must not be lost – a difficult balance to strike.

We hope to repeat the focus groups each year using a wider range of schools to chart the progress of our schools liaison policy and to forge closer relationships with our feeder schools. In addition, a similar process will be repeated with groups of unemployed adults and, hopefully, employees from our consultation committees.

ACKNOWLEDGEMENTS

We would like to thank the following: Alison Taylor, De Montfort University undergraduate; Peter Davies, The Staff College; Staff of the faculty of enterprise, marketing and the community; MASC – a joint venture of Maguire Associates and the Staff College: Maguire Associates is a market research company based in Massachusetts that has pioneered the application of the 'people-meter' electronic focus groups to education promotional materials. The Staff College is the UK's management development centre for further and higher education.

REFERENCE

Dearing, R. (1993) *The National Curriculum and its assessment. An interim report.* London: NCC and SEAC.

PART FIVE

Strategic Management

CHAPTER 18

The Deputy Head and Strategic Planning

RICHARD WEEKS

ABSTRACT

There has always been an opportunity for creative management in secondary schools. The management strategies I used in this project were formulated and are operable in the commercial world. Whilst the basic tenets of education and commerce are fundamentally different, it was, nevertheless, possible to adapt and modify strategic management practices to suit the purpose of school development. Through a carefully planned sequence of events, I was able to focus on how the educational process is perceived by pupils and parents. I then related this perception to those held by various professionals within the school and to a comprehensive examination of the current stage of development of the school. Analysis of this information allowed me to identify, with a greater degree of accuracy, what the future priorities should be for the school, and how they should be addressed.

INTRODUCTION

As deputy headteacher of Lakeside School and part of the senior management team (SMT), I have a concern for the future prosperity of the school. Prior to the Education Act 1988, our future was more or less assured by the actions of the local education authority (LEA). They gave us a student intake and a budget to work within and we didn't have to worry unduly about what effect our actions and their outcomes would have on the future. This situation has changed considerably. We have become increasingly accountable to our clients (parents and pupils); we compete directly for their custom (enrolment in our school); and rely heavily on the income which their attendance generates. Whilst striving to preserve educational and pedagogical issues as the domain of the teaching profession, the SMT have been compelled to listen more carefully to our 'consumers'. We need to find out what they want, to treat their views with respect and act appropriately in response to them. In business terms we have become 'market oriented'. I don't condemn this concept. I believe it has forced school management to become sharper and more focused and more supportive of the work of teachers and teaching teams. In turn it will, I believe, enhance the quality of the learning experience for the children.

As deputy head of Lakeside School I was conscious of these issues. I thought we were 'quite' a good school, with 'quite' good standards of academic and pastoral achievement and had within the local community 'quite' a good reputation. However, I had no factual evidence for these statements, just hearsay and the intuition that one acquires after serving in a school for 16 years. When giving thought to the following year's 'open evening', it was important to take account of our changed environment. A full intake was vital if we were to secure sufficient income to deliver the curriculum we had planned; and there were several other schools in the locality who were vying for the same intake.

It was agreed within the SMT that it would be valuable to undertake some formal research and planning to establish factual evidence. This would enable us to be in a better position both to attract a full intake and to offer them better-quality all-round educational provision. In business terms we needed to become more 'competitive'. As I was currently studying for an MBA in educational management, I offered to undertake the research. I received the full support of the headteacher who was fairly new to the post and anxious to ensure that the school was as attractive as possible to parents. My two senior deputy head colleagues, whilst not necessarily embracing the 'hard-nosed' business context within which I intended to work, did nevertheless support my actions. My job specification is fairly wide, allowing me sufficient scope for management creativity. I discussed procedures with the headteacher and established a business plan for the activity.

BACKGROUND

During the 1980s Michael Porter developed a doctrine for companies to analyse their actions and develop strategies which would give them a competitive edge (Porter, 1985). In the fast-changing world of education it is becoming apparent that some form of this approach is crucial for schools if they are to develop as successful and popular. It is from this base that I planned the work. I intended:

- to identify the current strategic position of the school. While there are many definitions of the term strategy, I defined it in the following way. Strategic position refers to the position that the school occupies in relation to its environment, that is, how well does the school function and how well does it compare with other schools in the same locality?
- through various techniques of analysis and evaluation, to decide what strategies the school needed to adopt in the future in order to increase its competitiveness within the local authority. In Porter's terms, to develop a business strategy.

Terminology such as this is often an anathema to members of the teaching profession. Consequently, there is a danger in presenting a school development package in this way. However, it is important to look beyond terminology to understand the concepts and the implications they may have. In real terms, the major issue was to ensure that the principles and processes were followed without adhering to commercial jargon. Accepting that schools now compete in a specific pupil intake market, it would seem prudent for SMTs to give some thought to their ability to compete in this market. This was my first objective. In addition, it was also my intention to establish exactly who our closest competitors were.

In commercial terms, the ability to compete is affected by criteria such as product, price, manufacturing and marketing techniques. In my context, however, whilst one assumes that factors such as exam results and facilities available are important, it was essential for me to establish the criteria for competition. Our current response to these criteria would determine our present level of competitiveness.

My second objective was to develop a business strategy. In these terms, the commercial and the educational contexts are no different. The intention is to formulate 'strategies' which allow the organization to compete as effectively as possible within the market. My focus was to use strategic planning techniques (described in more detail later) to establish future school policy.

METHOD

Before starting the work I considered three major factors. Firstly, from the outset it was vital that I offered certain assurances to the staff. I had to convince them of my principal motives. If my objectives in undertaking this strategic planning were solely to generate income or simply to become more market oriented, I would have had no support. I had to convince staff that the major purpose of the exercise was to enhance the quality of educational provision. This would be achieved by ensuring the future of the school through consolidating its popularity, its intake and, ultimately, its income generation.

Secondly, prior to the launch of the strategic planning programme, the headteacher and I discussed at length the cultural climate of our school. The work of Miles and Snow (1978) identified the varying nature and attitudes of individuals and managers within institutions. In our deliberations, we felt that ours was a school which possessed the personnel and the management framework which could accommodate such an activity. Lakeside School has a sufficiently proactive culture to rise to this challenge.

The third major factor is that of the key role of the project leader. Day (1992) asserts that the attitudes of the manager/innovator are crucial to the overall impact of culture and change. I felt that I had sufficient experience, genuine concern for the development of the school and sufficient past success in developing initiatives, to gain the general support of the staff. From this contextual basis, I felt that my actions would have credibility and that the outcomes would influence and affect future policy.

I did, however, recognize that the findings of my research might not be embraced by the school and that there might be difficulties in implementing the strategies identified. All too often in education we engage in elaborate research and development procedures, only to see the final recommendations not being implemented effectively. There are many reasons for this. These range from lack of staff ownership to an over-complex end product. I identified active implementation of the strategic plan as the major performance indicator when I came to assess the overall validity and success of the project.

In relating strategic planning to an educational situation, I chose to simplify procedures by applying only those most directly relevant to the planning process. I decided to carry out a competitive analysis followed by an environmental analysis. The results of these would enable me to produce a SWOT analysis (strengths, weaknesses, opportunities and threats) and finally a business strategy.

Competitive analysis

In introducing the topic to staff I was keen to reduce the business/market emphasis and to reassure them that what I was embarking on was more a systematic (yet subjective) approach to reviewing our circumstances. I then began work on the actual process by identifying the factors which influence parents when choosing a secondary school for their child. I will refer to these as critical success factors. This exercise would enable me to measure the strengths and weaknesses of Lakeside School and compare them with our nearest competitors. The first issue was how to identify with some degree of accuracy what the critical success factors were. The notion of what makes a good school is extremely subjective and I was conscious that perceptions of a good school can differ significantly depending upon whom you actually ask.

The major stakeholders in a school are the staff, students and parents and within each of these groups I expected a wide range of responses. Whilst it was clear that I could not approach everyone involved with the school, I attempted to lessen the impact of subjectivity by approaching a wide cross-section of people. I started with my senior management colleagues, and then moved on to teachers from different faculty areas. I chose those with differing years of teaching experience, in different posts within the formal hierarchy of the school. I then approached the students, choosing at random four classes in Year 8 since I assumed they would remember how they selected their secondary school. Each class was asked the same question: 'What issues did you and your parents feel were important when selecting your secondary school?' Their responses were similar to those factors which had already been listed by the SMT and the teachers. These activities allowed me to identify 12 key factors.

I was then able to draw up a questionnaire for parents (Figure 18.1). Along with an accompanying letter I distributed the questionnaire to all parents of current Year 7 students, with a 70 per cent completion rate.

My next task was to process all the returns to arrive at a final ranked list of critical success factors. I created a grid with the success factors down the side and a

Below is a list of factors which may be the criteria that parents use to select a secondary school. Please rank these in the order you used when you made your selection. For example, if you thought that a high level of discipline was the most important factor, then place a number 1 in the box, number your next important factor with a 2 and so on. If there are criteria that are not listed here but which you felt were important, please add them to the list, numbering them accordingly within the range of 1–12.

Facilities that the school has   [   ]

Reputation of the school within the local community   [   ]

The appearance and behaviour of students within the community   [   ]

Provision for children with special needs   [   ]

General appearance and cleanliness of the school   [   ]

Opportunities for extracurricular activities   [   ]

Past examination results   [   ]

The curriculum offered   [   ]

Distance from home to school   [   ]

Quality of the open evening   [   ]

The perceived friendly atmosphere of the school   [   ]

The perceived standards of discipline within the school   [   ]

Additional factors:

Should anyone be interested in the findings of this survey, please contact me at the school. Thank you for your help.

FIGURE 18.1   Questionnaire about parental preference when selecting a secondary school for their child.

ranking of 1 to 12 across the top and was then able to establish a ranked list.

It was clear that 'reputation of the school' was the number one choice and that 'quality of the open evening' was the least popular. Analysis of the final ranked list was very interesting. The standard assumption that 'past examination results' would be a most important criterion for parents was not borne out in my research. However, traditional attitudes towards work and behaviour were of major importance to the parents in the survey.

The vast majority of schools regard the 'open evening' as the single most important contributor to attracting new students. Consequently, schools generally invest a large amount of time, effort and resources into the occasion. From our survey it would appear that behaviour, standards of dress and attitudes of our children in the local community are the criteria many parents use in choosing a school. We recognized that other recent research had actually highlighted the opposite, that 'open evenings' were very influential in the eyes of parents. It is therefore feasible that I had failed to represent the real meaning of an 'open evening' to parents in the survey.

The next part of my research was to conduct a 'strategic group analysis', a concept first identified by Michael Hunt (1972). In a business sense this allows a company to identify the nature of the competition it faces, and who its most direct competitors are. In my own educational context I identified the characteristics of 'geographical location' and 'school type' within the LEA. This showed that we were located in an area within the authority where there was the highest density of schools of a similar type. These compete for students from a large catchment area of junior schools, and for many years there has been a lot of primary/secondary liaison activity by all the schools. More recently, this action has developed into a marketing drive by the secondaries since there were insufficient pupils to fill all the schools within the local authority. This information reinforced the fact that we did have close competition and that we needed to be a popular and successful school.

Having established a ranked order of critical success factors, and identified our closest competitors, the next task was to identify our school's strengths and weaknesses, in relation to the critical success factors, and to compare them against those of the three identified close competitors – this would provide me with my 'competitive analysis' (see Figure 18.2). The aim was to rank each of the competitors' schools out of a score of 10 (highest) on each success factor, so that direct comparisons could be made. There was a degree of subjectivity in this aspect of the exercise and I had to make every effort to minimize its impact in order to retain the validity of the exercise.

I laid out the critical success factors in ranked order and placed Lakeside School plus our three closest competitors next to them. I completed this exercise firstly by myself attempting to be as fair as possible. I began by scoring my school out of 10 on all the factors and then scoring the others by drawing direct comparisons with each in turn. Having done this, I then asked my senior colleagues to run through the exercise with me. I noted that there were only minor differences between our individual interpretations.

After assimilating the various pieces of information, I was then able to complete the competitive analysis. The results were illuminating. The indications were that we compared favourably with our competitors on the criteria identified from the research. Lack of facilities featured as a significantly weak area for us, as did the overall general appearance of the school. What was significant was the degree of similarity between ourselves and our nearest competitor school. We are geographically very close and the nature and status of our schools similar. We also draw from some of the same feeder schools.

This gave us a clear indication of the need to develop effective 'business' strategies. It was comforting to know that as a school we were already in a reasonably good competitive position. However, it was important we did not become complacent and that we maintained our 'competitive advantage' while addressing those areas where we were currently at a disadvantage. Having

CRITICAL SUCCESS FACTORS	LAKESIDE SCHOOL	SCHOOL T	SCHOOL G	SCHOOL J
Reputation of the school within the community	8	7	8	5
Perceived standard of discipline within the school	8	8	6	5
Past examination results	7	8	6	4
Facilities of the school	4	6	9	6
Appearance and behaviour of students within the community	7	7	5	5
Perceived friendly atmosphere of the school	9	9	5	5
Opportunities for extracurricular activities	7	7	8	6
The curriculum offered	8	8	8	8
Proximity of home to school	10	8	7	7
General appearance and cleanliness of school	8	9	9	7
Provision for children with special needs	9	9	8	8
Quality of the 'open evening'	9	8	9	8

Score: 10 = High

FIGURE 18.2 Competitive analysis.

completed the competitive analysis, I transferred the data into the strengths and weaknesses sections of the SWOT analysis.

Environmental analysis

The competitive analysis enabled us to identify the strengths and weaknesses of our school in relation to those of our competitors. The purpose of the environmental analysis is to identify the influences which provide either opportunities or threats for the school. The benefit of an environmental analysis is to enable organizations to keep a check on the important factors which may have an influence upon their future. In educational terms, this would include such issues as new government legislation (of which there is no shortage), population trends, the needs of the local community and changes in its socio-economic structure. Once again I chose to adopt a fairly simple procedure which would identify relevant information without gathering too much detail.

Johnson and Scholes (1989) refer to a STEP factor forecast, as a simple framework for undertaking such an audit of environmental influences. This allows the researcher to break down the influences of the environment into four factors – sociological, technological, economic and political. I felt this framework was appropriate for my work and each of my senior colleagues worked independently on a blank grid. We then met together to pool our final thoughts. Once again I collated the information to complete the final STEP forecast (Figure 18.3).

SOCIOLOGICAL	TECHNOLOGY
Growth in numbers coming through Primary School Urban Village School – heavy Community use Infant and Junior Schools on same campus 60% Asian intake & increasing Generally middle class (or aspiring)	Increased emphasis on use of Technology Increased student demand for Technological competency Increased community demand for access to Technology Courses and equipment
ECONOMIC	POLITICAL
LEA Funding Cuts LEA withdrawal of funding for Community Education Increased numbers coming to the school with inadequate resources to accomodate them Revenue from Leisure Services Sports Hall on Campus Private letting of facilities	Educational Reform Act – – National Curriculum – Local Financial Management – Increased powers to Governors – Open enrolment LEA Policies:– – Equal Opportunities – Behavioural – Attendance Increased tendency to publish Exam results and Exam leagues

FIGURE 18.3   STEP forecast for Lakeside School.

I then used the forecast to complete the opportunities and threats sections of the SWOT analysis. Accurate analysis of these factors required knowledge and judgement about a range of inter-related issues. It was our interpretation of these issues, in relation to circumstances unique to the school, that enabled us to make decisions. This type of 'internal forecasting' is an essential part of the process for any school embarking on such a course of action. Even if the factors under each heading were the same for two schools, analysis of them as opportunities and threats are likely to be quite different for each school. I completed this task with the Headteacher and we spent a lot of time discussing the implications of the factors. It became apparent that there were some factors present which could be interpreted as either threats or opportunities, depending upon how the school saw its future intentions.

In the forecast, I regarded all the 'sociological' factors as opportunities to enhance our intake. The recent withdrawal of LEA community funding meant that I could justifiably have placed the 'heavy community use' factor in the 'threats' column only. However, as the school management's intention was to maintain a commitment to further enhance our community use, I chose to view this also as an opportunity. 'Technological' issues (particularly those of resourcing) had been giving us cause for concern. However, we had been addressing these issues for 12 months – therefore it was feasible to view them now as further opportunities.

'Economic' issues were a great concern for us, therefore these factors featured as significant threats. 'Political' factors proved difficult to place. Development of the National Curriculum and the flexibility afforded us by the delegated budget were finally recognized as opportunities. Publication of exam results and league tables are new phenomena – we felt it was too early to establish whether this would be an opportunity or a threat so entered them in both columns.

The SWOT analysis

Johnson and Scholes (1989) highlight the value for a business to conduct a SWOT analysis. Through an identification of its strengths and weaknesses in relation to its competitors, and the opportunities and threats posed by its environmental influences, a company is then able to analyse its future business strategy. It was my intention to establish the same degree of information from my analysis. Having now completed all four columns of the analysis, I chose to fine tune them by weighting the entries. As can be seen from the completed analysis (Figure 18.4), the extent of the strength, weakness, opportunity or threat is identified by a 1, 2 or 3 with the latter being a substantial influence. The head and I ranked each factor and once again there was a degree of subjectivity involved.

STRENGTHS	WEAKNESSES
Reputation of the school (1)	Facilities that the school has (2)
Standards of discipline (1)	
Past examination results (2)	Facilities that the sixth form has (3)
Locality to catchment area (3)	
Quality of the open evening (1)	General appearance/cleanliness of
Friendly atmosphere of school (2)	the school (1)
Provision for children with special	
needs (1)	
Established 14–16 vocational	
programme (2)	
Established sixth form (2)	

OPPORTUNITIES	THREATS
Growth in numbers in primary schools (2)	LEA funding cuts (2)
Urban village school/heavy community use (2)	LEA withdrawal of funding for community use (3)
Infant/junior school on same campus	
50% Asian intake and increasing (1)	Increased numbers with
Increased emphasis/use and competency of technology (1)	inadequate resources (2)
Increased emphasis on 16-plus education (2)	16–18 provision in competitor schools and sixth-form
Fewer job opportunities (2)	college (3)
Revenue from lettings and sports hall (2)	
Education Reform Act/LEA policy (1)	Publishing exam results and league tables (2)
Publishing exam results and league tables (3)	

FIGURE 18.4 Environment SWOT analysis.

Competitive (business) strategy

Before analysing the SWOT and identifying a future strategy, it is vital that a school recognizes what its overall objectives are. These should be available through the school development plan. I noted that one of our prime objectives was to sustain six forms of entry which we had achieved for the first time in the previous year. Through the SWOT analysis and the observations made during the course of the analysis, it was possible for us to focus on a number of specific issues to achieve this (and other) objectives.

Research had shown that we were responding well to key educational issues and, in relation to other schools in the locality, we were in a strong market position. The strengths of Lakeside School had been identified as key factors for parents when making their choice of secondary school. Our place within the community was an opportunity for development. The main weaknesses and threats facing the school were ones of resourcing and, ironically, potential overpopulation.

I reported the results of the SWOT analysis and the summary of the findings of my research to the SMT. We gave thought specifically to identifying factors which would have a direct bearing on the quality of the educational experience we offered our students. In addition, we chose to address the issues which were not currently receiving any attention in strategic terms. The outcome of our deliberations was to arrive at six fairly precise objectives which we intended to pursue during the next two academic years (see Figure 18.5). The objectives were framed

---

OBJECTIVES

- Improve links with feeder primary schools

- Research and develop curriculum provision and monitor academic standards, in particular
    National Curriculum at Key Stage 4
    Cross-curricular issues

- Research and develop vocational courses at 16-plus

- Attract daytime users to leisure/academic/vocational courses

- Develop links with industry

- Upgrade facilities – enhance the quality of the learning environment, particularly for the sixth form

---

FIGURE 18.5 **Objectives.**

within the context of improving our provision and enhancing our competitiveness.

It is interesting to see that the objectives include primary and industry links, as well as adult links and varied curricular provision. These fitted well with our 'community' ideal. In real terms they added to the existing intentions identified in the school development plan and, more specifically, they added a sharper focus to our future strategy. The objectives which were identified responded directly to the outcome of the SWOT. It was at this point that the concept of cultural climate became important.

It is easy for school SMTs to sit round a table, and come up with marvellous ideas for enhancing the effectiveness of a school. The key issues are who will implement the ideas, and how well will this be done?

For each objective, with the aid of the key personnel involved, I drew up a development and implementation plan. I formed teams and team leaders and encouraged as much staff and pupil involvement as possible.

The extent to which these objectives would be realized depended on a number of variables. These relate to issues of personnel management, whether or not a 'change' culture exists within a school, and whether the developments were given a sufficiently high priority – particularly by the SMT. It was vital that they featured as priorities within the school development plan, and that this concept was acknowledged within the school as a tool for positive planned development.

After a period of 18 months I can see tangible indicators of some success being achieved in each of the six objectives. The processes involved in realizing these targets have also had their impact. There appears to be a growing sense of purpose and pride within the school, from both staff and students, and a real desire to continue moving forward. Although it has been informal, I have received positive feedback from some parents involved in the exercise. The new intake is at its highest ever, and the new sixth form is the largest it has ever been. What began in a business-oriented context has, by design, given clearly identifiable educational outcomes and benefits. This has, in turn, made us much more competitive and ensured a strong market position.

CONCLUSIONS

The successful outcome of the project was determined by certain factors, some of which could be shaped and influenced by the change manager, and others embedded in the nature and ethos of the school. The culture of a school needs to be able to accommodate the concepts behind such a venture and to embrace the change process itself. The formal hierarchical structure of some schools perpetuates bureaucratic processes, and members of such institutions may be disinclined to be involved in such a process or may feel tied down to a system which does not encourage them to be innovative. Schools, and particularly SMTs, must be committed to the idea of encouraging initiative and embracing failure.

It is important that a school recognizes its own unique circumstances. While some initiatives will be imposed from above, future planning for a school must be an internal affair. It is essential to plan according to the local environment, the nature of the pupils and the local community, and the values and attitudes of the staff.

Whilst the need for change is easily identified, establishing change is a much more difficult task. The value of a school development plan cannot be overstated. A regular and formal process of review and planning, identifying objectives and responding to them as a matter of course, is essential. Such a whole-school management approach, with everyone aware of the short-term goals of the school is much more likely to bring about positive and lasting change. Other factors can be directly influenced by the leader of the project. Examples of these are as follows:

- To implement a strategy drawn totally from commercial marketing techniques could have been disastrous. Teachers do not see themselves as industrialists, nor do they regard their institution and their professional activities as one which should be dictated by market forces. They do not think of students and parents as 'consumers', and they do not regard the outcomes of their creative labours as profit driven. They do, however, recognize the need for enhancing educational opportunities, the quality of provision and the quality of the learning environment. If such a project is to be successful it must adapt commercial marketing techniques to meet educational objectives.
- The person conducting the exercise needs to have a proven record of innovative practice. Support from staff is arrived at through the validity of the exercise and the esteem in which they hold the project leader.
- It is essential that staff involved feel a sense of ownership. If they are distanced from decision-making and action planning and consider they do not have the opportunity to express their views, it is unlikely their support and enthusiasm will be maintained. This became increasingly crucial when teams were formed to pursue the objectives which had been identified.
- SMT must lend the exercise their support. I also benefited from the full and active support of the headteacher.

Finally one's own enthusiasm, commitment and energy are quite clearly important. Whilst I identified with the business element of the task, the educational skills required for implementation were also of equal importance. In this case strategic and educational planning worked harmoniously together.

POSTSCRIPT

I would like to thank the senior management and staff of Lakeside School. Also Inger Boyett, course director, MBA, Nottingham University; Don Finlay, lecturer, MBA, Nottingham University; Janet Magee, for professional advice; and Audrey Bullard, for secretarial assistance.

REFERENCES

Day, C. (1992) *Promoting development culture in schools and colleges.* Nottingham University.
Hunt, M. S. (1972) Competition in the major house appliance industry 1960–1976. Doctoral dissertation, Harvard University.
Johnson, G. and Scholes, K. (1989) *Exploring corporate strategy – text and cases.* New York: Prentice Hall.
Miles, R. and Snow, C. (1978) *Organisational strategy, structure and process.* New York: McGraw Hill.
Porter, M. (1985) *Competitive advantage.* New York: Free Press.

CHAPTER 19

One School's Response to Parental Choice

ERIC MEADOWS

ABSTRACT

This case study looks at issues of responsiveness in a primary school faced with a falling roll. It shows the tension between values and professional judgement and market realities, with action being problematic since participants have differing needs and perceptions. The process began before the period described and it has not finished yet. The stages depicted span approximately one term each, over a period of a little more than a school year.

INTRODUCTION

The change agent has been headteacher for 10 years of Mareton County Primary School. This group 3 school has two forms of entry, and a capacity for 470 children with a present roll of 453. There is also a local education authority (LEA)-funded facility for 16 pupils with specific learning difficulties.

Until recently, Mareton experienced steadily increasing rolls. However, there was now a fall in numbers of entrants to the school, with consequent under-subscription, and some drift of children to other nearby schools, particularly a new church primary school. The roll was projected to fall to 430 in the next academic year. Several of the specific learning difficulty (SLD) facility children also had behavioural difficulties, which concerned some parents, who viewed it as the unnecessary importation of problems. There had been recent cases of children removed because of incidents between them and SLD children.

Mareton's natural catchment zone is bordered by main roads to east, west, and south, and a bypass and open downland to the north. The zone cannot sustain two forms of entry and the school depends upon attracting children from further away. Many parents are professionals, with two cars, and the means of shopping widely for the 'best' education. Many have high academic expectations. A proportion appreciated that the school was a 'caring' one, prepared to take on children with problems. Others seemed concerned only with their own children's academic progress.

The local birth-rate was buoyant and there was no evidence that the potential roll should fall. The five closest schools either had added further forms of entry in recent years or had the capacity to expand. Four of them had nursery classes and the fifth ran a thriving playgroup. This left Mareton, with no spare capacity, somewhat hemmed in. However, unlike four of these schools, Mareton had the perceived advantage to parents that it was an all-through primary school. Results and standards were comparable with the neighbouring schools.

Four classes were housed in two double-prefabs, one being 30 years old and in very poor condition. Some governors, staff and parents preferred that the accommodation used by the SLD facility be made available for a nursery class. The parent/staff association, the Friends of Mareton, was able to raise some £3,000 per year. The governors had set aside £10,000 for the specific purpose of building improvement.

A questionnaire seeking parental opinion, issued by the marketing committee to a random sample of about 20 per cent of the parents, with a 50 per cent return, revealed a desire for a nursery class from those with younger children. The school's general standards, its good communications, its friendly atmosphere and openness were all valued. The SLD facility was thought to attract too many difficult children. The uniform policy was regarded as too casual. There was some feeling that the school had grown too big too rapidly, with a consequent strain on accommodation and traffic and parking difficulties. There was general criticism about the condition of the old prefabs.

Despite the SLD facility occupying space which could otherwise be used for preschool provision, the head had been personally responsible for its creation and development. He was proud of the caring emphasis it promoted and was aware also that it contained teaching expertise from which the school benefited.

The roll seemed to be falling because of a combination of some of the more negative perceptions, coupled with increased competition from other schools, including the new church school, with streaming, and more formal uniform and discipline.

NATURE OF DESIRED CHANGE

The headteacher was concerned about the falling market share. In his judgement, a two-form entry school represented an optimum use of resources and, judging from the period when the school was smaller, mixed-year classes were unpopular both with parents and teachers.

The problems impacting to a greater or lesser extent on the falling roll could be grouped into related issues, each having an anticipated difficulty.

Nursery education

There was parental demand for a nursery class which was seen as an educational 'good' and a magnet. The neighbouring schools had such provision or, in one case, a playgroup. Few parents changed their child's school at five, if they were satisfied with the earlier experience. Relationships would have been formed by children and parents. A nursery place would be free of charge and it would enable both parents to work, vital for many of the families.

Despite educational and social advantages, parental demand and the realization of its importance in market appeal, there was no spare space. The local playgroups would regard any such development as a threat to their existence.

SLD facility

The facility contributed towards Mareton's caring image. However, there were negative parent perceptions, shared by some of the staff and governors: it did take up space which could be used for a nursery class, it did affect SAT results, and it contained disturbed children who took up more than their share of teacher time. The head saw no necessary dichotomy between a caring and an academic approach, and was not prepared to see the facility go. However, the antipathy shown by some parents was causing governors and staff to question whether the problems outweighed the advantages. The head knew those concerns had to be addressed.

Accommodation

Few regarded the school's accommodation as satisfactory. The roll had grown from 230 to 450 in ten years, without matching increase in physical resource. The hall was barely adequate. Toilets were hardly sufficient. One year group was housed in dilapidated prefabs. The infant playground was very small. The campus was sizeable but lacking in interest. Any improvement would be too expensive to be resourced from the school's own budget. LEA help was uncertain.

Traffic

The entrances to the school were along a narrow road, made more narrow by residents' parked cars. Problems to do with traffic flow and parental parking were annoying the local residents and also some of the older parents who remembered a smaller and therefore 'better' school. A one-way system and requests for more considerate parking by parents seemed the only improvements possible.

Uniform

School uniform was optional and worn by about half of the pupils. The head had an aversion to uniformity of any kind and favoured an individual approach to dress. He was not prepared to exert pressure for a more formal dress policy. With such diverging views, it seemed impossible to please everybody!

LITERATURE REVIEW

Drucker (1989) defines a manager as 'someone who achieves his or her objectives through other people's hands and minds'. Here there was the considerable challenge to win over the collective hands and minds of varied groups with views conflicting with those of the head. Two were inside the school: some staff and governors. Those outside were parents, residents, local playgroups and the LEA.

According to Newton and Tarrant (1992), 'the core function of leadership is change'. They agree with Kakabadse *et al.* (1988) who say that 'the more able managers seek to change their environment and adopt a more proactive approach', initiating, devising and implementing plans rather than simply implementing responses. They indicate the need for 'visionary objectives', sufficiently precise to give direction and guidance to further action. Fullan (1991) points to the importance of internalizing the change: 'You have to try to take people with you.' According to Handy (1976), a change agent diagnoses, examines the variables – their context, their interaction, how they may be influenced – and builds appropriate strategies, which include creating an awareness of the need for change . . . and also being prepared to accept a less than optimum strategy in the interests of achieving something rather than nothing.

Havelock (1970) sees the three primary change agent roles, not mutually exclusive, as catalyst, solution giver, and process helper. It is important to understand the process of change, the points of leverage, the most efficient channels, and the best times, places and circumstances for facilitating change.

Scott (1989) mentions four aspects of responsiveness – political authority, market, professional values and obligations, and the cultural imperatives of truth, rationality, and knowledge. This case study has mainly to do with market and professional responsiveness which, as shown, may conflict.

According to Gray (1989), educational institutions must respond to the needs and demands of a variety of clients (for example, parents and employers) and customers (students). Key words include 'responsiveness', 'market-oriented approach', 'choice', 'customer satisfaction', 'parent power' and 'competition'. But there is controversy as to who legitimately defines the needs of the client groups.

Hoy and Miskel (1989) discuss open systems theory and distinguish between general and specific environments, both of which influence internal structures and processes. General environments comprise broad factors, trends and conditions which potentially affect organizations, such as political structures, social and economic factors and demographic characteristics. Specific environments have immediate and direct effects on the organization and, in this case study, they include parents, other schools, residents, playgroup leaders and the LEA.

Internally, they include the staff, the governing body and the Friends of Mareton.

Bush (1989) makes the case for not relying exclusively on experience and common sense, but for developing a 'conceptual pluralism' – a systematic appreciation of theory which broadens the conceptual base for decision-making.

In taking a proactive stance to the challenges outlined above, the strategies used are based on some knowledge of the participants and the external and internal contextual factors, informed by the head's values and beliefs, his experience and whatever common sense he possesses, and some application of change theory. Informing the conceptual base is an acceptance that, like politics, management is the art of the possible.

Initially there was a clear 'visionary objective' (Newton and Tarrant, 1992) and the head was problem recognizer, solution giver and process helper (Havelock, 1970) all at the same time. This was partly because the various challenges became stronger around the time that the governing body was undergoing large-scale change. Changes in role emphasis, as the process continued, could be explained by reference to the contingency model (Lawrence and Lorsch, 1967), where managers act responsively, relating the decision-making process to the nature of the particular event or situation.

The study reveals strong and conflicting personal and professional views and concerns. Hoyle (1989), in a study of micropolitics in education, shows how the interests of individuals tend to coalesce, leading to the formation of interest sets.

The debate about the SLD facility is an indication of the differing expectations placed upon education institutions by consumers. Morrison and Ridley (1989) review educational ideologies – student, knowledge and society based – and discuss the conflicting demands faced by an institution which depends upon successfully serving a pluralist society.

THE EARLY STAGE IN THE CHANGE PROCESS

Nursery education

Plans to develop a nursery class had been proceeding for some years, with the previous governing body, who had agreed the objective. As other schools developed their own provision, demand intensified. An option being explored was combining the local public library, in the building, with the school library, so releasing space.

At this time about half of the governors reached the end of their term. The new governing body contained several new to governing, including the two teacher members. In the course of the unsuccessful negotiations with the public library service, an outline emerged for a relatively cheap addition to the main building, over an existing flat roof. The head, supported by some of the 'old' governors, but with the governing body as yet unconsulted, wrote asking parents to join in raising funds. He was influenced by the following factors:

- Building prices were depressed, there were several parent builders prepared to work at cost, and an architect/governor prepared to give his services.
- The Friends would be otherwise committed, having just been asked, with less than ideal timing, to finance playground improvements.
- The LEA could reasonably be asked to make a major contribution, in view of an earlier interest in matching funds and as it would avoid the necessity of carrying out expensive roof repair at the proposed site.
- Extra toilets could be incorporated.
- There were parent connections and it was possible that some sponsorship could be attracted.

SLD facility

Whilst making his commitment to special needs clear, the head decided to give more time to advertising the benefits of the additional resources, to associate care and good values, to demonstrate that caring was not incompatible with high standards, and to do more to celebrate successes, using the weekly parent update, the weekly open assembly, the governors' annual meeting with parents and as a focus for display within the school. He began to intervene in behavioural problems more directly, making it explicit that children have the right to be protected and to learn, and that teachers have a right to teach.

Accommodation

The Friends had long sought involvement in a major project. The head asked them to fund the campus development and, after determined selling including a parents' and governors' meeting, they agreed, aiming to complete within about three years, during which time the school could expect no further assistance.

The head encouraged the governors to persuade the LEA to replace the old prefabricated building. A survey report showing that repair was feasible was challenged. LEA capital programmes showed no intention to carry out such repair in the next year or two. A meeting with the chief education officer (CEO), the chair of governors and the head produced an awareness of other major problems facing the LEA, and a promise to look more closely at the condition of the prefab. To keep his options open, the head established that the cost of a triple prefab was not greatly more than that of a double.

Traffic

The premises committee renewed efforts to bring about a one-way system, but objections from sufficient local residents prevented this being approved. After consultations with the community policeman and the premises committee, the head asked parents to follow a voluntary one-way system. Some did so and there was slight improvement, but the voluntary system could not legally be enforced and created its own difficulties. The update was used to encourage parents to set down or collect children using other nearby roads, and to respect rights of residents when parking, but with mixed compliance the situation remained troubled.

Uniform

The marketing committee included governors who agreed philosophically with the head. It was accepted that the present casual approach was problematic, however, and they agreed to design a more attractive uniform which children would want to wear. The result was a choice of five colours with a discrete logo, and the wearing of uniform became widespread. Judging from random feedback, parents seemed well satisfied with the new policy.

THE SECOND STAGE

Concerns about the SLD facility persisted, and parent-governors were particularly targeted by disaffected parents. There were the continuing playground and classroom problems involving its children; and many parents asked why the facility should be housed within the main building, when two classes were having to manage in the old prefab. With opposition to do with nursery education, accommodation and traffic also coming together in an unanticipated way, there followed a painful period for the head and governors.

The Friends were disturbed that parents were now being asked to contribute towards nursery building, at a time when the committee was already working flat out to finance the ongoing campus work. Times were hard and parents could not be expected to be able to fund two such major projects. Many parents of older children objected to the idea of a nursery class, feeling that the site was already overcrowded and, if new money was available, it should be devoted to repairing or replacing the old prefabs, to enlarging the hall, to reducing class sizes and to extending playground space.

A petition was sent to the CEO, signed by parents, local residents, and playgroup leaders, objecting to the addition of a nursery class and to further growth of the school. Numerous individual letters were also sent. It was subsequently discovered that the main playgroup was behind much of this action. The CEO divulged that they had lobbied him and the local councillors. To add to the misery, the LEA published a paper showing Mareton as 23rd of 23 schools which had applied for a nursery class. The school was low on the social priority scale, unlike other schools had no room awaiting conversion, and objections received from within the community had influenced the education committee.

Some 'new' governors, worried about the stirring up of feelings, questioned being committed to a nursery class. Several had been approached by parents threatening to take their children away if one were added. To this the parent governors added their concerns about the SLD facility. At an ensuing meeting of the governing body, the head devoted considerable time and energy to reselling the idea of a nursery class, or at least some form of preschool provision. This involved persuading some that there was a solution for the infrastructure-related concerns and that, with the school's market situation, such provision was vital. He reiterated his commitment to the SLD facility, sharing his belief that present measures would work, given time. Some governors gave critical support, saying that they had sent their children to Mareton because it was a caring school.

In both matters, the head's task was made more difficult because it was known that some of the staff had views that differed from his. There was eventual agreement to support him, but it was hard won, and much could depend upon market outcomes.

THE FINAL STAGE IN THE CHANGE PROCESS

With regard to linked concerns about nursery education and accommodation, the head's first reaction was to try to correct what he saw as misinformation. For example, there was no new money to be used as the school wished.

In a letter to the chair of governors he wrote:

> Obviously opposition is to be expected from those with vested interest who feel threatened and it is also true that a proportion of those who most strongly want a nursery are as yet only potential parents of the school. . . . But the balance of educational opinion, both here and nationally, is strongly in favour.

He urged that governors 'seek to analyse the various currents of thought'. In his view, 'the governors have to be responsive, but also need to have a sense of purpose – a vision of the sort of school they wish Mareton to become'.

The marketing committee met to address the concerns and to frame a response to the parents. It was felt that not all governors were fully committed to the idea of a nursery class. Certainly several had continued to express sympathy towards some of the objections. It was decided to refer the matter back to yet another meeting of the governing body.

With his management team the head was preparing a new four-year school management plan, to be presented at this next meeting. They worked on a building development plan, the success of which depended upon replacement of the old prefab with a triple building, with toilets. In the extra classroom then available, a nursery class or playgroup could be housed. The site enabled the creation of a new small outdoor playspace and even a new school entrance, but from the same narrow road. The plan included a second phase, when resources permitted, for the building of a small hall over the flat roof originally earmarked for the nursery room, where there was adequate space.

The plan, which addressed the concerns to do with overcrowding in the main building, the old prefabs, and play and hall space, was accepted. The head then arranged a site meeting between architect/governor and county architect, to discuss the condition of the old building and its possible replacement with a triple prefab. The architects agreed that repair was not feasible and within a few weeks a plan had been produced for a replacement triple building. No agreement to replace had been reached, but there was a feeling of optimism.

The head and chair wrote jointly to the CEO, pointing out that there was an earmarked sum in the school's budget for building development, representing the difference between a double and a triple prefab. This resulted in a firm agreement to replace with a triple before the next school year commenced. The governors decided that, as the school did not rank high in the LEA's priority list and so would not be funded for a nursery class, the extra room would be used for playgroup development.

Serendipity then took a hand. The LEA announced that the nearest nursery school was to close since, with the saving of head and deputy salaries, for the same cost double the number of children could benefit from nursery education in school-attached classes. Mareton was in a good position to benefit, since the education committee had promised to place three new nursery classes in the local area.

In reaction to the abortive attempt to create a legal one-way system, residents had approached their county councillor, protesting that their life would be disrupted. They also told her that communications with the school were poor; they were not kept informed about its plans.

Learning this, the head looked again at the campus, which was bounded by housing on two sides and by the residents' road on a third. The road on the fourth side was part of a loop system, and little used for parking. He had a gateway constructed, in this fourth side, and two paths marked, leading to each of the playgrounds. Parents were encouraged to use this new entrance and the residents were informed. Many families approached from this direction, there was little trouble in setting down or picking up in the loop road, and difficulties in the school road eased a little more.

DISCUSSION AND ANALYSIS

The addition of a playgroup, and possibly a nursery class, looked likely to satisfy parental demand and thus weaken the market threat from local, rival schools. A nursery class could be vital, however. The revised siting, combined with the additional entrance, allayed parental fears of site congestion and also helped to alleviate resident concerns about traffic and parking. Since the new triple building would contain its own toilets, and was to be built mainly from LEA money, parents were shown that the needs of existing children were not being neglected. This process was helped by making public the school management plan with the intention to work towards an additional hall, and also by the Friends' previous agreement to resource the campus improvements.

Concerns over the SLD facility continued to trouble. It could not be ignored that some wanted Mareton to be an academic school with strong discipline (Morrison and Ridley, 1989). Unless the measures taken succeeded with the concerned parents, threat of removal or choosing another school remained (Westoby, 1989).

Although nearly every change seemed to be on the way towards achievement, the process was eventful and painful. In its course, residents and certain elements of the parent body and of the Friends were estranged or taken for granted.

It was unfortunate that it was necessary to convince some staff and governors of the value of the SLD facility and to persuade the governors to readopt the preschool/nursery target, at a time when internal energies needed to be concentrated to counter external threat.

Because perceptions and values varied, some of this was inevitable. As mentioned, the governing body changed radically at a crucial time, with several of the new governors unaware of the previous commitment to preschool provision, unsure of their own position, troubled by external protest, and aware that doubts had been expressed by a few of the staff, including the two new teacher-governors. The head's determination to see the changes through led at times to a naively optimistic approach to the change process, and a certain ignoring of democratic processes.

Playgroup relations represented the most unsuccessful element in the process, as it now seemed to be concluding. They feared that the competition would lead to their closure. Their community connections enabled them to organize a formidable coalition of interest sets (Hoyle, 1989), with parents of older children and residents. They successfully linked the traffic and perceived accommodation difficulties with the growth of the school and the proposed further growth, in the form of a nursery class. It was doubtful whether this conflict could have been avoided. However, playgroups offered only morning sessions and, together, they and the school could provide a comprehensive whole-day preschool system for the community and beyond. This remained a target for the head in the reconciliation period ahead.

Certain approaches were abandoned as the process unfolded, and others changed (Lawrence and Lorsch, 1967). This was because of strategic necessity: in order to get somewhere, flexibility and change of tactics were required, partly because not all elements and attitudes could be foreseen. As Handy (1976) mentions, it is important to have ambition, but it is also important to settle for what one can achieve. One lives in order to fight again. Looking at some of these:

- The nursery class became a playgroup, with possibility of further development.
- In the process, the site originally identified was changed, because of objections about overcrowding.
- Finance sought, rather optimistically, from parents and sponsors, was to come from the LEA, supplemented from the school's reserves.

- The attempt to bring about a compulsory one-way traffic system was replaced by a voluntary one.

These examples can be seen partly as a growth in situational understanding on the part of the head, and partly as a responsive application of the contingency theory (Bolman and Deal, 1989), according to which there is institutional dependence upon the environment.

CONCLUSIONS

The head set out to:

- Provide a nursery class. A classroom was to be gained for preschool use, possibly nursery use, at a cost of some strain with some parents and the Friends and worsening of relations with the local playgroups.
- Dispel the perception that the SLD facility represented more pain than gain. Given differing demands and expectations, the extent to which the problem had apparently been contained was deemed satisfactory by the head. The caring/ academic dialectic seemed quiet but dissatisfaction still simmered (Morrison and Ridley, 1989).
- Show agreement with parents that the old prefabricated classrooms were unacceptable and must be replaced. This was achieved, using the school management plan (SMP) as a strategic tool, linking prefab, nursery, toilets, and playground issues, at the same time obtaining commitment from the new and hesitant governors.
- Tackle traffic congestion. Other than a voluntary one-way system and continued appeals for polite parking, this could not yet be said to have succeeded. Much depended upon the effectiveness of the new school entrance. In the course of this, the degree to which residents were alienated was discovered, and thus efforts to bring about better relations could be commenced.
- Increase the wearing of school uniform. Most children now wore uniform and it was one which pleased almost everybody.

All these issues were linked with the worry over a falling market share. In this connection, no children had left recently for other school or facility-related reasons, and the roll was steady. The competition was intense, however, and the head intended to watch trends very carefully. He felt that the change process had brought a greater awareness to governors and staff.

If Mareton did finally receive its nursery class, it would be the result of chance as well as planned change. The closing of the nursery school had not been anticipated. It affected all schools seeking such development, with Mareton being geographically closest and therefore very likely to benefit. The school's long negotiations with the LEA had helped to build a favourable climate for such a change.

It was not the intention to create an opposing coalition of interest sets (Hoyle, 1989), to alienate playgroup leaders, residents, and some parents, including the parent – staff association. Nor was it foreseen that there would be internal debate with some of the teaching staff and with new and inexperienced governors.

In all cases but one, however, there was proof of the Confucian adage 'In every loss there is a gain.' The exception was school – playgroup relations where at least problems and concerns were out in the open. Any gain lay in the uncertain future, and it depended upon the forging of a partnership approach between rival institutions, operating in a similar market. The opportunities this could bring have already been mentioned.

The strengths of the performance of the head as change agent included thinking creatively when in crisis, as exemplified by his use of the school management plan and the notion of a new entrance, his power to influence, as in dealings with governors, his readiness to try to understand conflicting demands, as with the SLD facility, and his ability to divide opposition into manageable parts (Handy, 1976; Havelock, 1970). At times he felt alone and isolated in seeing the nature of the problems faced by the school. His 'visionary objective' (Newton and Tarrant, 1992) – the type of school he wanted Mareton to be – was not shared by all. But he showed vital change agent qualities of resolution and pertinacity.

His weaknesses included paying insufficient attention to communications with some of the participants in this process. It could not be right that residents were made to feel ignored by the school, that neither the Friends nor the majority of governors were consulted with before the first request for financial support was sent out. Nor was opposition envisaged from parents to the idea of a nursery. In such a vital yet difficult process, with many factions and vested interests, allies were necessary. For a time there were very few. These weaknesses stemmed from a certain 'pioneering naivety' and from a belief that time was short, change was necessary and someone had to drive it through regardless. This coupled with an absolute determination to see a nursery class at Mareton (Newton and Tarrant, 1992), led to overenthusiasm and end-gaming which, occasionally, deterred some of those on whom he depended.

RECOMMENDATIONS

The events, in what turned out to be a complex, unpredictable, and frustrating change process, with its share of disappointment and excitement, support Whitaker's (1993) assertion that the leader can aspire to little more than 'high-quality fumbling'. Nevertheless, reflection on the whole process reveals the undoubted need to plan, to inform, to involve and to share, to a far greater extent.

Collegiality (Bush, 1989) involves time and a search for understanding and shared values. The head felt the market situation to be such that things had to be done promptly. He never doubted his 'visionary objectives' (Newton and Tarrant, 1992) and frequently adopted a rather too bureaucratic style of leadership (Bush, 1989) with its attendant pitfalls. Perhaps, with a better balance between action and reflection, several of the difficulties encountered could have been avoided or managed more effectively, with a consequent improvement in the quality of the head's fumbling.

REFERENCES

Bolman, L. G. and Deal T. E. (1989) Organizations, technology and environment, in R. Glatter (Ed.) *Educational institutions and their environments: managing the boundaires*. Milton Keynes: Open University Press.

Bush, T. (1989) The nature of theory in educational management, in T. Bush (Ed.) *Managing education: theory and practice*. Milton Keynes: Open University Press.

Drucker, P. (1989) The spirit of performance, in C. Riches and C. Morgan (Eds) *Human resource management in education*. Milton Keynes: Open University Press.

Fullan, M. G. (1991) (with Stiegelbauer, S.) *The new meaning of educational change*. London: Cassell.

Gray, L. (1989) Marketing educational services, in R. Glatter (Ed.) *Educational institutions and their environments: managing the boundaries*. Milton Keynes: Open University Press.

Handy, C. (1976) *Understanding organisations*. London: Penguin Books.

Havelock, R. G. (1970) *A guide to innovation in education*. Michigan: Ann Arbor.

Hoy, W. K. and Miskel, C. G. (1989) Schools and their external environments, in R. Glatter (Ed.) *Educational institutions and their environments: managing the boundaries*. Milton Keynes: Open University Press.

Hoyle, E. (1989) The micropolitics of schools, in T. Bush (Ed.) *Managing education: theory and practice*. Milton Keynes: Open University Press.

Kakabadse, A., Ludlow, R. and Vinnicombe, S. (1988) *Working in organisations*. London: Penguin Books.

Lawrence, P. and Lorsch, J. (1967) *Organisations and environment*. Boston: Harvard Business School (quoted in Bolman, L. G. and Deal, T. E. (1989) see above).

Morrison, K. and Ridley, K. (1989) Ideological contexts in curriculum planning, in M. Preedy (Ed.) *Approaches to curriculum management*. Milton Keynes: Open University Press.

Newton, C. and Tarrant, T. (1992) *Managing change in schools*. London: Routledge.

Scott, P. (1989) Accountability, responsiveness and responsibility, in R. Glatter (Ed.) *Educational institutions and their environments: managing the boundaries*. Milton Keynes: Open University Press.

Westoby, A. (1989) Parental choice and voice under the 1988 Education Reform Act, in R. Glatter (Ed.) *Educational institutions and their environments: managing the boundaries*. Milton Keynes: Open University Press.

Whitaker, P. (1993) *Managing change in schools*. Buckingham: Open University Press.

CHAPTER 20

Strategic Planning in the Changing External Context

TERRY COWHAM

ABSTRACT

This case study investigates the process of developing strategic planning at SuperTec, a large further education college in the centre of a conurbation, which has recently been reorganized and, even more recently, incorporated. The study examines the developments in the context of external change, focused on the developing requirements of the Further Education Funding Council, at a time of rapid change and turbulence both for the college and for the sector in general. A theoretical perspective is provided to support the analysis taken from a number of sources which address theories and models of management applied to educational institutions. The events took place at a critical time for further education colleges during the first year of incorporation under the Further Education Funding Council (FEFC). This was a period of intense and rapid change.

INTRODUCTION

For this study I acted as an internal consultant, with the agreement of senior management, to investigate and report on the development of strategic planning at the college during the first 18 months of incorporation.

My role within the college is senior lecturer in the department of human resource development, which involves me in delivering in-house staff development programmes, as well as conducting training needs analysis and developing management training programmes for external clients. The department also operates EduCon, an educational consultancy service, as a commercial arm of its operation. While discussing my master's degree programme with my head of department, and the need to conduct a small-scale research programme, she suggested I contact the vice principal who has responsibility for curriculum and planning. He was enthusiastic about me conducting a piece of research into the college's approach to and progress with strategic planning, which would build on some of the support activities on management development, being provided by my department to the college managers. He proposed that I act as an internal consultant to advise senior management on the most effective communication and staff and management development strategies to use within the college. This suggestion was attractive because:

- it would be of value to the college, particularly in assessing the impact on staff across the institution, which would be directly relevant to the college's intention to apply for the Investors in People (IiP) standard;
- it would assist with my internal role concerned with in-house staff development;
- it would support the department's EduCon activities in providing training and consultancy to external agencies;
- it would provide me with an insight into the operation and role of college senior management, and would support my personal and professional development.

Having given the reasons for selecting this topic, it is important to describe the background to the college and its turbulent external environment. SuperTec is a large further education college sited on three campuses at the heart of a major conurbation. Each year the college enrols over 20,000 students, which equates to around 6,000 full-time equivalent (fte) students and employs 355 full-time academic staff with a similar number of support and ancillary staff. The college was formed from a major reorganization of further education in the city, required to achieve massive budget cuts which coincided with the implementation of the Education Reform Act in 1990. The reorganization was implemented in great haste and led to massive disruption of the service, casting to the elements any former attempts that had been made at strategic planning.

The college has a hierarchical management structure with:

- a principalship consisting of principal, deputy principal, vice principal and head of support services;
- a senior management team (SMT) consisting of the principalship and four directors each with functional responsibilities; three have a campus management responsibility and one is responsible for college marketing;
- 12 heads of department who manage independent cost centres, which are also units of curriculum delivery;
- four major support functions (finance, estates, personnel and management information services);
- sections, at subdepartmental level, headed by senior lecturers.

The process of formal strategic planning began at the college some 20 months after its establishment. The college governors saw a presentation given by a group of management consultants at a governor training event and then decided that the college needed a business plan. The whole governing body met with the senior management team and worked together on preparing a five-year plan at a residential weekend. The weekend coincided with the publication of the first circular, *92/01*, published by the newly established Further Education Funding Council. This circular indicated that colleges would be required to prepare strategic plans to share with the FEFC, and proposed a strategic planning framework (see Figure 20.1). The vice principal had taken responsibility for co-ordinating the preparation of the plan. He was concerned that the processes which had resulted in publication of the first version of the plan had created some resentment and tensions between the SMT and line managers. Line managers had felt excluded from the process and had no ownership of the plan. In an attempt to overcome this problem the SMT and line managers worked together at a second residential conference, to update the plan and to prepare annual operating statements. I was invited to attend this conference.

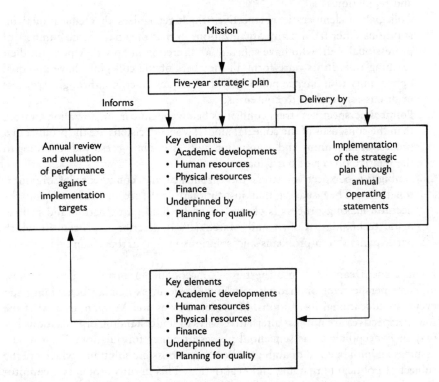

FIGURE 20.1   FEFC strategic planning model (FEFC, *Circular 92/01*).

The college was required to use the FEFC framework for planning, but it appeared to be simplistic and bureaucratic in its approach. A major issue for college managers is to bridge and manage the 'implementation gap' between the information and intentions as systematically stated in a plan, and the actual processes of staff and students learning and developing within the institution. This study is particularly concerned with how this issue was dealt with at SuperTec. It examines the changes that took place within the organizational culture of the institution and how they were affected by changes in the external environment.

LITERATURE

Davies and Morgan (1983), in their examination of the 'Management of higher education institutions in a period of contraction and uncertainty', attempt to provide an overarching theory which integrates four perspectives. These are:

1. **Bureaucratic**, which is the dominant theoretical perspective on organizations associated with the work of Max Weber. The perspective is based on a clear-cut division of labour, a hierarchical authority structure and system of rules and regulations.
2. **Collegial** or democratic perspective which recognizes that educational institutions differ from many organizations in that they have large numbers of professional staff, who have substantial discretion in how they perform their teaching role. In its pure form all members of the collegium have an equal opportunity to influence policies, with decisions emerging through a process of discussion leading to consensus.
3. **Political** perspectives stress conflict as being endemic in organizations, rather than the consensus of the collegial model, where decisions are the product of a process of bargaining and negotiation, with issues being resolved according to the relative power of participants.
4. **Ambiguity** perspectives stress the turbulence and complexity of organizational life. They suggest that institutional goals are unclear and that the decision-making process is characterized by fluid participation and problematic technology. Cohen and March (1974) describe a process in which participants dump problems and solutions into a 'garbage can'.

Bolman and Deal (1984) use the term 'conceptual pluralism' to describe how different perspectives or theories can have a role in explaining behaviours and events in educational institutions. However, Davies and Morgan argue that the four perspectives are not just alternative ways of understanding organizations but may be conceptualized as sequential phases of policy formulation. Their model assumes an initial period of ambiguity leading to possible solutions, which are the subject of political bargaining and negotiation. This in turn produces a compromise that is subject to a quasi-collegial process as activists engage in persuading other participants to adopt the proposal as official policy. The implementation of the policy forms a final bureaucratic phase.

In this study I investigate the applicability and operation of these models within the college and in its external interactions with FEFC. I adapted Davies and Morgan's approach to sequential phasing of policy formation to this context. I developed the hypothesis that the FEFC was imposing a highly systematic and bureaucratic planning structure on a varied sector, in a short time and was in danger of increasing the ambiguity of the sector.

Carlson (1975) drew a distinction between 'wild' and 'domesticated' organizations. 'Wild' organizations 'struggle for survival. Their existence is not guaranteed, and they do cease to exist. Support for them is closely tied to quality of performance. . . . Wild organisations are not protected at vulnerable points as are domesticated organisations' (p. 191). Whereas 'domesticated' organizations 'are fed and cared for. Existence is guaranteed' (p. 191).

It can be argued that central control and the use of rational procedures, which may be following political imperatives at the national level, is an attempt to standardize and 'tame' the sector which is generally noted for its 'wildness'. However, the pace of change introduced for 'domestication' appears to have the potential for driving it out of control and increasing its 'wildness'. I will use my analysis of circulars and the two conferences dealing with strategic planning and funding methodology to support this hypothesis.

The issue of management styles and strategies used for effecting change, as classified by Chin and Benne (1969), is referred to in the interview process undertaken with college managers. Chin and Benne identified the following strategies:

1. empirical–rational: attempting to convince people by rational means, appealing to reason and logic;
2. normative–re-educative: attempting to affect the norms, habits, and values of people and groups through education and training;
3. power-coercive: attempting to bring about change by political, economic, or other sanctions.

Tensions were identified between managers seeking to employ different styles and strategies, and there appears to be a relationship with the models referred to above.

METHODS

It was essential at an early stage to prepare an outline plan for collecting data. My data sources were:

- college reports and plans, and FEFC circulars and reports;
- interviews with college managers at different levels in the hierarchy;
- observation of meetings, conferences and staff development events;
- IiP survey of all staff.

The research plan was divided into three phases. These were planned out and Phase 1 is shown in Figure 20.2 as an example. Each phase was used to inform the activities to be undertaken in the next phase, as were developments in the external environment resulting from FEFC's developing policies, procedures and requirements. Before embarking on the research phases, I started a research diary to aid the processes of reflection and analysis of critical events.

Activity	Event/Individuals	Information sought
Semi-structured interview	Vice principal	Background information Attitudes and views
Observation Informal conversations	Residential conference: Involving SMT, HODS, 2 senior support staff, 2 governors	Group dynamics Attitudes and views Tensions and barriers Future policy
Semi-structured interviews	Principal Deputy principal	Attitudes and views Background information
Observation	Line managers' meeting	Group dynamics Attitudes and views Tensions and barriers Future policy
Semi-structured interviews	Head support services 2 directors	Attitudes and views Background information
Observation	SMT meeting	Group dynamics Attitudes and views Tensions and barriers Future policy
Semi-structured interviews	2 line managers	Attitudes and views
Review	Vice principal	Reflection Future action

FIGURE 20.2   Phase I of research plan.

The first phase was concerned with examining how the initial version of the college strategic plan was being developed and implemented. This phase involved preliminary reading, extensive and intensive observation and interviews.

In order to structure my observation sessions, I developed an observation schedule which summarized the purpose and outcomes of each session as well as the verbal and non-verbal contributions made by each participant.

For the interviews, I decided on a semi-structured approach. The outline questions used are listed in Figure 20.3. From the answers given to Question 5 on 'management culture' of the organization, I attempted to classify the response according to one of the four perspectives outlined in the previous section on Literature. Similarly for Question 6 on 'management style', I attempted to classify the response according to one of Chin and Benne's three strategies for managing change.

In the event it proved possible to meet the targets established in the first phase of the research plan. However, although I had realized that the topic was a challenging one I had not been prepared for the level of complexity encountered. A new circular, *92/18*, giving FEFC's requirements for Phase 1 strategic

---

(1)   Please describe your involvement, if any, in the development of the college strategic plan.

(2)   What are your views on:
      (a) the quality of the plan?
      (b) the processes involved in the plan?

(3)   Please try and assess (and qualify) what value, if any, you think the plan has to the organization in its:
      (a) external context
      (b) internal management processes and procedures

(4)   How have you used the plan yourself?

     Have you used it with your staff?

     In what way?

(5)   Please try and describe (in your own words) the predominant management culture of the organization and how it operates.

Interviewer classification and comment

      (i)   'Bureaucratic and hierarchical'
      (ii) 'Consultative and collegial'
      (iii) 'Competitive and political'
      (iv) 'Ambiguous and chaotic'

[Also explore which other(s) of the above apply and how.]

(6)   Please try and describe (in your own words) your (how others would see it) management style.

Interviewer classification and comment

      (i)   Power-coercive
      (ii) Normative–re-educative
      (iii) Empirical–rational

[Also explore which other(s) of the above apply and how.]

FIGURE 20.3   First-phase semi-structured interview schedule of questions.

planning and projected timescales and a book, *Funding Learning*, (FEFC 1992) describing proposals and options for a new funding methodology, had been issued. All the interviewees were very co-operative but the group tensions, conflicting attitudes and views which were revealed meant that analysing and processing the information proved to be a much greater task than I had anticipated. A backlog of incompletely processed information was created at the end of Phase 1. I decided to allow more time in my plan for reflection and analysis in Phase 2, which focused on departmental planning activities in response to and support of the college plan.

An important outcome of the strategic planning weekend and resulting second version of the plan was a commitment by the college to seeking the Investors in People (IiP) standard. The standard which is being promoted by the Employment Department and which features in the National Education and Training Targets (NETTs), requires organizations to commit themselves to development by developing their employees. It requires all employees to be aware of their organization's strategic plan and to have personal development plans which support the institutional plan. The IiP steering group, which I joined, prioritized a need to check the level of awareness and involvement in strategic planning at all levels across the college. It was decided to prepare a special edition of the college staff magazine, *TecView*, which would introduce the IiP project and include a survey on awareness, knowledge of and attitude to college strategic planning. I was given the responsibility for conducting the survey as part of this project.

The material provided by the survey would provide the opportunity to triangulate the data with that provided by interview and observation. However, I had realized that my attempts to triangulate data were complicated by the changing nature of the external and internal environments. This is expressed in Figure 20.4 which shows an outer data triangulation operating in the context of an inner triangle of change affecting both the external and internal environments.

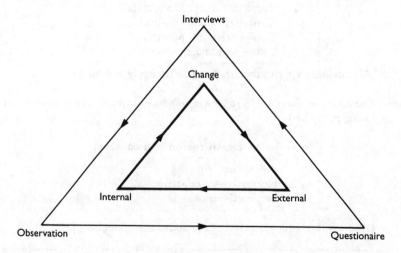

FIGURE 20.4 Outer data triangulation in the context of inner triangle of change.

The idea provided the focus for the third phase of the project which was planned to address:

- an analysis of the attitudes and issues uncovered in Phases 1 and 2;
- an assessment of development and changes, particularly arising from review of annual operating statements;
- the IiP survey of staff understanding and attitudes to strategic planning across the college;
- an analysis of changes in the external environment, arising from the developing requirements of FEFC and the likely impact on planning within SuperTec.

DATA PRESENTATION AND ANALYSIS

This section is divided into the following five subsections:

1. First-phase interviews.
2. Observation of internal processes.
3. IiP survey.
4. Second-phase interviews – assessing changed views and attitudes.
5. Observation of external processes – from FEFC conferences.

First-phase interviews

It became clear that there were significant differences in attitudes and approach between the eight senior managers of the college. This perhaps reflected the recent history of the college and its experiences under the local authority, which had militated against rational planning and provided a highly politicized context. The principal acknowledged this when talking about his approach to managing the college:

> I will often drop an initiative like a pebble, into a pool of managers to see who runs with it and who is most successful. . . . I don't have a great deal of time for meetings, which are just talking shops, and prefer clear accountability and action. . . . I suppose that I would be seen as being mainly 'power-coercive' in my approach, although I always like to maintain a level of unpredictability in my dealings and am essentially pragmatic.

The deputy principal stated, 'Managers should know their responsibilities and get on with them. Essentially I believe in strong central direction and have been called a Stalinist, which I guess is fairly accurate.'

Both the vice principal and head of support services tended to express some frustration with a predominantly political style of operation. The head of support services stated, 'It's very frustrating that nothing ever gets properly written down or discussed. I try and keep my operation running as a 'tight ship' and clear from external interference. I believe it's important to build a strong and loyal team, but I'm very much the boss.' The vice principal was clear that he was intent on trying to change the culture of the college and to use strategic planning as a vehicle for doing this:

> I believe that organizations should practise what they preach and as our mission is primarily educational, that we must focus on developing and training our staff which requires being explicit in what we say we are going to do, how we are going to do it and how we assess if we are being successful. We have to try to be more collegial which requires normative–re-educative strategies where time allows. I want to try and use the pressures for external change as a means of achieving internal change in improving our quality.

I was very surprised to find this ambiguity of approach right at the top of the college's hierarchy. It appeared as if there were value conflicts, which would lead to political differences in the approach to the style and culture employed in managing the college.

The interviews with the four directors confirmed these tensions and reflected similar differences in style, approach and affinity to those exhibited by the principalship. The overall impression of the predominant culture of the college was that it was 'competitive and political', resulting in many instances of 'organized anarchy' (Cohen and March, 1976).

Views on the activity of preparing the strategic plan were themselves both interesting and illuminating. The principal had seen preparing the plan as something of a threat to his autonomy, but also as a chore. However, he had been surprised at how well his senior managers worked as a team when preparing the plan and hoped to make use of this again in the future. The deputy principal was generally cynical on planning processes in a context of turbulence and change, but recognized the necessity of having a plan to meet external accountability requirements. The head of support services was relieved that the college now had an official plan, which was available for governors and external agencies. The vice principal, who had responsibility for co-ordinating strategic planning, spoke of his concerns over the requirements of FEFC and the need for the development of management processes to introduce a culture of planning, review and evaluation.

Following the observation sessions, I selected and interviewed four out of the 12 line managers. It became clear that they resented the directors and that this tension was increased by the way in which the first version of the strategic plan had been produced. Considerable work had been undertaken by the vice principal to develop ownership of the plan by group work at the second residential conference. The group dynamics of the line managers seemed to indicate that they fell into three groups:

- a sharing group who appeared to be primarily collegial in their focus;
- a group who tended to be either reactive or assertive in their behaviour

depending on the circumstances and to be primarily bureaucratic in their focus;
- a smaller group who appeared to address issues obliquely, and while sharing no group identity tended to be primarily political in their focus.

In my interviews I was able to select two managers from the first group and one from each of the other groups. The interviews confirmed the assumptions, made through observation, on the predominant style of the managers selected. There was general agreement that the predominant culture of the organization was 'competitive and political', which sometimes led to 'ambiguity and chaos'. When questioned about the development of strategic planning, the managers said that their initial concerns were that the college's approach to planning would be 'bureaucratic and hierarchical'. This was a particularly emphatic view, expressed by the managers who were observed to be most collegial in their behaviour. However, these fears had largely been allayed by the residential weekend, which appeared to those interviewed to provide the potential for the college becoming more collegial in its culture.

Observation of internal processes

The observation of internal workshops and meetings proved to be both fascinating and complex. Having an observation schedule proved to be absolutely essential in the collection of data. An interesting feature was that the behaviour and contribution made by managers seemed to be markedly different during planning seminars from that displayed in meetings. There was a clear development of collegial behaviour in the former while the latter appeared to confirm the 'competitive and political' features of the organization. The classification of the line managers into collegial, bureaucratic and political (as above) was first identified through observation. It appeared that managers from the collegial group tended to take positive and leading roles in planning developments, but to be much more reactive in management meetings with a reversal of roles with the other two groups. A potential gender issue was identified with the ratio of female managers being significantly higher in the collegial group. It was interesting to note that when FEFC matters were discussed at management meetings, the tone of the meetings invariably changed when opened to discussion, with a more collegial emphasis being demonstrated. However, interpretation of FEFC policy and how it might be applied internally, tended to introduce insecurity and fear in managers and a retreat into more traditional behaviour modes. This was particularly noticeable as the pace of external change quickened in the latter stages of the project.

The meeting which led to the establishment of the IiP steering group was preceded by a presentation from an officer of the local Training and Enterprise Council (TEC). This appeared to provide an interesting combination of bureaucratic tendencies in the organization leading to an aspiration for collegiality. The pursuit of a potentially prestigious award was in the main bureaucratic, but achieving the standard requires the organization to focus on sharing values in its processes and procedures. This interesting combination led to an almost unanimous agreement from college managers that the college should pursue the IiP standard.

The different styles of departmental meetings attended depended on whether they were dealing directly with the plan or with curriculum development as a consequence of the plan. In the former case, two meetings were selected, one with a head of department who showed a collegial approach and the other with a head of department using a bureaucratic style. In the latter case a meeting was held which introduced the plan as 'tablets of stone' dispensed from on high, with a set of operating statements prepared by the head for comment. The meeting item on planning was short and generated little comment of discussion. A much more interactive style was employed by the collegial head of department. Small teams were established to draft annual operating statements for the department. Curriculum meetings were more open ended, generally collegial in their style, and much more positive in outcome.

IiP survey

The survey was administered through the personnel depart and went out with a special report on the IiP project. This ensured a 93 per cent response rate with follow-up being undertaken with the non-respondents. The level of ignorance of the plan was greatest among support staff who had not generally been involved in the formal preparation of an action plan. There was a high degree of correlation between the level of awareness and involvement with the strategic plan and the management style exhibited by the departmental manager. Departments with managers exhibiting primarily 'political' behaviour showed the lowest level of awareness and involvement. The converse was true with staff in 'collegial' departments.

Second-phase interviews

Significant changes noted in the second-phase interviews indicated a much higher degree of uniformity on ownership of the plan and the importance of the plan in dealing with the requirements of the FEFC. However, the more positive nature of the responses to the strategic plan was mirrored by a much greater level of disillusionment with the role and requirements of the FEFC, which were alluded to a much greater number of times than in the first-phase interviews. The FEFC was seen as being both highly interventionist and impractical in its dealings with the college and sector in general.

Interestingly, a perceptible change was noted in management culture and management style. A higher degree of collegiality was recorded although some of this was inspired by the perception of the FEFC as a common foe which united the college managers in opposition to its oversimplistic and bureaucratic processes and policies. It was also noteworthy that the consensus of opinion on management style being employed for managing change was moving away from 'power-coercive' towards 'empirical–rational'.

Observation of external processes

The increasingly negative reactions of college managers to the FEFC were also reflected in observations at two external conferences dealing with 'Funding Methodology' and 'Second-Phase Strategic Plans'. In both conferences college managers expressed grave concern over FEFC's simplistic approach towards dealing with a highly complex sector. One principal of a large college stated in obvious frustration to FEFC officers: 'Do you realize that between us we are engaged in the highly structured planning of chaos?' My conclusion was that at a national level there are clear indications of an oversimplistic bureaucratic approach generating ambiguity and leading, in Cohen and March's (1974) terms, directly to 'the garbage can'.

CONCLUSIONS

From the analysis made in the previous section, it seems clear that in the context of the external and internal environments of SuperTec, it is possible to find evidence of the operation of the four management perspectives, which were introduced earlier. Also, over the period of the study it is possible to detect clear changes in the operation and effect of the different models which supports Davies and Morgan's (1983) view that the theories can be integrated. I have been able to represent the theories as operating as phases, differentially in the internal and external environment of SuperTec. My thesis is that during the period of time of the study there is a complementary relationship between the perspectives operating in the external and internal environments, as expressed in Figure 20.5.

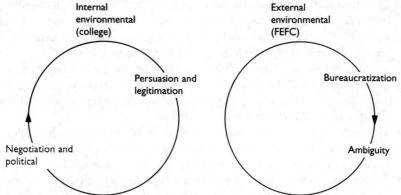

FIGURE 20.5 Processes operating on management in the context of planning at SuperTec (adapted from Davies and Morgan, 1983).

A move from a political culture towards collegiality was identified in the internal environment, both through observation and the management interviews. At the same time a move from bureaucratization to the unintended and ambiguous effects of the 'garbage can' was detected in the external environment. Thus in the diagram two parallel cycles are shown, with the internal cycle moving from 'negotiation and political' to 'persuasion and legitimation', and the external cycle moving from 'bureaucratization' to 'ambiguity'. It would be interesting, but beyond the scope of this study, to investigate over a longer period of time whether all four perspectives would appear in each cycle and with what phasing. The primary focus on issues concerned with the nature and role of strategic planning at the institutional level regrettably left little opportunity for further exploration of Carlson's (1975) classification of 'wildness' and 'domestication'. However, the evidence obtained is generally supportive of the hypothesis that the FEFC is in danger of increasing the 'wildness' of the sector, through increased ambiguity. Information was obtained on the issues and tensions of management styles for effecting change, and how change in the external environment might affect the management styles employed to achieve consequent internal change.

RECOMMENDATIONS

The recommendations made to the management of SuperTec, on the conclusion of this study, were that much has been gained within the college from the development of strategic planning, which should be continued with and built upon. More specifically:

- The foreseeable future for colleges will be extremely turbulent and threatening. This must be planned for in the strategies for the management of change within the college.
- The management strategies for dealing with the unstable and threatening external environment should be both practical and pragmatic, focusing on: (i) seeking to be cautious in external dealings with the FEFC, by fulfilling their bureaucratic requirements, even if they seem to be unrealistic and unreasonable, and aiming for the 'middle of the pack' in terms of what other institutions may seek to do; and (ii) acknowledging, but minimizing, the external threat to the internal operation of the college, by building on the development towards 'collegiality', which has been achieved through the strategic planning exercise and extending efforts to promote a culture of openness and information sharing, such as through the IiP initiative.
- To work with the senior management team on addressing the policy issues arising from FEFC requirements, beginning with a planning day to address the updating of the strategic plan in order to produce version 3.
- To continue to focus line management's attention on curriculum change. This could be done by building on the work undertaken on the planning day which addressed curriculum planning and student needs, with further planning days

on modularizing the curriculum and accommodating growth in student participation.

• To build on the process of continuous monitoring, review and evaluation developed with the preparation of action plans expressed as annual operating statements.

REFERENCES

Bolman, L. G. and Deal, T. E. (1984) *Modern approaches to understanding and managing organisations*. San Francisco: Jossey Bass.

Bush, T. (1989) The nature of theory in educational management, in T. Bush (Ed.) *Managing education: theory and practice*. Milton Keynes: Open University Press.

Carlson, R. (1975) Environmental constraints and organisational consequences: the public school and its clients, in J. Baldridge and T. Deal (Eds) *Managing change in educational organisations*. Berkeley: McCutchen.

Chin, R. and Benne, K. (1969) General strategies for effecting changes in human systems, in W. G. Bennis, K. Benne and R. Chin (Eds) *The planning of change*. New York: Holt, Rinehart & Winston.

Cohen, M. and March, J. (1986) Leadership and ambiguity, reprinted in T. Bush (Ed.) *Managing education: theory and practice* (1989). Milton Keynes: Open University Press.

Davies, J. and Morgan, A. (1983) Management of higher education institutions in a period of contraction and uncertainty. (Reprinted in T. Bush (Ed.) *Managing education: theory and practice* (1989). Milton Keynes: Open University Press.)

Further Education Funding Council (FEFC) (1992/93) *Circular 92/01: Preparing for incorporation; Circular 92/11: College strategic plans; Funding learning; Circular 92/18: Requirements for college strategic plans; Circular 93/14: Recurrent funding methodology 1994/95; Circular 93/16: Recurrent funding methodology 1994/95: allocation mechanism; Circular 93/20: Recurrent funding methodology 1994/95: funding categories.*

Index